Not Guilty

BE FREE TO EXPERIENCE GOD'S LOVE

Devotional Commentary
on the Book of Romans

Brian & Candice Simmons

BroadStreet
PUBLISHING

BroadStreet Publishing® Group, LLC
Savage, Minnesota, USA
BroadStreetPublishing.com

Stock or custom editions of BroadStreet Publishing titles may be purchased in bulk for educational, business, ministry, fundraising, or sales promotional use. For information, please email orders@broadstreetpublishing.com.

Cover and interior by Garborg Design Works | garborgdesign.com

Printed in China

23 24 25 26 27 5 4 3 2 1

Contents

Foreword

I first met Brian Simmons in a refugee camp in Bethlehem. We were ministering to orphans and widows, singing praises to God and blessing dear ones. I met a man who was opening the gates of his heart to be a vessel of love to strangers whom others would deem worthless. I met a man who would give his last dollar to a hungry child in need. I met a man who surrendered his life, becoming a missionary in the jungle and risking even his family, to follow the call of God. I met a man who lived out the romance of the book of Romans.

Since that time in Israel, ministering and worshiping the Lord side by side, I have come to call Brian a dear friend. The Lord Jesus himself said you would know true and false teachers by their fruit. I have personally seen the fruit of Brian's life, and I hope to imitate him as he imitates Christ.

Brian's devotional commentary and study guide through the book of Romans is a precious gift to the body of Christ. Not only does Brian lay out striking biblical truth throughout his writing, but he also includes amazing questions to help you go deeper into the glorious work that is the letter to the Romans. Each lesson's impactful activations will challenge and equip you to use what you are reading in your life. This combination of balanced truth and practical application is what makes *Not Guilty: Be Free to Experience God's Love* a standout among devotional commentaries on this deeply important book of the Bible.

There are so many moments that I could hold up where Brian brilliantly opens the mind to the Scriptures with his revelatory teaching gift. Here are just a few of my favorites. Speaking of how our knowledge of salvation should spur us to righteous living, Brian says, "You have nothing to *fear*, only something to *expect*: deeper communion with him. This is the heavenly transaction that took place when you trusted in Christ for salvation by grace through faith. Now, live like it!" In addressing the tension of how we are to embrace our new identity in Christ without ignoring our present

4

tense issues, Brian exhorts us, "Have you settled for less? Have you been in a wrestling match with sin (bad habits, bad attitudes, bad behavior) instead of reckoning yourself dead to it? Our Lord Jesus has paved the path to freedom for us, and we walk it through sweet surrender. This is how we take up our cross and follow him." And finally, underscoring the truth of how the author himself lives his life, Brian speaks, in that potent way only he can, of our freedom to worship the Lord. He says, "Our freedom is complete, for 'if the Son sets you free from sin, then become a true son and be unquestionably free!' (John 8:36). We are not just free *from something*, but we are also free *to do something*—to worship God with our whole lives."

That is who Brian is, a wholehearted worshiper of God. I am so grateful for this offering in the form of a devotional commentary. I will be recommending it to the church that I lead and any and every believer who wishes to walk in the true freedom that is expressed in Paul's letter to the Roman church. What an amazing time we are living in to have such powerful teachers of the Word! I implore you to embrace these truths, walk in their tension, and give your whole life in worship to the only one found worthy. May the Lamb himself open the scroll of your heart as you read this work. Amen.

Caleb Hyers
Senior Leader of The Resting Place Family
trpfamily.org

Major Purpose and Themes

Introduction

Introduction to the Book of Romans

Grace and Glory!

The book of Romans is perhaps the greatest piece of theological literature in history and the greatest expression of Paul's unique spiritual genius. There has never been a letter like it. The sheer scope and magnificence of Romans set it apart. The closest comparison would be Isaiah, and thus Romans can be viewed as the "Isaiah" of the New Testament and vice versa.

Truly Holy Spirit inspired, Romans is a masterpiece treatise of church doctrine. We thank God for Paul's obedience and dedication to writing it for us, but we wholly recognize only God could author such a treasure chest of theology. You will be stirred, challenged, and perhaps even corrected as you read this enlightening letter.

Paul's gospel was the gospel of grace and glory, which is the beautiful and much-needed major theme of this book. As believers in Christ, we are more than just dedicated disciples; we are desperate lovers. We intensely long for deep connection with the one who made us and made us his. And, once we have been brought into that communion with him, we recognize how we need to learn and grow! We need a solid, systematic, and stable theology, and Romans gives us that.

Key Verses

The key verses of this book are Romans 8:15–16. This passage focuses our heart on the thrust of Paul's gospel: our new life in Christ is empowered by the Spirit, not human effort, and by his Spirit we experience God's love and are enfolded into his family.

> You did not receive the "spirit of religious duty," leading you back into the fear of never being good enough. But you have received the "Spirit of full acceptance," enfolding you into the family of God. And you will never feel orphaned, for as he rises up within us, our spirits join him in saying the words of tender affection, "Beloved Father!" For the Holy Spirit makes God's fatherhood real to us as he whispers into our innermost being, "You are God's beloved child!" (Romans 8:15–16)

Why You Should Read Romans

Romans is full of revelatory truth with the power to transform us. The revelation of righteousness by faith, not works, which Paul heralded in Romans, is a lightning bolt of truth that breaks the power of darkness and releases the power of light into our lives.

The Power of the Gospel

Romans is power packed. Literally. There is revelation-light in Romans that can and should bring a revolution to our lives. In fact, two major revivals of church history were born out of the revelation of righteousness found in Romans: the Protestant Reformation and the Wesleyan Revival. Catch the fire of truth and grace for yourself as you read through Paul's masterpiece.

You can imagine the joy that came over the church at Rome when they read Paul's letter. You, too, will be blessed as you read the anointed words found herein. The romance of Romans will fill you with freedom. Freedom from sin. Freedom from self. Freedom from dead works. A new freedom is coming into your spirit as you embrace the truth of Romans.

The Purity of the Gospel

Concerning this epistle, in his work, *Preface to the Letter of St. Paul to the Romans*, Martin Luther declared it to be the "purest gospel." He further encouraged every Christian to consume it "as though it were the daily bread of the soul." Because history has proven our humanistic desire to want to add to the pure gospel, we take Luther's encouragement to heart. The law said "do," but the gospel says "done"; there is nothing more to add to its perfection. Faith alone in Christ alone is enough, and that is truly good news.[1]

The Peace of the Gospel

The love of God is so rich; it leaves our hearts full of heaven. When we believe in Jesus Christ, he pours his Holy Spirit into our hearts until every sense of abandonment leaves us. We become children of God, sons and daughters of glory, who follow the Lamb. Peace becomes our new normal.

Do you want to be enriched and discover the heavenly treasures of faith, grace, true righteousness, peace, and power? Plug into the book of Romans, and you'll never feel the same again. Truth always sets the heart free, and nothing can free you more than the truth found in Romans. Grace and glory are waiting for you to unwrap and make your own. Live in the truths of Romans and watch how God's love sets you free.

Purpose

The most important letter in the world was written to the most important city in the world. Because Rome was the power center of the known world when Paul penned this letter, it was the most

---

1   Martin Luther, *Preface to the Letter of St. Paul to the Romans*, trans. Andrew Thornton (Manchester, NH: Saint Anselm College Humanities Program, 1983), https://www.ccel.org/l/luther/romans/pref_romans.html.

influential city on earth at that time. Although Paul had not yet been to Rome, he would one day be martyred there. So Paul wrote to these Roman Christians an important epistle filled with rich doctrines of our faith that reveal God's heart for his people and what must be our proper response to such sacrificial love. Paul's theology flows from the romance of God toward us. Intimacy longs for understanding and oneness. And to be intimate with the God of glory requires that we understand his heart and join him in every way. As a result of Paul's writing, we can determine the following purposes:

1. Paul wrote Romans to communicate the grand themes of God's grace and glory encapsulated in the gospel. No one comes into glory except by the grace of God that fills believers with his righteousness. The works of religion and our clumsy attempts to please God are unable to make us holy. But God is so kind, compassionate, and gracious that he shares his righteousness with all who receive his Son, Jesus Christ. He causes his faith-filled ones to be made holy by his grace and glory. Paul wrote his letter to clearly articulate this message, to explain why he preached it, and to show how it should affect Christians in their daily life and community.

   • God's grace is an inexhaustible subject. It seems too good to be true...but it is true! God is good, and he wants us fully immersed in the revelation of his covering of grace and love. His grace truly is sufficient. Paul learned this first-hand when God spoke to him saying, "My grace is always more than enough for you, and my power finds its full expression through your weakness" (2 Corinthians 12:9). The other great theme of Romans is glory. Without the understanding of grace, we will never experience his glory. Glory is his plan for you, dear friend! In Adam, we all sinned (Romans 5:12) and fell short of God's glory (3:23), but now in Christ, we are restored and glorified: "Having determined our destiny ahead of time, he called us to himself and transferred his perfect righteousness to everyone he called. And those who possess his perfect righteousness he co-glorified with his Son!" (Romans 8:30).

- The longing of every human soul is unconditional love—that's grace—and to be changed—that's glory. Forgiveness is only half of the salvation package. Transformation is also provided. We are meant to grow and go from glory to glory to glory. The psalmist expressed this transcendent longing with these words: "Here's the one thing I crave from YAHWEH, the one thing I seek above all else: I want to live with him every moment in his house, beholding the marvelous beauty of YAHWEH, filled with awe, delighting in his glory and grace. I want to contemplate in his temple" (Psalm 27:4).

- Paul was hoping that Rome would be his "base of operations" in the West (like Antioch had been for him in the East and Ephesus had been for him in Asia Minor). Consequently, he wrote this letter, explaining his gospel carefully and fully, in the hopes that the Roman Christians would embrace him and his message completely. Further, since his life had already been in much danger from the Jews (Acts 17:5, 13 and 20:3), Paul may have sensed the need to pen his thoughts about the gospel in a systematic way. Paul was, of course, a missionary. At the time of his writing of Romans, he was in Corinth. He wrote this letter and sent it to the Roman believers by way of Phoebe, who was one of the outstanding women in the church of Cenchrea, a port city near Corinth.

2. Paul wrote Romans in part to address some conflicts within the church over nonessential matters of differing opinions. Paul did what is good for us all to do—he refocused hearts

onto what matters most: God's love, grace, and goodness. God's love is supreme over "nonessential truths."

Twelve Major Themes

- **The Gospel:** You could summarize the entire book of Romans with this one word: *gospel*. In the opening sentence, Paul explains that God had set him apart with the mission to unveil "God's wonderful gospel" (1:1), which Paul preaches as salvation by grace through faith alone. This is one way of explaining the gospel. Here are some others: the revelation of God's Son, the wonderful message of Jesus, the joyful message of God's liberating power unleashed within us through Christ, the message of Christ's goodness.

- **Good News:** We know the gospel, but we still need some good news. Romans is full of the good news that encourages our soul.

- **Salvation:** God's salvation (Greek *soteria*) is purely by grace. There can be no mixture (grace plus anything else); otherwise, it is no longer grace. Salvation is wondrous in its cost as it cost God everything and costs us nothing.

- **The Love of God:** Romans 5 reveals how we receive "the endless love of God cascading into our hearts" (5:5). What love! His love never ends and will never fail us.

- **Justification:** This is our new reality in Christ. We are just, as if we had never sinned. When God looks at us, he sees Jesus. He sees us clean, holy, and beautiful.

He sees us justified—a legal term that means "not guilty."

- **The Righteousness of God:** We can't get any more righteous than we are right now. Our righteousness is not of our own making; it is of God and God alone. He has made us righteous. He has actually made us the righteousness of God in Christ Jesus (2 Corinthians 5:21).

- **The Law:** Many have noted that Paul's relationship with the law is complicated. In Romans, Paul says, "The law is holy and its commandments are correct and for our good" (Romans 7:12). It was given to us for our benefit and intended to bring life, but instead, it brought death (v. 10). Paul concluded, "God achieved what the law was unable to accomplish, because the law was limited by the weakness of human nature" (8:3). Through Christ, God achieved what we could not: Christ perfectly fulfilled every requirement of the law so that now "we are free to live, not according to our flesh, but by the dynamic power of the Holy Spirit!" (v. 4). 8:4

- **The Flesh versus the Spirit:** One of the most interesting comparisons Paul makes is between our old life in "the flesh" versus our new life in the "life-giving Spirit." He offers this comparison as an exhortation to live the kind of life God desires from his children— not in the morally fallen way we once lived but in the new way as true children of God "who are moved by the impulses of the Holy Spirit" (v. 14).

- **The Destiny of Israel:** As a parenthetical insert in chapters 9–11, Paul addresses the question of where natural Israel fits in God's heart and plan. In this portion, we see Paul's great compassion for his own people as well as God's faithfulness and loyal love.

- **In Christ:** Paul sees Christians living "in Christ." Although used more frequently in Ephesians, Paul uses this phrase, or one equivalent to it, *twenty-nine* times in Romans. The phrases are used with different connotations, depending on the context. Sometimes they express the instrumentality of Christ's activity (3:24; 8:39); sometimes they express the intimate relation of Christians and Christ, who live a sort of symbiosis (6:11). "In Christ" is the fulfillment of Jesus' own High Priestly prayer from John 17. We are in him. There is now no justifiable accusing voice coming against us because we are "in Christ." Paul states it powerfully with these words, "So now the case is closed. There remains no accusing voice of condemnation against those who are joined in life-union with Jesus, the Anointed One" (Romans 8:1).

- **Grace:** The radical gospel of grace, as it is found throughout Scripture, has always had its critics. One prominent leader told me a few years ago that he's convinced that by trusting in God's justifying and preserving grace, I would end up living a life of sin before long—and possibly lose my salvation and be consigned to hell. Similarly, Paul anticipated that reaction from the religious community of his own day after he said, "Wherever sin increased, there was more than enough of God's grace to triumph all the more!" (5:20). So he asked the question he expected us to ask: "Do we persist in sin so that God's kindness and grace will increase?" (6:1). Meaning, should we sin so that we can receive more grace? In other words, "If people believed what you just said in Romans 5, Paul, wouldn't they take advantage of the situation and live like the devil, knowing they were 'safe and secure from all alarm'?" That's a fair question. But it reveals a basic misunderstanding of the nature of God's saving grace. Paul's response is unmistakable: "What a terrible thought! We have died to sin once and for all, as a dead man passes away from this life. So how could we live under sin's rule a moment longer?" (v. 2).

- **Glory:** We have the hope of glory within us. We are not just saved *from something*. We are also saved *unto something*—Christlikeness. In the example of Christ, we must take up the cross and die to ourselves to achieve the glory found in Christ. We must daily put to death the flesh's fears and worries and desires. The flesh wants only to glorify itself. This death of self leads to life in Christ! The glory of our Christlikeness is worth celebrating. As Paul says in Romans 5:2, "Our faith guarantees us permanent access into this marvelous kindness that has given us a perfect relationship with God. What incredible joy bursts forth within us as we keep on celebrating our hope of experiencing God's glory!" We, as well as all of creation, have an expectation of unveiled glory. This expectation gave Paul the perseverance to endure his earthly suffering: "I am convinced that any suffering we endure is less than nothing compared to the magnitude of glory that is about to be unveiled within us" (8:18). Romans encourages Christians that they will participate in God's glory.

Key Terms in Romans

There is some confusion within the body of Christ over these three important experiences: justification, sanctification, and glorification. We need good, sound teaching to help us not be wishy-washy in our understanding of these foundational biblical topics. We need to know, really know, these fundamentals:

1. Who we are in Christ
2. Who he is in us
3. What his atonement accomplished for us
4. What his resurrection accomplished for us

Here is a chart that defines and describes each term.

Justification	Sanctification	Glorification
Past	Present	Future
We have been saved from the penalty of sin	We are being saved from the power of sin	We will be saved from the presence of sin
One-time experience	Life-long experience	Eternal experience
Positional	Continual	Final
God's work for us	God's work in us	God's work to us
Perfect in this life	Not perfect in this life	Perfect in the next life

Sanctification

We are holy and being made holy. This is mind-blowing, so we have to get God's thoughts, his mind, on this. To him, right now and forever, we are perfect and perfectly positioned "in Christ." Done! And yet, we are still in the process of becoming more like Jesus every day.

The conclusion is this: We are perfect and perfectly loved while we are being made perfect. We don't do our good works in order to be made holy; we do them *because* we are being made holy. As Luther said, we are simultaneously saint and sinner during the process of sanctification. Christians live in a tension between what was achieved by the cross and what will be fulfilled with the second coming. Sanctification is a "God-concept" that we believe by faith, even if our human minds can't quite understand it. It is *by faith* that these truths are *activated* in our lives.

Justification

Before God, we are clean because of the blood of Jesus. We have been declared "not guilty," and our new reality in Christ is that we now live just as if we had never sinned. Clean, pure, free—this is what Jesus has made us. We are eternally justified!

The conclusion is this: we have been made righteous and declared innocent by the judge of the universe. The only one qualified to condemn us, God himself, bore our guilt at Calvary. Therefore, we will never be judged for our sins and do not have to strive for victory. Instead, we live from the victory Christ won for us on the cross.

Glorification

We focus on our justification and sanctification quite a bit but not as much on our glorification. Why is that? The grace that delivers us from sin is also taking us to glory.

The conclusion is this: The finished work of the cross not only saved us from sin and sin's effects but also brought us into God's glory. Sin has been dealt with; the price is paid. Therefore, sin should not get our focus—glory should. Glory is our destiny.

"Both/And"

The Western mindset struggles to try and file truths as "either/or," but the Hebraic mindset operates in terms of "both/and." This will stretch our thinking but will also align us with the heart and mind of God. His thoughts are higher than ours. In a "divine ambiguity," God will mingle truths. For example, we are both filled and being filled. We are both holy and being made holy. We are both thirsty and satisfied. We are both hungry and full. We are both strong in him and boasting in our weakness. We are both perfect and not yet perfect. We are both at rest in Christ and at work for Christ. We are both seated in heaven and taking our stand on the earth in the evil day. You get the idea! We must simply embrace and enjoy the mystery.

Romans in Church History

Romans, a Masterpiece of Christian Doctrine

The acceptance of this great book as Pauline is rarely disputed due to its testimony by the apostolic fathers and its inclusion in early listings of New Testament books. We can date this letter to about AD 55. While preaching in Corinth, Paul dictated the letter to Tertius (Romans 16:22) and entrusted it to Phoebe (v. 1) to deliver it to the Roman believers. Romans has been described as Paul's Song of Songs because it is a letter that so beautifully expresses the unconditional love of God, and the keynote of Romans is "no condemnation!" "There is now no condemnation for those who are in Christ Jesus" (8:1 NIV).

- *No Condemnation*

    o To Roman culture, it was very common to issue legal verdicts with this very pronouncement: "No condemnation!"

    o This pronouncement, therefore, from the apostle Paul was bombastic in its effect. Heaven has pronounced you not guilty! Free and clear! You have been justified in Christ.

    o In fact, Paul emphatically charges his readers: "Who then is left to condemn us?" (8:34). What a question! Who indeed?

- *In Christ Jesus*

    o In him, the debt is cancelled. In him, we are pardoned and accepted. Our new identity is *in Christ*.

Romans' Effect on Theologians

- "This letter is truly the most important piece in the New Testament." —Martin Luther[2]

- "It is impossible to read or to meditate on this letter too much or too well. The more one deals with it, the more precious it becomes and the better it tastes." —Martin Luther[3]

- "No man verily can read it too oft, or study it too well; for the more it is studied, the easier it is; the more it is chewed, the pleasanter it is; and the more groundly it is searched, the preciouser things are found in it." —William Tyndale[4]

- "The Epistle to the Romans is the cathedral of the Christian faith." —Frédéric Louis Godet, nineteenth-century Swiss theologian[5]

Famous Historical Testimonials

In 386, Augustine, feeling cold and far from God, read in Romans 13:13–14 these heart-stirring words:

> We must live honorably, surrounded by the light of this new day, not in the darkness of drunkenness and debauchery, not in promiscuity and sensuality, not being argumentative or jealous of others. Instead fully immerse yourselves into the Lord Jesus, the Anointed One, and don't waste even a

---

2   Luther, *Preface to the Letter.*
3   Luther, *Preface to the Letter.*
4   "A Prologue upon the Epistle of Saint Paul to the Romans," Tyndale's Prologue to the Epistle of Paul to the Romans, accessed December 3, 2021, http://www.bible-researcher.com/romansprologue.html.
5   Frédéric Louis Godet, "The Epistle of St. Paul to the Romans," StudyLight.org, accessed December 3, 2021, https://www.studylight.org/commentaries/eng/gsc/romans.html.

moment's thought on your former identity to awaken its selfish desires.

God's power released through his illuminating Word gripped Augustine, and he gave his whole life to Jesus Christ at that moment.

In August 1513, a monk by the name of Martin Luther, though a teacher of God's Word, found his life empty and in disorder. In particular, he felt confused about how God's righteousness could do anything but condemn. Luther's search led him to Romans 1:17, which says,

> This gospel unveils a continual revelation of God's righteousness—a perfect righteousness given to us when we believe. And it moves us from receiving life through faith, to the power of living by faith. This is what the Scripture means when it says: "We are right with God through life-giving faith!" [6]

About this verse, Luther later said: "Night and day I pondered until…I grasped the truth that the righteousness of God is that righteousness whereby, through grace and sheer mercy, he justifies us by faith. Therefore I felt myself to be reborn and to have gone through open doors into paradise…This passage of Paul became to me a gateway into heaven." [7] This truth changed Martin Luther's heart and life, and from there, the Reformation spread throughout the world.

In May 1738, John Wesley, a failed minister and missionary, went to a small Bible study. Someone read from Martin Luther's *Commentary on Romans*, and John later described the impact this reading had on his life in his journal: "While he was describing the change, which God works in the heart through faith in Christ, I felt my heart strangely warmed. I felt I did trust in Christ, Christ alone,

---

6   David Guzik, "Romans 1—The Human Race Guilty before God," Enduring Word, accessed December 3, 2021, https://enduringword.com/bible-commentary/romans-1.
7   Guzik, "Romans 1."

for my salvation, and an assurance was given me that he had taken my sins away, even mine."[8] John Wesley went on to be a leader in the Great Awakening that swept through England and its thirteen American colonies.

Romans Releases Reformation

One of the unique aspects of Romans among all other New Testament books is its history of sparking revival and reformation. The powerful truths of Romans spawned two major spiritual awakenings that have literally changed the world.

The Protestant Reformation

Martin Luther led this great movement in the 1500s. Luther encountered the revelation-truth of salvation by grace through faith and broke out of the empty form and ritual of the church of his day, forming the Protestant church movement. It was a truth rediscovered from Romans ("The just shall live by faith" 1:17 KJV) that sparked this raging inferno we ourselves are a part of.

The Wesleyan Revival

This sweeping revival of the 1700s was also born out of the revelation of righteousness found in Romans. Its focus was the relationship between grace, faith, and holiness of heart and life. We will never outgrow the wonder, beauty, and simplicity of our great salvation.

Expect Revival and Reformation

As you apply yourself to the study of this great book, you, too, can expect a reformation. Expect revival fire. God's power will surely influence you and make timeless truths come alive within you. Through our own individual revival and reformation, God will use us to bring his passion and fire to the world around us and ignite a great awakening. *Expect him!*

8   John Wesley, "'I Felt My Heart Strangely Warmed,'" in *The Journal of John Wesley*, ed. Percy Livingstone Parker (Chicago, IL: Moody Press, 1951), https://www.ccel.org/ccel/wesley/journal.vi.ii.xvi.html.

Let's Go Deeper!

Questions

1. Throughout our study of Romans, we will be discussing foundational truths concerning justification, sanctification, and glorification. (Refer to the chart in this lesson.) How would you answer these questions?

   - *Who are we in Christ?*

   - *Who is he in us?*

   - *What did his atonement accomplish for us?*

   - *What did his resurrection accomplish for us?*

2. There are two realities we all long for: unconditional love and transformation, or grace and glory. How do they work together, and why must we not have one without the other?

3. Romans is power packed. Within it are truths that can revolutionize you. Take some time for reflection and prayerfully list the results you want in your life through this study.

4. The key verses of Romans are 8:15–16. Write them down, and spend time daily committing these to memory, hiding them in your heart.

5. Many major doctrinal issues are addressed in Romans. Some may be new to you or even contrary to what you have

learned. Prayerfully commit to the Lord to have an open mind and heart to his transforming truth.

Deeper Still!

Activations

The Good News of Grace and Glory

The Greek word for gospel is *euangelion*, which simply means "good news." Acts 20:24 and Galatians 1:6 both use the terms "gospel" and "grace" interchangeably.

- "But whether I live or die is not important, for I don't esteem my life as indispensable. It's more important for me to fulfill my destiny and to finish the ministry my Lord Jesus has assigned to me, which is to faithfully preach the wonderful news of God's grace" (Acts 20:24).

- "I am shocked over how quickly you have strayed away from the One who called you in the grace of Christ. I'm astounded that you now embrace a distorted gospel!" (Galatians 1:6).

When you understand the gospel as the grace of God, it will release the power of God into your life. That's huge! Paul uses the word *gospel* as shorthand for the amazing, joyful message of God's saving work through Jesus Christ. The entire Christian message is wrapped up in this one theme: the good news of God's grace. The gospel is the message about how God has acted in the world to rescue humanity from sin and death through the life, death, and resurrection of Jesus. So when Paul says "gospel," he means all of that.

There was a tendency in the early days of the church, as well as throughout church history, to stray from the simplicity of grace. Friends, let's keep it simple. Have you been trusting in your works? Have you been striving against sinful habits? Today is your day to relinquish to God every heavy burden and every weight of sin.

Simple surrender will usher in the tidal wave of God's grace upon your life for real transformation and increasing glory.

Let's Pray

Lord, bring me back to the joy of my salvation, the joy that flows from your fountain of pure grace. I let go of all self-righteousness and all trust in my own good works. I repent of striving to please you or earn your love in any way. I surrender all, Lord—all of my life for all of yours. Bring me back to the simplicity of the gospel of grace. Help me to abide under that waterfall, letting your grace and glory cascade into me, washing away every lie and every excuse. Through this study in Romans, God, I ask you to cause me to become rooted and grounded fully and only in your loving grace. These things I ask in Jesus' beautiful name. Amen.

The Power of Grace

Introduction

God's Great Grace

Grace has been described as "God's riches at Christ's expense," but really, grace is indescribable. *Hesed* is the Hebrew word most often translated as "loving-kindness" or "mercy" and probably best represents God's grace toward us. Though Paul uses the Greek *charis*, often translated "grace," his use of the word reflects his Semitic roots and the depths of God's love that *hesed* conveys. Translators have had difficulty giving *hesed* a proper English equivalent, but it is the word for God's covenant love that prevails. He will never quit on us. His love holds on and on and on…and on! Past our faults or failures right into eternity. That is *hesed,* and that is grace. It is God's default setting when it comes to his children.

When we deserve a lecture, we get his kiss. When we are at our very worst and in our greatest weakness, God's love is at its greatest potency. In fact, it's through his love that his grace is glorified. "For it was always in his perfect plan to adopt us as his delightful children, through our union with Jesus, the Anointed One, so that his tremendous love that cascades over us would glorify his grace—for the same love he has for his Beloved, Jesus, he has for us. And this unfolding plan brings him great pleasure!" (Ephesians 1:5–6). Grace is so rich and deep and multifaceted.

We could study the rest of our lifetime, digging into the bounty of grace, and never hit the bottom.

For our study of Romans, we will focus on the truth that grace cannot be mixed with works. Grace cannot be diluted or mingled with anything of our own strength or merit; otherwise, it ceases to be grace. The works we do are *empowered by* grace not *combined with* grace in order to earn blessings from God. Grace is pure and holy. It cannot be earned or merited. It is more than we deserve and more than we could ever have hoped for. Grace is God's kiss reserved for his dear children, and oh, how he loves to lavish his grace upon us!

Understanding the Power of Grace in Romans

1. There is a relationship between *grace* and *mercy*.

   - Grace gives us what we don't deserve (blessing).

   - Mercy doesn't give us what we do deserve (punishment).

God is full of mercy. Therefore, it is always good to ask for mercy. "Have mercy!" is a simple yet powerful prayer, and intercession is, in essence, the cry for mercy on someone else's behalf. We need mercy, and God is rich in mercy. He is love—he "is merciful and gracious, slow to anger and abounding in compassion and lovingkindness" (Psalm 103:8 AMP).

2. There is a relationship between *grace* and *justification*.

   - Like grace, justification is unearned and free.

If there were a way to earn freedom from the consequences of our sinful actions, then Jesus' sacrifice was unnecessary. However, it was necessary, and just as grace is a free gift, so is our justification. We could never make ourselves guiltless, "yet through his powerful declaration of acquittal, God freely gives away his righteousness. His gift of love and favor now cascades over us, all because Jesus, the Anointed One, has liberated us from the guilt, punishment, and power of sin!" (Romans 3:24).

3. There is *no* relationship between *grace* and *wages*.

- We minister to God and for God as privileged servants.

- We aren't exchanging our service for a wage from God because we belong to him. He deserves our all.

Our lives are as sacrificial love offerings, surrendered to God for his pleasure and purpose. Jesus declared this dynamic relationship by saying, "All who belong to you [Father] now belong to me as well, and my glory is revealed through their surrendered lives" (John 17:10). And he further stated, "So learn this lesson: After doing all that is commanded of you, simply say, 'We are mere servants, undeserving of special praise, for we are just doing what is expected of us and fulfilling our duties'" (Luke 17:10). We, therefore, serve out of love and devotion, not for wages. After all, there is nothing we did to earn his grace.

4. There is *no* relationship between *grace* and *debt*.

- God doesn't owe us anything.

5. There is *no* relationship between *grace* and *reward*.

There are certainly rewards in this kingdom life. The Bible refers to many crowns, but our eternal salvation is not such a reward. Salvation by grace is a gift, not the result of self-effort: "So no one will ever be able to boast, for salvation is never a reward for good works or human striving" (Ephesians 2:9). And the Holy Spirit is poured out as a gift from heaven, not an earned credit: "So answer me this: Did the Holy Spirit come to you as a reward for keeping Jewish laws? No, you received him as a gift because you believed in the Messiah" (Galatians 3:2).

6. There is *no* relationship between *grace* and *boasting*.

- If we were to stop and account for our assets, we would have to readily confess that anything good about us came from God.

- There is simply no room for boasting, not before others and especially not before God.

Paul, more than most, understood this important truth. From a human perspective, he had many reasons to boast, yet his confession was this: "God's amazing grace has made me who I am! And his grace to me was not fruitless. In fact, I worked harder than all the rest, yet not in my own strength but God's, for his empowering grace is poured out upon me" (1 Corinthians 15:10).

This was a truth for which Paul suffered much persecution and laid down his life. He was passionate about protecting the pure grace gospel unadulterated by a "works mentality." His love for Jesus compelled him to exalt Christ's work, not ours, as the focus of all our boasting. "Where, then, is there room for boasting? Do our works bring God's acceptance? Not at all! It was not our works of keeping the law but our faith in his finished work that makes us right with God" (Romans 3:27). Grace produces works out of gratefulness; works should not come from our need to boast or to earn a gift God gives freely.

"Hyper-Grace"

Hyper-grace refers to the nature of God's grace as being "hyper," which means "over, above, beyond." There is a lot of talk and concern about the concept of "hyper-grace" in our day. From a godly desire to avoid cheap grace and to preach a true gospel that produces transformed lives, some fear a false grace message that condones or winks at sinful living. In his 1937 book, *The Cost of Discipleship*, theologian Dietrich Bonhoeffer first defined cheap grace as "the grace we bestow upon ourselves" when we "preach of forgiveness without requiring repentance."[9] He goes on to say, "Cheap grace is grace without discipleship, grace without the cross, grace without Jesus Christ, living and incarnate."[10] However, we mustn't go to the

---

9   Dietrich Bonhoeffer, *The Cost of Discipleship*, trans. R. H. Fuller and Irmgard Booth (New York: Touchstone, 1995), 44.
10   Bonhoeffer, *The Cost of Discipleship*, 45.

extreme of making grace something other than it is: lavish, extreme, and unlimited. So let's tackle this issue from the perspective of God's Word as hyper-grace is actually a biblical concept.

1. God's Grace, Love, and Power Are Limitless

God's limitless grace is revealed in three forms.

- *Huper-ballo*—"to transcend, surpass, exceed, excel" (see Ephesians 2:7)
- *Huper-perisseuo*—"super-abound, abound much more, exceeding" (see Romans 5:20)
- *Huper-pleonazo*—"super-abound, to be exceedingly abundant" (see 1 Timothy 1:14)

When we soberly consider the depravity of our past sins, God's abundant grace is so lovely. Where would we be without such love, and why would we ever want to diminish or limit such grace? Jesus' work on Calvary was enough. *His* resurrection was also *ours*. Because of his death and resurrection, we are free indeed. We have salvation as well as the power for transformation all wrapped up in the wondrous package of God's amazing grace.

2. True Hyper-Grace Is Not Sloppy Grace

Upon the Reformer's rediscovery of the biblical doctrine of grace, someone once questioned Martin Luther, saying, "If this is true, a person could simply live as he pleased!"

"Indeed!" Luther replied. "Now, what pleases you?"[11]

The biblical reality, therefore, is that God's grace *is* extreme and abundant. Some fear the message of *huper*-grace will encourage Christians to live sinful lives. This would effectively turn God's truly hyper-grace into sloppy or cheap grace that says, "No big deal! I can sin. I'm under grace!"

---

11 "Gospel of Grace," Bible.org, accessed December 3, 2021, https://bible.org/illustration/gospel-grace.

However, true grace stirs us to greater devotion, purity, love, and passion for holiness in our pursuit of intimacy with God. We *greatly need* hyper-grace. But not so we can just skate by in life, barely making it, looking and acting like the world. We need abundant grace to walk in the abundant life Christ died to give us. Grace empowers us to walk in purity. Paul said it this way, "But God's amazing grace has made me who I am!" (1 Corinthians 15:10).

3. Saving Grace Is Also a Teaching Grace

Romans 6 really addresses this issue, and we will discuss it further when we get there in our study, but Paul succinctly puts it this way: "We have died to sin once and for all, as a dead man passes away from this life. So how could we live under sin's rule a moment longer?" (v. 2). In other words, how can we live in sin knowing that Jesus died to free us? It is a rhetorical question, friends. Grace empowers us and teaches us to live worthy of Jesus.

When addressing Titus, Paul reveals how this grace is a daily part of a Christian's life: "This same grace teaches us how to live each day as we turn our backs on ungodliness and indulgent lifestyles, and it equips us to live self-controlled, upright, godly lives in this present age" (Titus 2:12).

The bottom line is that lovers of God don't want to *do* anything or *have* anything that hurts their intimacy with Jesus. Grace enables us in our godly pursuit of his beautiful heart. More grace means more purity. So we say, "Give us more grace, Lord!"

4. Biblical Advocates of *Huper*-Grace

John the Beloved—"From the overflow of his fullness we received grace heaped upon more grace!" (John 1:16).

- John's revelation of Jesus is that Jesus Christ is grace personified. He is grace with skin on. Grace is the fullness of Jesus' nature—it's who he is. He is full of grace and mercy, and out of his fullness, we are filled.

The Apostle Peter—"Then, after your brief suffering, the God of all loving grace, who has called you to share in his eternal glory in Christ, will personally and powerfully restore you and make you stronger than ever. Yes, he will set you firmly in place and build you up" (1 Peter 5:10).

- Peter's revelation of God was that he is "the God of all loving grace." Do you know him that way? Oh, how he wants you to!

- Peter understood that we "continue to grow and increase in God's grace" (2 Peter 3:18). We are on a beautiful journey of discovery into the gracious nature of God. It will never ever end, and he will just become more and more lovely to our hearts.

James (Jacob), the Brother of Jesus—"He continues to pour out more and more grace upon us. For it says, 'God resists you when you are proud but continually pours out grace when you are humble'" (James [Jacob] 4:6).

- To James, God is the one who gives us more and more and more grace! He "pours out grace" upon humble hearts who come to his throne of grace (Hebrews 4:16).

The Prophet Zechariah—"What are you, you great mountain? Before Zerubbabel you will become a plain; and he will bring out the top stone with shouts of 'Grace, grace to it!'" (Zechariah 4:7 NASB).

- To Zechariah, God is a master builder who is establishing his house, his people, by the power of his grace.

- No matter what mountain of impossibility and resistance seems to block your path or promise, God's unrelenting grace will overcome it.

The Prophet Joel—"'Tear your heart and not merely your garments.' Now return to the LORD your God, for He is gracious and compassionate, slow to anger, abounding in mercy and relenting of catastrophe" (Joel 2:13 NASB).

- Joel had a revelation of the gracious God who is willing and ready to receive every repentant heart. Our cry for mercy will touch his gracious heart.

Moses—"Then the LORD passed by in front of him and proclaimed, 'The LORD, the LORD God, compassionate and merciful, slow to anger, and abounding in faithfulness and truth'" (Exodus 34:6 NASB).

- Moses knew him as the great forgiver—so slow to anger. He never holds a grudge. He overflows with grace, *hesed*.

- Moses deeply understood the grace nature of the great I AM.

Oh, the Endless Grace of God!

Grace…Well, it is hyper, friends. It is extreme, and praise God for that! His grace pursues us like a persistent lover. It is relentless until it overtakes us. His loving grace woos us into his arms, and he never lets us go. Grace draws us, saves us, and keeps us. Grace plus nothing is more than enough! His grace revealed through his love is so endless that nothing in the universe can weaken or lessen it:

Who could ever divorce us from the endless love of God's Anointed One? Absolutely no one! For nothing in the universe has the power to diminish his love toward us. Troubles, pressures, and problems are unable to come between us and heaven's love. What about persecutions, deprivations, dangers, and death threats? No, for they are all impotent to hinder omnipotent love. (Romans 8:35)

Overview of Romans

Basic Outline of Romans

1. The Grace of God—Chapters 1–8
2. The Destiny of Israel—Chapters 9–11
3. Relationships—Chapters 12–16

In-Depth Outline of Romans

Section 1: Introduction (1:1–17)

I. Paul offers a brief summary of the gospel message.

- Jesus Christ is the focus of the gospel.

- Paul is qualified to proclaim the gospel.

II. Paul longs to visit the church in Rome for the purpose of mutual encouragement.

III. The gospel reveals God's power for salvation and righteousness.

Section 2: Why We Need the Gospel (1:18–4:25)

I. Theme: All people have a need for justification before God.

- The natural world reveals the existence of God as Creator; therefore, people are without excuse.

- The gentiles are sinful and have earned God's wrath (1:18–32).

- The Jews are sinful and have earned God's wrath (2:1–29).

- Circumcision and obeying the law are not enough to appease God's wrath for sin.

II. Theme: Justification is a gift from God.

- All people (Jews and gentiles) are powerless against sin. No one is righteous before God based on their own merit (3:1–20).
- People don't have to earn forgiveness because God has granted us justification as a gift.
- We can receive this gift only through faith (3:21–31).
- Abraham was an example of someone who received righteousness through faith, not through his own works (4:1–25).

Section 3: The Blessings We Receive through the Gospel (5:1–8:39)

I. The gospel brings peace, righteousness, and joy (5:1–11).

II. The gospel allows us to escape the consequences of sin (5:12–21).

III. The gospel frees us from slavery to sin (6:1–23).

IV. The gospel frees us from slavery to the law (7:1–25).

V. The gospel offers us a righteous life through the Spirit (8:1–17).

VI. The gospel offers us ultimate victory over sin and death (8:18–39).

Section 4: The Gospel and the Israelites (9:1–11:36)

I. Both Israel and the church have always been part of God's plan.

II. Israel has missed the point concerning God's law.

III. God still has plans for the Israelites, his people.

Section 5: Transformation by the Power of the Gospel (12:1–15:13)

I. Theme: The gospel results in spiritual transformation for God's people.

II. Theme: The gospel is the primary concern for followers of Jesus.

Section 6: Conclusion (15:14–16:27)

I. Paul details his travel plans, including a hoped-for visit to Rome (15:14–33).

II. Paul concludes with personal greetings for various people and groups within the church at Rome (16:1–27).

Let's Go Deeper!

Questions

1. What truth from this lesson affected you most and why?

2. Has this teaching changed your concept of grace in any way? How so? How will this new understanding affect your daily life? (Be specific.)

3. Have you limited God's grace toward yourself or others? How so?

4. Read Luke 15:11–32. Can you see yourself in this story? In what way? What does this story reveal about the nature of the Father? What message about God's unlimited, boundless, and overflowing grace is revealed in this story?

5. Read 1 Peter 5:10 and 2 Peter 3:18. Describe Peter's personal understanding of Jesus' grace. What does it mean to you that you "grow in grace and intimacy" with the Lord? How have you experienced the connection between grace and intimacy?

Deeper Still!

Activations

His Throne of Grace
Grace is described in this lesson as being God's default setting. When we deserve a lecture, he gives us a kiss.

- "You kissed my heart with forgiveness, in spite of all I've done. You've healed me inside and out from every disease" (Psalm 103:3).

- "But Christ proved God's passionate love for us by dying in our place while we were still lost and ungodly!" (Romans 5:8).

We are the blessed ones! We are the well and truly loved children of God. For us, mercy triumphs over and over and over and over…for all eternity. The Father has set his holy affection upon us and adopted us into his family. Grace has placed us eternally in Christ.

Jesus, our Lord, is not ashamed to call us brothers and sisters. Just like in the story of the prodigal son, when we show up at the door needing more grace and love, God doesn't have to check our account to see if we are overdrawn. No, there is enough grace within the beautiful heart of God to cover all of our withdrawals. Our brother, Jesus, beckons us to come and draw near.

> So now we draw near freely and boldly to where grace is enthroned, to receive mercy's kiss and discover the grace we urgently need to strengthen us in our time of weakness. (Hebrews 4:16)

You are under his canopy of amazing grace. Grace has fully *saved* you. Therefore, you are saved from all sin, healed from all infirmity, and delivered from all demonic power forever. Rest in his grace and receive his mercy-kiss (Psalm 119:75–77). The highest price of all was paid to give you the greatest gift of all: God's undiluted grace.

1. Spend some quality time soaking in this truth—saying it, praying it, and praising God for it.
2. Creatively express in some way the revelation of grace you received through this lesson. Here are some examples: journal it, sing it, dance it, paint or draw it, explain it to another person, or put it to poetry.

Let's Pray

Lord, help me to rely fully on your great grace. Help me also to be more gracious and more graceful to others. Lord, let grace, loving-kindness, and faithful covenant love be the hallmark and the fragrance of my life…like it is of yours. Help me be a faithful witness and ambassador of the pure, unadulterated grace of God. Amen.

Paul and His Mission

(Romans 1:1–10)

The Power of the Gospel (Romans 1:1–7)

Introduction to Paul's Credentials

Paul begins Romans with one of his longest prescripts. He spends seven verses introducing himself before he launches into the body of the letter itself.

Paul

Who is this man? Paul's amazing transformation from a persecutor of Christians to a powerful missionary to the gentiles is a picture of the work of grace in his own life. In his day, no one thought of Paul as particularly important. He wasn't the emperor; Nero was. Today, however, we can argue, even by secular standards, that Paul was one of the most influential of all Roman citizens because of his response to God's calling for his life.

When we, too, have an encounter as Paul did with the risen Lord Jesus, we realize Jesus is the only worthy One. We fully dedicate our lives to exalt him and increase his fame throughout the earth so that all may truly see the beautiful One and make him their holy pursuit as well.

Verse 1 (and 7)

> Paul, a loving and loyal servant of the Anointed One, Jesus. He called me to be his apostle and set me apart with a mission to reveal God's wonderful gospel. (7) I write to all his beloved chosen ones in Rome, for you are also called as holy ones. May his joyous grace and total well-being, flowing from our Father and the Lord Jesus Christ, rest upon you.

Paul, a Servant

Paul refers to himself as a *doulos* in the Greek, which is a servant who serves out of love and not duty. Historically, a *doulos* slave would not claim his freedom in the year of jubilee (when slaves were, by law, set free) but would instead choose to remain in loving service to his master. This is Paul's heart.

The Old Testament servant who wanted to remain in service to his master was bound only by love, not law or duty. A provision was made for this unique devotion: "But if the servant declares, 'I love my master and my wife and children and do not want to go free,' then his master must take him before the judges. He shall take him to the door or the doorpost and pierce his ear with an awl. Then he will be his servant for life" (Exodus 21:5–6 NIV).

As we lower our lives in humility and love, knocking upon the "gate"—Jesus Christ is the Gateway (John 10:9)—he pierces our hearts, and his truth transforms us into his "servant for life," a loving slave, his devoted *doulos*.

Paul, an Apostle

The word *apostle* means "one who is sent with authority." First servant, then apostle. First *identity*, then *ministry*. We need this truth in our heart, don't we? You're not an apostle (or any type of true leader) if you're not first a *doulos*. Paul was called as an apostle and set apart, but the preparation for his mission (taking the wonderful news of salvation to the gentiles) took place over a period of many years.

Paul is also making the case that he is a real apostle. Many in the early church didn't see him this way because he wasn't one of the Twelve or Matthias, who replaced Judas. They saw him as a latecomer with less authority. However, Paul wasn't using this word in the generic sense or assuming a title that wasn't his to take: Jesus himself set Paul apart to be Jesus' authoritative representative and to share the gospel with the gentiles.

Christ, "the Anointed One"

"Christ" is not Jesus' last name; it is a title, a term for the Messiah. Jesus is the Anointed One, the fulfillment of the three Old Testament offices that God anointed (selected and set apart for special service).

- *Prophet* (Psalm 105:15; Deuteronomy 18:18; and fulfilled in John 7:40)

- *Priest* (Exodus 29:7; Leviticus 4:3; Psalm 110:4; and fulfilled in Hebrews 6:19–20)

- *King* (1 Samuel 2:10; Psalm 2:2, 6; and fulfilled in Mark 15:26 and Revelation 19:16)

A Preacher of the Wonderful News

Paul was "set apart," which means "permanently divided off from." (This is the root word for "pharisee," a separated one, and some see this as Paul hinting that his time as a Pharisee was all in God's plan to train him and prepare him for the gospel of grace and glory.) Paul knew he was unique and separated for a special ministry for God, just as the Levites were separated from the other tribes for priestly service.

Verse 2

My commission is to preach the good news. Yet it is not entirely new, but the fulfillment of the hope promised to us through his prophets in the sacred Scriptures.

Commissioned to Preach

Preaching may not always be popular, but God, indeed, calls preachers. We need the fiery, thundering voices of radical, sold-out, "John the Baptizer" preachers in every generation. God's wisdom is higher than human wisdom, and he has chosen the simple method of preaching to call lost hearts home: "For in his wisdom, God designed that all the world's wisdom would be insufficient to lead people to the discovery of himself. He took great delight in baffling the wisdom of the world by using the simplicity of preaching the story of the cross in order to save those who believe it" (1 Corinthians 1:21).

The Gospel

- *Gospel* means "the good news."

  o It is the message that Christ died for our sins, was buried and rose again, and now is able to save all who trust him (1 Corinthians 15:1–4).

- It is the gospel of God (Romans 1:1).

  o It originates with God; it was not invented by people.

- It is the gospel of Christ (Romans 1:16).

  o It centers on Christ, the Savior.

- Paul also calls it "the gospel of [God's] Son" (Romans 1:9).

  o This indicates that Jesus Christ is God.

- Paul called it "my gospel" (Romans 16:25–26).

  o By this, he meant to indicate the special emphasis he gave in his ministry to the doctrine of the church and the place of the gentiles in the plan of God.

- The gospel is not a new message.

> o It was promised in the Old Testament, beginning in Genesis 3:15.
>
> o The prophet Isaiah certainly preached the gospel in passages such as Isaiah 1:18, and chapters 53 and 55.
>
> o The salvation we enjoy today was promised by the prophets though they did not fully understand all that they were preaching and writing (1 Peter 1:10–12).

Verses 3–4

> For the gospel is all about God's Son. As a man he descended from David's royal lineage, but as the mighty Son of God he was raised from the dead and miraculously set apart with a display of triumphant power supplied by the Spirit of Holiness. And now Jesus is our Lord and our Messiah.

Son of David, Son of God

To prove Jesus' messiahship, Paul highlights his natural lineage as being from the family of David, as well as showing Jesus to be God's own Son through his resurrection and his "triumphant power."

Missionary to the Gentiles

There were both Jews and gentiles in the house churches of Rome because Paul addresses both in this letter.

- Jews: Romans 2:17–29; 4:1; 7:1.

- Gentiles: Romans 1:13; 11:13–24; 15:15–21.

The churches in Rome were not founded by Peter or any other apostle. If they had been, Paul would not have planned to visit Rome because his policy was to minister only where no other apostle had gone (Romans 15:20–21).

Verse 5

> Through him grace cascaded into us, empowering us with the gift of apostleship, so that we can win people from every nation into the obedience that comes from faith, to bring honor to his name.

A Faithful Commitment

In the Hebraic mindset, there is no such thing as a belief without a corresponding obedience to that belief. As Christians, we are disciples of Christ; we are faithfully obedient to him. *Faith empowers us to walk in obedience.*

Paul's mission was to lead people into the obedience that comes from faith (v. 5). I liken this to "lightning and thunder"—faith is the lightning bolt, and obedience is the thunder.

Verse 6

> And you are among the chosen ones who are called to belong to Jesus, the Anointed One.

"The Call"

In these first verses, notice the repetition of the word *called*: Paul was called to be an apostle; the believers were the called of Jesus Christ; and they were also called saints. (Note: They weren't called *to be* saints—they already *were* saints. A saint is a set-apart one, and the person who trusts Jesus Christ is set apart and is a saint.)

Salvation is not something that we do for God; it is God who calls us in his grace (2 Thessalonians 2:13–14). When you trust Christ, you are saved by his grace, and you experience his peace.

Paul's Passion and Prayer for the Roman Believers (Romans 1:8–10)

Paul Was Thankful and Prayerful

The Christians in Rome did not know of Paul's prayer support, but the Lord knew about it and honored it. I wonder how many of us are fully aware of the people who are praying for us. One of the burdens of Paul's prayer was that God would permit him to visit Rome and minister to the churches there. He would have visited them sooner, but his missionary work had kept him busy (Romans 15:15–33). He was about to leave Corinth for Jerusalem to deliver the special offering received from the gentile churches for the poor Jewish saints. He hoped he would be able to travel from Jerusalem to Rome and then on to Spain, and he was hoping for a prosperous journey.

Actually, Paul's journey was very perilous, and he arrived in Rome a *prisoner* as well as a *preacher*. In Jerusalem he was arrested in the temple, falsely accused by the Jewish authorities, and eventually sent to Rome as the emperor's prisoner to be tried before Caesar. When Paul wrote this letter, he had no idea that he would go through imprisonment and even a shipwreck before arriving in Rome. At the close of the letter (Romans 15:30–33), he asked the believers in Rome to pray for him as he contemplated this trip, and it is a good thing that they did pray!

Verse 8

> I give thanks to God for all of you, because the testimony of your faith is spreading throughout the world.

"All of You"

All means all! We can learn from Paul the beauty of selfless, unconditional love no matter people's condition or behavior.

Their Testimony

The church of Rome, which consisted of many house churches, was famous "throughout the world" for strong, persistent faith.

Verse 9

> And God knows that I pray for you continually and at all times. For I serve and worship him with my spirit in the gospel of his Son.

"Continually"

What a powerful reality. How would our lives, families, ministries, and relationships excel if we have the habit of continual prayer? When we really get a revelation of the power of prayer, we will become more devoted to it like Paul was. God moves when we pray. Through prayer we have access to the power of God, and prayer makes the way for God to act and do the impossible.

A Heart for Others

Two of the most powerful things we can do for others are to celebrate them with true thankfulness for who they are and to pray for them with genuine love. How very powerful the church of Jesus Christ would be if we all took this posture toward others!

Choose Thankfulness

None of us has arrived. We all need to learn and grow. But still we choose a posture of thankfulness to God for the work he has already done and for his faithfulness that will cause him to complete that work. We thank God, and we ask for more—for ourselves and for our fellow believers.

"With My Spirit"

Think of all that the great apostle Paul accomplished in his *doulos* ministry to the King, and he says it all flowed from his spirit. There is a key here for us: we can worship, seek, serve, pray, and minister from our spirit, not our own strength or might.

Verse 10

> My desire and constant prayer is that I would succeed in
> coming to you, according to the plan and timing of God.

Paul's Visit to Rome

Even though Paul prayed and desired to visit the church in Rome
to minister to them, his eventual journey to Rome came because of
his arrest for the gospel's sake. According to church tradition, Rome
was probably the end of Paul's earthly journey. Many believe he was
beheaded while imprisoned in Rome.

Although Paul wrote this magnificent letter to the Romans
from Corinth, he assured them that his great desire was to visit
them personally as soon as he was able. He wanted them to know
how dear they were to him. The Christian faith is not one of avoidance; it is a missionary faith that requires us to go where we are
called despite any possible dangers.

Paul was a fiery servant of God and lover of God's people! We
can learn so much by making his life and ministry a focus of study.
Lord, enflame our hearts with this same love, in Jesus' name. Amen.

Let's Go Deeper!

Questions

1. Paul refers to himself as a *doulos*, a loving servant to Christ.
   In God's "upside-down kingdom," the path to greatness is
   servitude. Read John 13:1–17. Jesus is the pattern Son, and
   Paul is the pattern man. How does their example of humble service speak to your heart? How does it compare with
   concepts of ministry in our day?

2. Paul declared he was commissioned to preach the gospel (v. 2). You, as Christ's disciple, have also received this commission (Mark 16:15). Take a little self-evaluation and inventory. How prepared are *you* to share the gospel? (Read 1 Corinthians 15:1–4 for a short and clear "heart of the gospel.") Paul called it "my gospel." How prepared are you to share *your* gospel?

3. In this study, we have discussed how grace seems too good to be true, and yet it is true. Have you limited grace in your heart? Have you been trusting in your works to "add to" his grace? It's time to take the limits off. How will a fuller understanding of the magnitude of God's grace affect your life? (See 1 Corinthians 15:10; 2 Timothy 2:1; and Ephesians 2:8–9.)

4. What concepts are included in the title "Son of God" (Romans 1:3–4)? (Are we not all sons and daughters of God?)

5. In verse 3, Jesus is said to be in the lineage of David or "the seed of David." Jesus was the "seed of the woman" in Genesis 3:15, the "seed of Abraham" in Galatians 3:16, and here in Romans 1, the "seed of David." (See also Acts 13:16–41.) How does this prove God fulfilled his promises through the birth and life of Jesus Christ?

Deeper Still!

Activations

Romans is a profound book. It is considered by many to be the chief book of the New Testament. Its power is evidenced by the world-changing revivals and reform that it has sparked globally.

Friend, are you ready for your own personal revival and reformation? Be encouraged to open your heart wide to see what you've not seen before and experience more than you have previously in your walk with God. Let go of the ways you've limited the power of God and the abundance of his grace. Allow God to burst your bubbles like he did for Luther, Wesley, Augustine, and countless devoted saints throughout human history.

This is your moment, your season to be ignited by heaven with fresh fire and passion. Precious promises have been given to those who will simply open their hearts for more. So, open wide!

Read Exodus 16:33 and Revelation 2:17. Not all the manna went away with the wilderness journey. Who has access to this special portion of hidden manna? What might it represent? (See Psalm 119:18; Psalm 119:162; Proverbs 2:3–10; Matthew 13:11; and Luke 8:17.)

Let's Pray

> *Father, I come humbly before your throne today and ask*
> *for life-changing encounters with you through this study*
> *of Romans. Lord, I ask you to bring reformation and*
> *transformation in my life. I open up my heart for more of*
> *you, God, and I ask for your fire of revival to ignite me. I*
> *want to burn with love for you because you are worthy of*
> *such devotion and passion. In Jesus' name, I pray. Amen.*

Without Excuse

(Romans 1:11–2:29)

Proclaiming the Power of the Gospels (Romans 1:11–17)

Paul's Love and Apostolic Care

Because of Paul's loving and personal words, one might come to the logical conclusion that Paul himself planted the church in Rome, but he did not. His great love for the Christians at Rome came not because he birthed this church but because he was birthing it in prayer through his intercession. He volunteered, as it were, to carry the yoke of the Lord in prayer for these saints and, therefore, was filled by the Holy Spirit with God's love for them. This power and love fill all those who make themselves available.

Verses 11–12

I yearn to come and be face-to-face with you and get to know you. For I long to impart to you some spiritual gift that will empower you to stand strong in your faith. Now, this means that when we come together and are side by side, something wonderful will be released. We can expect to be co-encouraged and co-comforted by each other's faith!

Love

The measure of your love is the extent of the measure of your authority in ministry. True ministry only results from true love. We can't "drum up" that love, but we can offer our lives to God to be dispensers of his divine love. We can choose, like Paul, to make ourselves vessels of love. When we make that choice, God's love comes flooding in: "We can now experience the endless love of God cascading into our hearts through the Holy Spirit who lives in us!" (Romans 5:5).

"Side by Side"

did not focus on self

This is the pastoral heart in Paul, the great missionary. Some of the saints in Rome were very dear to Paul, such as Priscilla and Aquila (16:3–4), who risked their lives for him; the "much loved" Persis (v. 12); and others who had labored and suffered with Paul. But he also loved the believers who he did not know, and he longed to be able to share some spiritual gift with them. He was looking forward to a time of mutual blessing in the love of Christ.

Paul Longed for a Spiritual Harvest among Them

In these next verses, the earnest heart of the apostle Paul is on full display. His passion for souls, his love for God's people, and his mission to establish the church through his apostolic gifting compelled him to minister to the believers in Rome.

Verse 13

> So, my dear brothers and sisters, please don't interpret my failure to visit you as indifference, because many times I've intended to come but have not been released to do so up to now. For I long to enjoy a harvest of spiritual fruit among you, like I have experienced among the nations.

"Harvest"

This was the delightful goal: a harvest of souls, spiritual fruit, and lives set free! We are heaven's harvesters, and wherever we go, we should long for and expect an ingathering for God of greater fruit-fulness and greater intimacy with God. All hands are needed, no matter who you are or what you feel holds you back. You don't have to be an expert for God to use you in life-changing ways.

Verse 14

> Love obligates me to preach to everyone, to those who are among the elite and those who are among the outcasts, to those who are wise and educated as well as to those who are foolish and unlearned.

"Love Obligates Me"

As the apostle to the gentiles, Paul had an obligation to minister in Rome. He would have fulfilled that obligation sooner, but his other labors had hindered him. Sometimes Paul was hindered because of the work of Satan (1 Thessalonians 2:17–20), but in this case, he was hindered because of the work of the Lord. Paul understood that God opens and closes doors for a reason. There was so much to do in Asia Minor and Greece that he could not immediately spare time for Rome.

Paul Was Eager to See Them

In verse 15, the word translated as "excited" means "eager, with a ready mind." Paul was not eager to die—though he was prepared to die. He was eager to visit Rome so that he might minister to the believers there. It was not the eagerness of a sightseer, but the eagerness of a soul-winner. Also, this letter was his "letter of intro-duction" that prepared the believers in Rome for his visit. No doubt, the false teachers had already gotten to Rome and were seeking to poison the Christians against Paul (see Romans 3:8). Some would accuse him of being anti-law. Others would say he was a traitor to the Jewish nation. Still others would twist his teaching about grace and try to prove that he taught loose living. No wonder Paul was eager to get to Rome! He wanted to share with them the fullness of the gospel of Christ.

Verse 15

> This is why I am so excited about coming to preach the wonderful message of Jesus to you in Rome!

Excited and Eager

There is just something remarkable about a heart that loves to win souls. You can't keep them quiet about God or his goodness. They leak the fragrance and love of Christ everywhere they go. They truly go forth bearing precious seed to sow, sometimes with weeping, but one thing they will never regret is sharing the gospel with others. There is great reward and blessing attached to the labor of sowing God's Word.

> They may weep as they go out carrying their seed to sow,
> but they will return with joyful laughter and shouting with
>   gladness
> as they bring back armloads of blessing and a harvest
>   overflowing! (Psalm 126:6)

After reading the evidence of Paul's concern for the Christians at Rome, these saints could not but give thanks to God for the apostle Paul and his burden to come and minister to them.

Paul's Unshakable Confidence

With undiluted passion and determination, Paul boldly upholds the pure gospel of grace. He is supremely confident in the power of the gospel to transform lives. Having lived most of his life steeped in a religious mindset that focused on outward works to earn righteousness, Paul passionately proclaims the message of the righteousness that only comes by faith. This gospel truth (v. 17) is the one that turned the world upside down in the days of Martin Luther: the just shall live by faith. It truly is "liberating power unleashed in us through Christ!" (v. 16).

Verses 16-17

I refuse to be ashamed of the wonderful message of God's liberating power unleashed in us through Christ! For I am thrilled to preach that everyone who believes is saved—the Jew first, and then people everywhere! This gospel unveils a continual revelation of God's righteousness—a perfect righteousness given to us when we believe. And it moves us from receiving life through faith, to the power of living by faith. This is what the Scripture means when it says:

"We are right with God through life-giving faith!"

The Gospel Is Power

Why be ashamed of power? Power is the one thing that Rome boasted of the most. Greece might have its philosophy, but Rome had its power. The fear of Rome hovered over the empire like a cloud. Were they not the conquerors? Were not the Roman legions stationed all over the known world? But with all of her military power, Rome was still a weak nation. The philosopher Seneca called the city of Rome "a cesspool of iniquity," and the writer Juvenal called it a "filthy sewer into which the dregs of the empire flood."[12]

No wonder Paul was not ashamed. He was taking to sinful Rome the *one message* that had the power to change men's lives. He had seen the gospel work in other wicked cities, such as Corinth and Ephesus, and he was confident that it would work in Rome as well. It had transformed his own life, and he knew it could transform the lives of others.

The Operation, Outreach, and Outcome of the Gospel

- *The Operation of the Gospel:* power of God (v. 16)

  o There is no need to add to the gospel.

---

12   Warren W. Wiersbe, *The Bible Exposition Commentary, vol. 1: The New Testament* (Colorado Spring, CO: Cook Communications Ministries, 2001), 517.

o The pure gospel is the power of God for salvation.

- *The Outreach of the Gospel:* everyone who believes

  o The gospel is not *exclusive.* It is not for a favored few; it is for *whosoever* will believe.

  o "And he said to them, 'As you go into all the world, preach openly the wonderful news of the gospel to the entire human race!'" (Mark 16:15).

  o "And it's true: 'Everyone who calls on the Lord's name will experience new life'" (Romans 10:13).

- *The Outcome of the Gospel:* salvation, deliverance, wholeness, righteousness, faith (Romans 1:16–17)

  o All God requires of us is to *believe.* He doesn't ask us to *behave;* he asks us to believe.

  o Grace will change behavior.

  o No matter where you are in your believing, God is moving you to a greater place of faith. He is taking every one of us from faith to faith.

The Just Shall Live by Faith

In all, there are more than sixty references to faith or unbelief in Romans. The truth of "the just shall live by faith" appears in four distinct passages in most English translations—first in Habakkuk and then three times in the New Testament. It's important to note that Hebrew does not have a word for "cognitive assent" or "intellectual belief," and the word often translated as *faith* is more action orientated than the English word.

1. "Behold the proud, his soul is not upright in him; but the just shall live by his faith" (Habakkuk 2:4 NKJV).
2. "It is obvious that no one achieves the righteousness of God by attempting to keep the law, for it is written: 'The one

who is in a right relationship with God will live by faith!'"
(Galatians 3:11).

3. "And he also says, 'My righteous ones will live from my faith. But if fear holds them back, my soul is not content with them!'" (Hebrews 10:38).

4. "We are right with God through life-giving faith!" (Romans 1:17).

As revealed in these verses, Paul emphasized different aspects of this profound truth in Romans, Galatians, and Hebrews.

- Romans amplifies "the righteous!"

- Galatians underscores "shall live!"

- Hebrews emphasizes "by faith!"

God Is Both Just and the Justifier

1. *The Problem*—The problem of "How can a holy God ever forgive sinners and still be holy?" is answered in the gospel. Through the death and resurrection of Christ, God is seen to be both *just* and the *justifier* (Romans 3:26).

2. *The Solution*—The gospel reveals a righteousness that is by faith. In the Old Testament, righteousness was by works, but sinners soon discovered they could not obey God's law and meet his righteous demands.

3. *The Final Verdict*—When you study Romans, in a sense, you walk into a courtroom.

First, Paul called Jews and gentiles to the stand and found both guilty before God. Then he explained God's marvelous way of salvation: justification by faith. At this point, he answered his accusers and defended God's salvation. They claimed, "This plan of salvation will encourage people to sin!" and "It is against the very law of God!" But Paul refuted them and, in so doing, explained how Christians can experience victory, liberty, and security because they have been declared "not guilty!"

Righteousness

Romans 1:17 is a key verse. In it, Paul announces the theme: the righteousness of God. The word *righteousness* is used in one way or another over sixty times in this letter (righteous, just, and justified). God's righteousness is revealed in the gospel; for in the death of Christ, God revealed his righteousness by punishing sin, and in the resurrection of Christ, he revealed his righteousness by making salvation available to the believing sinner. There are three ways we can see God's righteousness:

- An *attribute* of God—the righteousness that *belongs to God*

- A *gift* he gives—the righteousness *from God*

- An *activity* of God—actively brought into your life *by God*

Eternal Focus

In verses 16 and 17, we see Paul's passion for souls. Let's make our hearts open and available to be containers of that same holy passion. Only two things are eternal: the Word of God and souls. Scripture proclaims, "The Word of the Lord endures forever! And this is the Word that was announced to you!" (1 Peter 1:25). Let's focus our lives with a view to eternity and live for what matters most.

Jesus lived his short life on earth with just such a passionate focus. He walked this world with a steadfast vision for the salvation of souls and the coming of the kingdom. He wants us to live with the same eternal perspective, and so he taught us, "There is a day coming when everyone who has ever died will hear my voice calling them back to life, and they will come out of their graves! Those who have done what is good will experience a resurrection to eternal life. And those who have practiced evil will taste the resurrection of judgment!" (John 5:28–29).

The Gentile World Is Guilty before God (Romans 1:18–32)

A Gospel for the Guilty

Telling people the good news of the gospel often means telling them the bad news that they are sinners in need of a Savior. Warning people is our loving responsibility. People need to know that heaven is real and that hell is also real. We all will stand before an awesome God one day. Better to do so trusting in the precious blood of Jesus than in human reasoning or self-righteousness. You can read all the self-help books in the entire world but "there is none righteous, no, not one" (Romans 3:10 NKJV), and the cure for man's guilt and sin is not a program or philosophy. *It is three nails.* The pure gospel is the power of God for salvation.

Intelligence

Newsflash: humanity is not *evolving* but rather is *devolving*. In fact, the depravity of human hearts works actively against the knowledge of God, trying to smother it. Rebellion is at the core of the fallen human nature, and it does not love the light but rather hides from it and tries to hide it. Human history *began* with people knowing God. It is not the story of a beast that worshiped idols and then evolved into a person worshiping one God. Sadly, human history is just the opposite: people knew God but turned from the truth and rejected God.

Verse 18

> For God in heaven unveils his holy anger breaking forth against every form of sin, both toward ungodliness that lives in hearts and evil actions. For the wickedness of humanity deliberately smothers the truth and keeps people from acknowledging the truth about God.

God's Wrath against Sin

God's anger is upon sin in all its forms of ungodliness and evil actions. Even though it may seem as if he is ignoring wickedness, he is not. All who are unsaved are under his wrath and condemnation. They experience the weight of guilt that can only be escaped at the cross and remedied by the blood of Jesus.

Verse 19

> In reality, the truth of God is known instinctively, for God has embedded this knowledge inside every human heart.

Embedded Truth

We are *hardwired* by God to recognize the truth of who God is. That is why we are without excuse. We all need salvation and forgiveness. Creation's glory also leaves humans without excuse. God's truth is available and revealed in the world he has made. So what about those who have never heard? There is a sense in which everyone has already heard. (The heavens declare it, according to Psalm 19.) But we have turned away from God and his truth.

Ignorance

First, Paul explained why intelligence is not an excuse, and he now describes why ignorance is not an excuse. People knew God (this is clear), but they did not want to commune with God or honor him as God. Instead of being thankful for all that God had given them, humans refused to thank God or give him the glory he deserves. People were willing to use God's gifts, but they were not willing to worship and praise God for his gifts. The result was an empty mind and a darkened heart. The worshiper became the philosopher, but this empty wisdom only revealed humanity's foolishness.

Verse 20

> Opposition to truth cannot be excused on the basis of igno-
> rance, because from the creation of the world, the invisible

qualities of God's nature have been made visible, such as his eternal power and transcendence. He has made his wonderful attributes easily perceived, for seeing the visible makes us understand the invisible. So then, this leaves everyone without excuse.

The Nature of God Is Made Visible

The qualities of God's beautiful nature, who he really is, is made known and visible to those who seek and look for him. He makes himself visible to us through his eternal power and his transcendence.

Verses 21–23

Throughout human history the fingerprints of God were upon them, yet they refused to honor him as God or even be thankful for his kindness. Instead, they entertained corrupt and foolish thoughts about what God was like. This left them with nothing but misguided hearts, steeped in moral darkness. Although claiming to be wise, they were in fact shallow fools. For only a fool would trade the unfading splendor of the immortal God to worship the fading image of other humans, idols made to look like people, animals, birds, and even creeping reptiles!

The Issue of Idolatry

Mankind did not get tricked into idol worship. We chose it by pushing aside the embedded knowledge of God within us and embracing a foolish, sinful, and futile false reality. Atheism as well as idolatry both require a foolish heart. (See Psalm 14:1 and 53:1.)

Created to Worship

Having suppressed God's truth and refusing to acknowledge God's glory, humanity was left without a god...and that's a problem, for mankind is created to worship. *We must worship something.* If we will not worship the true God, we will worship a false god even if we must manufacture one. The psalmist describes man's innate quest for an object of worship with these words:

> Their possessions will never satisfy.
> Their lifeless and futile works cannot bring life to them!
> Their things can't talk to them or answer their prayers.
> Blind men can only create blind things.
> Those deaf to God can only make a deaf image.
> Dead men can only create dead idols.
> And everyone who trusts in these powerless, dead things
> will be just like what they worship—powerless and dead!
> (Psalm 135:16–18)

(See also Deuteronomy 27:15; Isaiah 44:15; and Habakkuk 2:18.)

Making Idols

Romans actually lists the forms these idols take people, animals, birds, and reptiles.

Interestingly, human beings top the list. We are quite prone to turn to self-worship and man-worship when we will not give God the glory due his name. This worship of self and humanity is depicted in Revelation as the worship of the beast: "Everyone on earth will worship the wild beast—those whose names have not been written from the foundation of the world in the Book of the Life of the Lamb who was slain...This will require wisdom to understand: Let the one with insight interpret the number of the wild beast, for it is humanity's number—666" (Revelation 13:8, 18).

Indulgence

From idolatry to immorality is just one short step. If people are their own gods, then they can do whatever they please and fulfill any desires without fear of judgment. God lifted his hand and gave them over to their desires, which brought them into even deeper darkness.

Verses 24–27

> This is why God lifted off his restraining hand and let them have full expression of their sinful and shameful desires. They were given over to moral depravity, dishonoring their bodies by sexual perversion among themselves—all because they traded the truth of God for a lie. They worshiped and served the things God made rather than the God who made all things—glory and praises to him forever and ever! Amen!
>
> For this reason God gave them over to their own disgraceful and vile passions. Enflamed with lust for one another, men and women ignored the natural order and exchanged normal sexual relations for homosexuality. Women engaged in lesbian conduct, and men committed shameful acts with men, receiving in themselves the due penalty for their deviation.

Trading Truth for Lies

We reach the climax of man's battle with God's truth when humanity exchanges the truth of God for "a lie," abandoning truth completely. In total delusion, people are their own gods, and they worship and serve themselves and not the Creator. This is the same lie Eve heard from Satan in the garden: "You will be like God" (Genesis 3:5). Satan has always wanted the worship that belongs only to God (Isaiah 14:12–15 and Matthew 4:8–10), and through idolatry, he receives that worship because "when an unbeliever offers a sacrifice to an idol, it is not offered to the true God but to a demon. I don't want you to be participants with demons!" (1 Corinthians 10:20).

Self-Deification Results in Self-Indulgence

If you become your own god, you have no limitations or boundaries outside your own choosing. The result of this self-deification is *self-indulgence,* and here in verses 26–27, Paul mentions a vile sin that was rampant in his day and has become increasingly prevalent in our own day: homosexuality.

This sin is repeatedly condemned in Scripture (Genesis 18:20ff; 1 Corinthians 6:9–10; and Jude 7). Paul characterizes it as "vile" and "disgraceful" as well as against "natural order." Not only were the men guilty, but the women were as well.

"Gave Them Over"

Because of their sin, "God gave them over" to their sin (reiterated three times in Romans 1:24, 26, 28), which means that he permitted them to go on in their sins and reap the sad consequences. They received "in themselves the due penalty for their deviation" (v. 27). This reveals the meaning of Romans 1:18, "The wrath of God is being revealed from heaven" (literal translation). God revealed his wrath not by sending fire from heaven but by abandoning sinful humans to their lustful ways. But there was yet one more stage in their devolution.

Impenitence

Further degradation made them impenitent, unwilling to repent. Can you see the downward spiral? This is the path of sin. It promises fulfillment but leads only to futility. It promises pleasure but leads only to perdition. It promises solace but leads only to spiritual slavery.

Verses 28–32

> And because they thought it was worthless to embrace the true knowledge of God, God gave them over to a worthless mind-set, to break all rules of proper conduct. Their sinful lives became full of every kind of evil, wicked schemes, greed, and cruelty. Their hearts overflowed with jealous cravings, and with conflict and strife, which drove them into hateful arguments and murder. They are deceitful liars full of hostility. They are gossips who love to spread malicious slander. With inflated egos they hurl hateful insults

at God, yet they are nothing more than arrogant boasters. They are rebels against their parents and totally immoral. They are senseless, faithless, ruthless, heartless, and completely merciless. Although they are fully aware of God's laws and proper order, and knowing that those who do all of these things deserve to die, yet they still go headlong into darkness, encouraging others to do the same and applauding them when they do!

Sin Results in a Worthless Mindset

When people began to feel the tragic consequences of their sins, you would think they would have repented and sought God, but just the opposite was true. Because they were abandoned by God, they could only become worse. People did not even want to retain God in their knowledge! So, "God gave them over" this time to a "worthless mind-set" (Romans 1:28), which means a mind that cannot form right judgments. They now abandoned themselves to sin. Paul names twenty-four specific sins, all of which are with us still today. (For other such lists, see Mark 7:20–23; Galatians 5:19–21; 1 Timothy 1:9–10; and 2 Timothy 3:2–5.)

Leading Others Also into Darkness

This is the final step of humanity's devolution. People not only committed these sins in open defiance of God but also encouraged others into sin and applauded them when they succumbed. *How far humanity fell.* We began in the garden, glorifying God and clothed in glory, but ended up exchanging that glory for idols. We began knowing God but ended refusing to keep the knowledge of God in our mind and heart. We began as the highest of God's creatures, made in the image of God, but we ended lower than the beasts and insects because we worshiped them as gods.

This is the verdict: "This leaves everyone without excuse" (Romans 1:20).

Guilty before God (Romans 2)

Jews and Gentiles

Some Bible scholars disagree about whom Paul was addressing in this section of Romans. All of Paul's congregations were likely blends of pure gentiles, God-fearing gentiles, Jews who didn't believe Jesus was the Messiah, Jews who did believe in Jesus, and a wide range in between. Those who say this section was directed toward the Jews point out that Paul's discussion of the law in Romans 2:12–16 would have been more meaningful to a Jew than to a gentile, and in Romans 2:17, he openly addressed his reader as "a Jew." Those who believe Paul was addressing gentiles mention that he addressed those "people who don't possess the law" in Romans 2:14.

Convincing some Jews of their guiltiness would not be an easy task since disobedience to God was one sin they did not want to confess. The Old Testament prophets were *persecuted* for accusing Israel of its sins, and Jesus was *crucified* for the same reason! Paul therefore "summoned" witnesses into the "courtroom" to prove the Jewish nation was as guilty as the gentiles. Their testimony is irrefutable.

We can just nearly hear the applause from some Jews as Paul goes through this list of sins, for they would heartily agree with this condemnation of the "gentile dogs." Some may have found it easy to dismiss Paul's previous list of sins, saying "This doesn't apply to me." They would never believe they were equally guilty...until Paul proved otherwise. It's important not to stereotype; not all Jews rejected Jesus or judged the gentiles, just as not all gentiles committed evil acts or practiced paganism. Jesus himself was a Jew, and so was Paul. Paul's goal in Romans, especially in this chapter, is to show the universal need for Jesus' sacrifice and the Christian faith while remaining true to the Jews and the promises God made to them.

Verses 1–3

> No matter who you are, before you judge the wickedness of others, you had better remember this: you are also without excuse, for you too are guilty of the same kind of things! When you judge others, and then do the same things they do, you condemn yourself. We know that God's judgment falls upon those who practice these things. God is always right, because he has all the facts. And no matter who you think you are, when you judge others who do these things and then do the same things yourself, what makes you think that you will escape God's judgment?

"No Matter Who You Think You Are"

Paul used this judgmental, "holier than thou" attitude to prove the guilt of the Jews, for the very things they condemned in the gentiles, they themselves were practicing. Many thought that they were free from judgment because they were God's chosen people. But Paul affirmed that God's election of the Jews made their responsibility and accountability *even greater.*

A Righteous Judgment

God's judgment is according to truth. He does not have one standard for Jews and another for gentiles. One who reads the list of sins in Romans 1:29–32 cannot escape the fact that each person is guilty of at least one of them. There are sins that contaminate "body and spirit" (2 Corinthians 7:1). There are "prodigal sons" and "elder brothers" (Luke 15:11–32). In condemning the gentiles for their sins, the Jews were really condemning themselves. As the old saying puts it, "When you point one of your fingers at somebody else, the other three fingers are pointing back at you."

The Purpose of the Law

The law is good! One purpose of the law is to expose the sin in our hearts and lead us to Christ, who offers us the only remedy for our sin: the cross. However, the law has no power to transform us or to remove wickedness. No, its only power is in revealing how much we need God's grace. Grace is what liberates the human heart.

Greater Blessing Means Greater Responsibility

Instead of their covenant with God shielding them and somehow qualifying them for special treatment from God, the blessings that the nation of Israel received from him gave them a *greater responsibility* to obey him and glorify him.

Verses 4–5

> Do the riches of his extraordinary kindness make you take him for granted and despise him? Haven't you experienced how kind and understanding he has been to you? Don't mistake his tolerance for acceptance. Do you realize that all the wealth of his extravagant kindness is meant to melt your heart and lead you into repentance? But because of your calloused heart and refusal to change direction, you are piling up wrath for yourself in the day of wrath, when God's righteous judgment is revealed.

His Kindness Is Meant to Melt Our Hearts

In his goodness, God had given Israel great spiritual and material riches. For example:

- A wonderful land
- A righteous law
- A temple
- A priesthood
- God's providential care
- Divine protection

God had patiently endured Israel's many sins and rebellions and had even sent them his Son to be their Messiah. Even after Israel crucified Christ, God gave them nearly forty more years of grace, withholding his judgment. It is not the judgment of God but the goodness of God that leads humans to repentance. His kindness woos us and melts our hearts. However, Israel did not repent.

Verses 6–11

For:

He will give to each one in return for what he has done.

For those living in constant goodness and doing what pleases him, seeking an unfading glory and honor and imperishable virtue, will experience eternal life. But those governed by selfishness and self-promotion, whose hearts are unresponsive to God's truth and would rather embrace unrighteousness, will experience the fullness of wrath.

Anyone who does evil can expect tribulation and distress—to the Jew first and also to the non-Jew. But when we do what pleases God, we can expect unfading glory, true honor, and a continual peace—to the Jew first and also to the non-Jew, for God sees us all without partiality.

All Humanity Is Facing the Judgment of God

In Romans 2:6–11, Paul was not teaching salvation by human goodness or human effort. He was explaining another basic principle of God's judgment: God judges according to deeds, just as he judges according to truth. Paul was dealing here with the consistent actions of a person's life, the total effect of his character and conduct. For example, David committed some terrible sins, but the total emphasis of his life was obedience to God. Judas confessed his sin and supplied the money for buying a cemetery for strangers, yet the total emphasis of his life was disobedience and unbelief.

True saving faith results in obedience and godly living even though there may be occasional falls. When God measured the deeds of the Jews, he found them to be as wicked as those of the gentiles. The fact that Jews occasionally celebrated a feast or even regularly honored the Sabbath day did not change the fact that without accepting Jesus as the Messiah, their consistent daily life was one of disobedience to God. God's blessings did not lead them to repentance.

God's Law

No matter our ethnicity (Jew or non-Jew) or our spiritual upbringing, we are all accountable for our behavior before a holy God. Will we stand before him trusting in our own goodness? This is the heart of the matter. Paul states the deeply penetrating and hard truth that only "doing all that the law says" (v. 13) makes us right before God. Such a statement forces us to evaluate where we stand in relation to God's law. Are we still working hard to keep it perfectly, or are we resting in the finished work of the cross?

Verses 12-13

> When people who have never been exposed to the laws of Moses commit sin, they will still perish for what they do. And those who are under the law of Moses and fail to obey it are condemned by the law. For it's not merely knowing the law that makes you right with God, but doing all that the law says that will cause God to pronounce you innocent.

With or without the Law

In verse 12, Paul divides all of humanity into two classes:

1. Those without the law—gentiles
2. Those under the law—Jews

Paul explained that the Jewish law only made the guilt of Israel that much greater. God did not give the law to the gentiles, and therefore, they would not be judged by the law. However, they were still without excuse.

Perfect Law-Keeping Is Impossible

It's not possession of the law that matters but doing the law. Having the law is a good thing, but one must obey it. This, then, presents the great dilemma: no one is righteous. With or without the law, we all need Christ.

God's Judgment

Not every person is raised to obey the Mosaic law or the Ten Commandments. They obey the "law" of their God-given conscience. This moral law, written on their hearts, guides them. Still, in either case, no one can fully keep the law. The law (moral or Mosaic) only reveals our sinful state and our need for salvation from God's judgment.

Verses 14–16

> For example, whenever people who don't possess the law as their birthright commit sin, it still confirms that a "law" is present in their conscience. For when they instinctively do what the law requires, that becomes a "law" to govern them, even though they don't have Mosaic law. It demonstrates that the requirements of the law are woven into their hearts. They know what is right and wrong, for their conscience validates this "law" in their heart. Their thoughts correct them in one instance and commend them in another.
> So this judgment will be revealed on the day when God, through Jesus the Messiah, judges the hidden secrets of people's hearts. And their response to my gospel will be the standard of judgment used in that day.

The Witness of the Human Conscience

The gentiles had "the requirements of the law...woven into their hearts" (v. 15). Wherever you go, you find people with an inner sense of right and wrong. This "inner judge" the Bible calls "conscience." You find among all cultures a sense of sin, a fear of judgment, and an attempt to atone for sins and appease whatever gods are feared. While gentiles don't have *the* Law (Torah), they do have a "law" written in their hearts. There is a witness from God left inside the human heart.

Secrets of the Heart

The Jews looked on the gentiles as blind, in the dark, foolish, immature, and ignorant. But if God found the "deprived" gentiles guilty, how much more guilty were the "privileged" Jews! God not only judges according to truth (Romans 2:2) and according to men's deeds (v. 6), but he also judges "the secrets of people's hearts" (v. 16). He sees what is in the soul of men, and therefore, his judgment is true.

The Jewish Religion Will Not Save You

No punches are pulled in the next portion of Scripture. Paul is humble, but he is straightforward and bold. He understood from his own past life the pride that ruled in the heart of many Jewish people. They excelled in having a "holier than thou" attitude toward "lesser" gentiles but failed to see their own sinful reality. Jesus is the only solution to our sinful condition. Many Jews refused to face this truth, so in these next verses, they get a forceful, blunt, and some might even say rude awakening.

Verses 17–24

> Now, you claim to be a Jew because you lean upon your trust in the law and boast in your relationship with God. And you claim to know the will of God, and to have the moral high ground because you've been taught the law of Moses. You are also confident that you are a qualified guide to those who are "blind," a shining light to those who live in darkness. You are confident that you are a true teacher of the foolish and immature, all because you have the treasury of truth and knowledge in the law of Moses. So let me ask you this: Why don't you practice what you preach? You preach, "Don't steal!" but are you a thief? You

are swift to tell others, "Don't commit adultery!" but are you guilty of adultery? You say, "I hate idolatry and false gods!" but do you withhold from the true God what is due him? Even though you boast in the law, you dishonor God, the Lawgiver, when you break it! For your actions seem to fulfill what is written:

> "God's precious name is cursed among the nations because of you."

The Offense of the Cross

This accusation was extremely offensive to any Jew who walked in great spiritual pride. They boasted in their relationship with God, but Paul reveals that they trusted in form and ritual but lacked in fire and relationship. They did not want to bow to the truth that their self-righteousness was filthy before God's holiness. Jesus described them this way:

> Great sorrow awaits you religious scholars and Pharisees—frauds and imposters! You are nothing more than tombs painted over with white paint—tombs that look shining and beautiful on the outside but filled with rotting corpses on the inside. Outwardly you masquerade as righteous people, but inside your hearts you are full of hypocrisy and lawlessness. (Matthew 23:27–28)

These people had a religion of outward action, not inward attitude. They may have been moral on the outside, but what about the heart? Our Lord's indictment of the Pharisees in Matthew 23 illustrates this principle perfectly. God not only sees the deeds, but he also sees the "true thoughts and secret motives of our hearts" (Hebrews 4:12). It is possible for someone to be guilty of theft, adultery, and idolatry (Romans 2:21–22) even if no one saw him or her commit these sins outwardly. In the Sermon on the Mount, we are told that such sins can be committed *in the heart.*

Bringing Defamation to God's Name

Instead of glorifying God among the gentiles, some Jews were dishonoring God, and in verse 24, Paul quoted Isaiah 52:5 to prove his point. The pagan gentiles had daily contact with the Jews in business and other activities, and they were not fooled by the Jews' devotion to the law. The very law that the Jews claimed to obey only exposed them.

Circumcision

No outward act, ritual, sacrament, or performance can ever make us holy or justified before God. Any outworking must only come from an inner working of God's grace. Circumcision is an outward sign of an inward covenant, much like a wedding ring a husband or wife wears in our day. The ring doesn't make a person married but is merely an outward designation of an inward reality. God always wants our heart. He wants to circumcise our hearts through new birth into the life of Christ by the power of the Holy Spirit.

Verses 25–29

> You trust in the covenant sign of circumcision, yet circumcision only has value if you faithfully keep the teachings of the law. But if you violate the law, you have invalidated your circumcision. And if the uncircumcised one faithfully keeps the law, won't his obedience make him more "Jewish" than the actual rite of circumcision? And won't the one who has never had the knife cut his foreskin be your judge when you break the law? You are not a Jew if it's only superficial— for it's more than the surgical cut of a knife that makes you Jewish. But you are Jewish because of the inward act of spiritual circumcision—a radical change that lays bare your heart. It's not by the principle of the written code, but by power of the Holy Spirit. For then your praise will not come from people, but from God himself!

A Covenant Sign for Israel

In the Jewish world of Paul's day, the two things that identified the Jewish people were the law and circumcision. This was the great mark of the covenant, and it had its beginning with Abraham, the father of the Jewish nation (Genesis 17). To the Jews, the gentiles were "uncircumcised dogs." The tragedy is that some Jews depended on this physical mark instead of the spiritual reality it represented (Deuteronomy 10:16; Jeremiah 9:26; Ezekiel 44:9). A true Jew is one who has had an inward spiritual experience in the heart and not merely an outward physical operation. People today make this same mistake with reference to water baptism, the Lord's Supper, or even church membership.

Covenant Must Not Be Superficial

God judges according to "the hidden secrets of people's hearts" (2:16). He is not impressed with mere outward formalities. An obedient gentile with no circumcision would be more acceptable than a disobedient Jew with circumcision. In fact, a disobedient Jew turns his circumcision into uncircumcision in God's sight, for God looks at the heart. Many Jews praised each other for their obedience to the law, but the important thing is the praise that comes from God and not human praise (2:29). When you think about the fact that even the name "Jew" comes from *Judah*, which means "praise," this statement takes on new meaning (Genesis 29:35 and 49:8). Sincere worship is what God desires from us. Jesus said the Father longs for our true adoration, Spirit to spirit:

> From now on, worshiping the Father will not be a matter of the right place but with a right heart. For God is a Spirit, and he longs to have sincere worshipers who adore him in the realm of the Spirit and in truth. (John 4:23–24)

Let's Go Deeper!

Questions

1. Paul gives us the example of combining prayer with thanksgiving. Read Colossians 1:3; Psalm 100:4; Philemon 1:4; and Philippians 4:6. What happens when we pray with gratitude? How does thanksgiving affect our hearts and prayer life?

2. Paul's incredible passion for soul-winning is an example for us to follow. He confessed, "Love obligates me" (Romans 1:14) and said, "This is why I am so excited about coming to preach the wonderful message of Jesus to you in Rome!" (v. 15). Where did Paul's love and passion for souls come from? Is that same fiery love and passion available to you? How do you think his love and passion helped people to receive his message?

3. Paul was bold even in the face of the greatest persecution because he knew the gospel was full of power. He said, "It [the gospel] moves us from receiving life through faith, to the power of living by faith" (v. 17). The power for *salvation* as well as *transformation* is contained in the gospel message—*grace and glory*! Why do you think it is important that both aspects are proclaimed and understood?

4. Paul teaches in 1:18–19 that God's truth is embedded in every human heart and revealed through his invisible qualities seen in the visible creation. In light of this truth, why isn't there anyone anywhere who is excused from both the judgment and the mercy of God? What does it mean to be "without excuse" (1:20), and why is this important for how we understand the gospel?

5. After studying Romans 1 and 2, write a brief character sketch of the apostle Paul. Include his attitudes, passions, heart for people and for God, and other details. Describe what you learned from his example and then turn that into a prayer for your own life.

Deeper Still!

Activations

Christ, the Solid Rock

We sing a beautiful hymn that states, "My hope is built on nothing less than Jesus' blood and righteousness."[13] Often though, we do inwardly trust in our own works of righteousness to some degree. This misplaced trust gets exposed…when we fail. Our failures, big or small, reveal to what degree we have really anchored our souls in

---

13   Edward Mote, "My Hope Is Built on Nothing Less," Hymnary, accessed April 4, 2022, https://hymnary.org/text/my_hope_is_built_on_nothing_less.

the finished work of the cross rather than our own ability to behave perfectly. Belief trumps behavior. What a weight and burden we choose to bear when we are not wholly trusting in "Jesus' blood and righteousness"!

Ask the Lord to reveal any ways that you are putting trust in your own righteousness—your good works, good behavior, or good intentions. Then repent and lay those false gods down.

Let's Pray

Lord, I thank you for the cross. I thank you for the blood you shed for me. I confess my trust in you and you alone. I desire to walk uprightly before you, Lord, because I love you so much, but I confess I am only justified in your sight as a result of faith, for "the just shall live by faith." Lord, let this reality be broadcasted through my life everywhere I go so that others can also put their hope in your salvation and your grace. Amen.

The Righteousness of God

(Romans 3:1–24)

Paul's "Courtroom Drama" Continues (Romans 3:1–8)

The Jews Are Guilty

Up to this point, Paul has been systematically and decisively removing every excuse for any person's sin (whether Jew or gentile), powerfully presenting a detailed list of sins that come out of the human heart against God and must be judged. Before a holy God, we will all stand, and it is better to do so clothed in Christ rather than in our own self-righteousness.

All of Paul's four witnesses agreed: the Jews were guilty before God. In Romans 3:1–8, Paul sums up the argument and refutes those Jews who tried to debate with him. They raise three questions. Paul expertly and wisely brings truth to each question and shuts down the debate.

Verses 1–8

> So then what is the importance of circumcision, and what advantage is there of being a Jew? Actually, there are numerous advantages. Most important, God distinguished

the Jews from all other people by entrusting them with the revelation of his prophetic promises. But what if some were unfaithful to their divine calling? Does their unbelief weaken God's faithfulness? Absolutely not! God will always be proven faithful and true to his word, while people are proven to be liars. This will fulfill what was written in the Scriptures:

Your words will always be vindicated
and you will rise victorious
when you are being tried by your critics!

But what if our wrong shows how right God is? Doesn't our bad serve the purpose of making God look good? (Of course, I'm only speaking from a human viewpoint.) Would that infer that God is unfair when he displays his anger against wrongdoing? Absolutely not! For if that were the case, how could God be the righteous judge of all the earth?

So, if my lie brings into sharp contrast the brightness of God's truth, and if my lie accentuates his glory, then why should I be condemned as a sinner? Is it proper for us to sin, just so good things may come? May it never be! Yet there are some who slander us and claim that is what we teach. They deserve to be condemned for even saying it!

The Debate

Paul refutes each argument raised by some Jews in their attempt to debate the accusation Paul has raised against them:

1. *"What advantage is it to be a Jew?"* Reply: Every advantage. God granted them his Word.
2. *"Will Jewish unbelief cancel God's faithfulness?"* Reply: Absolutely not. Instead, Jewish unbelief establishes God's faithfulness.

3. *"If our sin commends his righteousness, how can he judge us?"* Reply: We do not do evil so that good may come of it. God judges the world righteously.

Hamartiology and Hamartano

Hamartiology is the study of sin.

- Even though this is not an uplifting topic, it is important because we benefit from a greater understanding of the workings and results of sin.

Hamartano is one of the seven aspects of sin, and it means "missing the mark."

- The picture would be that of an archer whose arrow goes awry. For us and our understanding of sin, this helps give clarity to what happens when we "miss the mark."

- So, what is "the mark"? This question is powerfully answered for us in Romans 6. The mark is the glory of God. Sin is anything that falls short of the glory of God. Our mark, our holy goal, is glory!

- The clear and tragic loss that occurred in the garden of Eden was *glory*. Praise God we are restored in Christ! In him, we are glorified.

Soteriology

Soteriology is the study of salvation.

- The Greek word for "salvation" is *soteria*. It is for our entire being—body, soul (thoughts, feelings, choices), and spirit.

- The Bible is clear: it is not by our works of righteousness but solely by grace that God has saved us.

Help for the Helpless

We often hear the sentiment, "God helps those who help themselves," but the opposite is true. *God helps the helpless.* The only "hoop" you have to jump through or requirement you have to fulfill in order to be saved is simple faith in a simple gospel.

Saving faith is not embracing facts or dogma but rather embracing the person and work of Jesus Christ. Trusting in Jesus is the basis of our salvation. He alone is the way, the truth, and the life!

The Whole World Stands Guilty (Romans 3:9–20)

Universal Sinfulness

In these next few verses, Paul quotes verse after verse from the Old Testament to make the point clear that every person is *sinful* before God. Christianity is not a New Age theology of fanning into flame some mystical spark of divinity within humanity. No, without God, we are lost and sinful. We simply must have a savior. This "bad news" makes the "good news" *really good.* Praise the Lord forever and ever for coming to save us from our sin.

Verses 9–12

> So, are we to conclude then that we Jews are superior to all others? Certainly not! For we have already proven that both Jews and gentiles are all under the bondage of sin. And the Scriptures agree, for it is written:
>
> > There is no one who always does what is right,
> > no, not even one!
> > There is no one with true spiritual insight,
> > and there is no one who seeks after God alone.
> > All have deliberately wandered from God's ways.
> > All have become depraved and unfit.
> > Kindness has disappeared from them all,
> > not even one is good.

"No One"

Note the repetition of the words "no one" and "all," which in themselves assert the universality of human guilt. These verses indicate that the whole of man's inner being is controlled by sin:

- *His will*—"no one who does what is right"
- *His mind*—"no one with true spiritual insight"
- *His heart*—"no one who seeks after God alone"

"No God!"

Paul's first quotation is from Psalm 14:1–3 and 53:3. Psalm 14 begins with, "The fool hath said in his heart, there is no God" (KJV). Such a statement denies the indescribable gifts God gives us and reveals the human pride, which says that all we have achieved, we have done by our own efforts.

The Sinner, Head to Toe

In Romans 3:13–18, Paul gives us an "X-ray" study of the lost sinner, from head to foot. To support this thorough study, Paul quotes many Old Testament verses. The quotations are as follows: verse 13 and Psalm 5:9; verse 13 and Psalm 140:3; verse 14 and Psalm 10:7; verses 15–17 and Isaiah 59:7–8; and verse 18 and Psalm 36:1. These verses should be read in their contexts for the full effect.

Verses 13–14

> Their words release a stench,
> like the smell of death—foul and filthy!
> Deceitful lies roll off their tongues.
> The venom of a viper drips from their lips.
> Bitter profanity flows from their mouths,
> only meant to cut and harm.

The Sinner's Mouth

In these verses, Paul emphasizes human speech—the throat, tongue, lips, and mouth. The connection between words and character is seen in Matthew 12:34: "For what has been stored up in your hearts will be heard in the overflow of your words!" The sinner is spiritually dead by nature (Ephesians 2:1–3); therefore, only death can come out of his mouth. The *condemned mouth* can become a *converted mouth* and acknowledge that "Jesus Christ is Lord" (Romans 10:9–10). Ultimately, our words are quite significant to our spiritual progress as Jesus indicated when he said, "Your very words will be used as evidence, and your words will declare you either innocent or guilty" (Matthew 12:37).

Verses 15–16

> They are infatuated with violence and murder.
> They release ruin and misery wherever they go.

The Sinner's Feet

Here Paul pictures the sinner's feet. Just as *his words* are deceitful, so *his ways* are destructive. The Christian's feet are shod with the gospel of peace (Ephesians 6:15), but the lost sinner brings death, destruction, and misery wherever he goes. These tragedies may not occur immediately, but they will come inevitably. The lost sinner is on the broad road that leads to destruction (Matthew 7:13–14); he needs to repent, trust Jesus Christ, and get on the narrow road that leads to life. According to the psalmist, the promise for such a life is delight: "What delight comes to the one who follows God's ways! He won't walk in step with the wicked, nor share the sinner's way, nor be found sitting in the scorner's seat" (Psalm 1:1).

Verse 17

> They never experience the path of peace.

The Sinner's Mind

Romans 3:17 deals with the sinner's mind: he does not know the way of God's peace. This is what caused Jesus to weep over Jerusalem (Luke 19:41–44). The sinner does not want to know God's truth (Romans 1:21, 25, and 28); he prefers to believe Satan's lie. God's way of *peace* is through Jesus Christ:

> Our faith in Jesus transfers God's righteousness to us and he now declares us flawless in his eyes. This means we can now enjoy true and lasting peace with God, all because of what our Lord Jesus, the Anointed One, has done for us. (Romans 5:1)

Verse 18

> They shut their eyes to the awe-inspiring God!

The Sinner's Eyes

The sinner's arrogant *pride* is described in Romans 3:18, which cites Psalm 36:1: "The rebellion of sin speaks as an oracle of God, speaking deeply to the conscience of wicked men. Yet they are still eager to sin, for the fear of God is not before their eyes." The entire psalm should be read to get the full picture. The ignorance mentioned in Romans 3:17 is caused by the pride of verse 18, for it is "the fear of the Lord" that is the beginning of knowledge (Proverbs 1:7 NIV).

The Purpose of the Law

Through the law, no one can be made perfect. Salvation has always been by faith. However, the law clearly shows us God's perfection and therefore our need. Before the law was given, sin existed, but it was only after the law came that sin could be clearly specified and measured. By the law's illumination, we can know how sinful we really are and how far we fall from God's righteousness.

Verse 19

Now, we realize that everything the law says is addressed to those who are under its authority. This is for two reasons: So that every excuse will be silenced, with no boasting of innocence. And so that the entire world will be held accountable to God's standards.

The Law Holds Everyone Accountable

These quotations from God's law, the Old Testament Scriptures, lead to one conclusion: the whole world is guilty before God. There may be those who want to argue, but every mouth is stopped. There is no debate or defense. The whole world is guilty, Jews and gentiles.

- The Jews stand condemned by the law of which they boast.

- The gentiles stand condemned on the basis of creation and conscience.

Verse 20

For by the merit of observing the law no one earns the status of being declared righteous before God, for it is the law that fully exposes and unmasks the reality of sin.

The Law Exposes Sin's Reality

The word *for* in Romans 3:20 carries the meaning of *because* and gives the reason why the whole world is guilty. No flesh can obey God's law and be justified (declared righteous) in his sight. It is true that the doers of the law are justified (Romans 2:13), but nobody can do what the law demands. This inability to keep the law is one way that humans know they are sinners. As it says in Galatians 3:24, "The law was our guardian until Christ came so that we would be saved by faith" (Galatians 3:24).

When they try to obey the law, they fail miserably and need to cry out for God's mercy. Neither Jew nor gentile can obey God's law;

therefore, God must save sinners by some other way. The explanation of that "way" occupies Paul for the rest of his letter to the Roman church.

"New Perspective" Theology on the Law

In recent years, there has been a new thinking that has arisen in the church regarding the law and its purpose. It basically adheres to an idea that it is only the man-made traditions added by Jews to the law that are bad, but the Ten Commandments are still effective to produce righteousness. This thinking can subtly bring back into play a works mentality (which carnal people are prone to). The Ten Commandments reveal our sinfulness and keep us from straying, but they cannot save us. We must really safeguard the purity of the gospel message.

Again, it is faith alone in Christ alone. Anything that dilutes the grace gospel should be held suspect. Salvation is from God as proclaimed in Revelation: "And they shouted out with a passionate voice: 'Salvation belongs to our God seated on the throne and to the Lamb!'" (7:10). Our only "job" is *receiving* his salvation. It is a gift, and gifts are not ever earned. Otherwise, it is not a gift at all.

The Penal Substitutionary Atonement

Jesus paid it all! The Father laid upon Christ the punishment that brought us peace and right-standing with God. He who knew no sin became sin in order to make us righteous. He took our place! Jesus willingly endured being forsaken as a guilt offering because of love:

- "This is how we have discovered love's reality: Jesus sacrificed his life for us. Because of this great love, we should be willing to lay down our lives for one another" (1 John 3:16).

- "For the greatest love of all is a love that sacrifices all. And this great love is demonstrated when a person sacrifices his life for his friends" (John 15:13).

- "The very next day, John saw Jesus coming to him to be baptized, and John cried out, 'Look! There he is—God's Lamb! He takes away the sin of the entire world!'" (John 1:29).

- "Continue to walk surrendered to the extravagant love of Christ, for he surrendered his life as a sacrifice for us. His great love for us was pleasing to God, like an aroma of adoration—a sweet healing fragrance" (Ephesians 5:2).

The Gospel Reveals God's Righteousness (Romans 3:21–24)

Abraham Is Justified by Faith

We recognize Abraham as the father of faith. He believed God, and that belief made him righteous before a righteous, holy God. We have all become children of Abraham because we have been grafted into the family of God (discussed later in Romans 9–11). "And so the blessing of Abraham's faith is now our blessing too!" (Galatians 3:9). We all like the benefits and blessings that come to us through Abraham's relationship with God, but few would invite the tests of Abraham. He is an example to us of a man of faith, the pioneer of faith. His life is truly worthy of deep study and reflection. The testimony of God is that Abraham "became known as the *lover* of God!" (James [Jacob] 2:23, emphasis added).

Verses 21–22

> But now, independently of the law, the righteousness of God is tangible and brought to light through Jesus, the Anointed One. This is the righteousness that the Scriptures prophesied would come. It is God's righteousness made visible through the faithfulness of Jesus Christ. And now all who believe in him receive that gift. For there is really no difference between us.

"Independently of the Law"

Under the Old Testament law, righteousness came by *behaving*, but under the gospel, righteousness comes by *believing*. The law itself reveals the righteousness of God because the law is "holy and its commandments are correct and for our good" (Romans 7:12). Even though the law bore witness to this gospel righteousness, *it could not provide it.*

- Beginning at Genesis 3:15 and continuing through the entire Old Testament, witness is given to salvation by faith in Christ. The Old Testament sacrifices, the prophecies, the types, and the great "Gospel Scriptures" (such as Isaiah 53) all bore witness to this truth. The law could *witness* to God's righteousness, but it could not *provide* God's righteousness for sinful people. Only Jesus Christ could do that. (See Galatians 2:21.)

- "This means that the covenant between God and Abraham was fulfilled in Messiah and cannot be altered. Yet the written law was not even given to Moses until 430 years after God had 'signed' his contract with Abraham! The law, then, doesn't supersede the promise since the royal proclamation was given before the law. If that were the case, it would have nullified what God said to Abraham. We receive all the promises because of the Promised One—not because we keep the law!" (Galatians 3:17–18).

Faith in Christ/Faithfulness of Christ

1. *We Trust in Christ's Faithfulness*—Faith is only as good as its object. All people trust something, even if only themselves, but the Christian trusts Christ.

   - Law righteousness:

     o Is a reward for works

> o Exhibits trust in self

- Gospel righteousness:

  > o Is a gift through faith

  > o Exhibits trust in God

2. *We Have Complete Faith in Christ*—Many people say, "I believe in God," but this intellectual consent is not what saves us. It is personal, individual faith in Jesus Christ that saves and justifies the lost sinner. Even the demons from hell believe in God and tremble, yet this does not save them. It is a "believing *into* him" that saves us—this encompasses embracing him, accepting him as truth, being in union with him, and having an inner confidence that he is more than enough. In Greek, this phrase is a genitive absolute. This common grammatical form has a unique two-way switch. We have faith in Christ *and* the faith of Christ.

   - "You can believe all you want that there is one true God, that's wonderful! But even the demons know this and tremble with fear before him, yet they're unchanged— they remain demons" (James [Jacob] 2:19).

   - "Faith, then, is birthed in a heart that responds to God's anointed utterance of the Anointed One" (Romans 10:17).

Verses 23–24

For we all have sinned and are in need of the glory of God. Yet through his powerful declaration of acquittal, God freely gives away his righteousness. His gift of love and favor now cascades over us, all because Jesus, the Anointed One, has liberated us from the guilt, punishment, and power of sin!

Salvation for All

God gave his law to the Jews, not to the gentiles. However, the good news of salvation through Christ is offered to all humanity. All need to be saved. There is no difference between the Jew and the gentile when it comes to condemnation. "All have sinned and are coming short of the glory of God" (Romans 3:23, literal translation). God declared all humanity guilty so that he might offer to all his free gift of salvation.

"Gift"

The Greek word for "gift" is *dorea,* which also means "present," "legacy," or "privilege." Gifts are freely given, never earned, and they touch us deeply.

God Freely Gives His Righteousness

God has two kinds of attributes:

- Absolute—what he is in himself
- Relative—how he relates to the world and to men

One of his absolute attributes is love: "God is love" (1 John 4:8). When God relates that love to you and me, it becomes grace and mercy. God in his mercy does not give us what we do deserve, and God in grace gives us what we do not deserve.

The Greek word seen as "freely" in verse 24 is translated as "for no reason" in John 15:25. We are justified for no reason, without a cause. There is no cause—*no reason*—in us that would merit the salvation of God!

It is all grace.

Let's Go Deeper!

Questions

1. How did this lesson affect you most? What is something new you learned? What questions were sparked?

2. Salvation does not come through a mental assent and consent to a set of facts. Salvation and regeneration must be *by faith*. True faith (Greek *pistis*) has a number of components: acceptance, embracing something (or someone) as truth, union with God and his Word, and an inner confidence that God alone is enough. Have you experienced this saving faith? What were the effects in your life?

3. The pure gospel is faith alone in Christ alone. Even repentance is a gift from God. You don't add to your salvation at all. There is not one thing people can do to save themselves. Only grace will bring a person to salvation. Read Ephesians 2:1–5; Acts 5:31; 11:18; 2 Timothy 2:25; John 15:16; and Revelation 7:10. What do these verses reveal about salvation, the gift of repentance, and the work of grace?

4. Read Hebrews 4:9–10; 12:2; and Philippians 1:6. Who started your love story with God? Who will finish it?

5. When measured by God's perfect righteousness, no human being is sinless. People have gone astray and have become unprofitable both to themselves and to God. Our Lord's parables in Luke 15 illustrate this perfectly. Take some time to read through and meditate on those parables. Jot down the truths the Holy Spirit reveals to you through them about:

- *His heart and his nature:*

- *His love for you:*

- *His passionate pursuit of you:*

- *His passionate pursuit of others:*

Deeper Still!

Activations

The "Thirty-Seconds Challenge"
You were challenged in this lesson! Can you share the gospel in thirty seconds? Become an expert in sharing the *simple* gospel. Do your research, write out, rehearse, and then "Go ye!" into your world and preach the good news. There is no better messenger than you and no better time than the present. You are a carrier of the glory and a dispenser of the divine. It's time to share your story with the world. Indeed:

> You must continually bring healing to lepers and to those who are sick, and make it your habit to break off the demonic presence from people, and raise the dead back to life. Freely you have received the power of the kingdom, so freely release it to others. (Matthew 10:8)

Let's Pray

Lord, I am so grateful for my salvation! My sin was so great, but your grace was greater. Now, Lord, I want to share that salvation hope everywhere your hand leads me. Help me to freely give what you have so generously given to me. I pray this in Jesus' holy name. Amen.

Faith Alone in Christ Alone

(Romans 3:25–4:17)

Unadulterated Grace (Romans 3:25–31)

The Sufficiency of Jesus' Sacrifice

Distorted grace or diluted grace is *no longer grace.* Don't accept a different gospel of distorted grace. Don't receive the lie that you can add something to the finished work of the cross. We won't ever "get over" the cross. The cross is the epicenter of the universe. Jesus, the slain Lamb pictured in the book of Revelation, is forever seated on the throne of heaven, and *all worship* centers on him, the crucified One, the Lamb of God. We won't someday, in the great by-and-by, reminisce about the good ol' days when we focused on Calvary, the blood, and God's amazing grace. No, the wonderful cross and its message of saving grace is ever the theme of our hearts and the key to our eternal salvation.

Verses 25–26

> Jesus' God-given destiny was to be the sacrifice to take away
> sins, and now he is our mercy seat because of his death on
> the cross. We come to him for mercy, for God has made a
> provision for us to be forgiven by faith in the sacred blood
> of Jesus. This is the perfect demonstration of God's justice,

because until now, he had been so patient—holding back his justice out of his tolerance for us. So he covered over the sins of those who lived prior to Jesus' sacrifice. And when the season of tolerance came to an end, there was only one possible way for God to give away his righteousness and still be true to both his justice and his mercy—to offer up his own Son. So now, because we stand on the faithfulness of Jesus, God declares us righteous in his eyes!

Perfect Justice

God must be perfectly consistent with himself. He cannot break his own law or violate his own nature. "God is love" (1 John 4:8), and "God is pure light" (1:5). A God of love wants to forgive sinners, but a God of holiness must punish sin and uphold his righteous law.

- How can God be both "just and the justifier"? *The answer is in Jesus Christ.*

- When Jesus suffered the wrath of God on the cross for the sins of the world, he fully met the demands of God's law and fully expressed the love of God's heart.

Mercy and Justice Kissed at Calvary

The animal sacrifices in the Old Testament never took away sin, but when Jesus died, he reached all the way back to Adam and took care of those sins. No one (including Satan) could accuse God of being unjust or unfair because of his seeming passing over of sins in the Old Testament time. Through the cross, Jesus paid the full penalty for all sin for all humans of every time and every place.

With *one drop* of his sacred blood, sin's power was broken. We enter into that freedom only by grace through faith in the finished work of the cross. Oh, the wonderful cross!

- "For here is the way God loved the world—he gave his only, unique Son as a gift. So now everyone who believes in him will never perish but experience everlasting life. God did not send his Son into the world to judge and condemn the world, but to be its Savior and rescue it!" (John 3:16–17).

- "Your glorious throne rests on a foundation of righteousness and just verdicts. Grace and truth are the attendants who go before you" (Psalm 89:14).

- "Your mercy and your truth have married each other. Your righteousness and peace have kissed" (Psalm 85:10).

"Mercy Seat"

The term "mercy seat" can also be translated as "propitiation." Propitiation is defined as God's wrath being satisfied or appeased. Christians believe this appeasement occurred with the death of Jesus on the cross. The mercy seat becomes a symbol for the sacrificial, redemptive work of Christ. The mercy seat was the lid to the ark of the covenant, which was carried throughout the wilderness for years and finally found a home in the temple in Jerusalem. "Blood of mercy" was sprinkled on the mercy seat (or "place of satisfaction") yearly on the Day of Atonement. This covered the sins of the people until Jesus sprinkled his blood on the mercy seat in heaven. The mercy seat was not seen by the people because only the high priest went into the holy of holies to sprinkle blood upon the mercy seat. Yet Jesus was publicly offered as the satisfaction for sin's consequences.

"Covered Over"

This phrase can also be "passed over" or "released" (or let it be). This is the only place this Greek word *paresis* is found in the New Testament.

Boasting in the Law Is Excluded

At the core of any worldly religious system is pride. Christianity is distinct from any other religion because the supreme focus is on the greatness of God's faithful love and mercy. Jesus Christ is love. The cross is love exemplified. And the Bible itself is a love story. Surely, there is no room for boasting there, for the only proper response is thankful worship as we simply receive his covering love.

Verses 27–28

> Where, then, is there room for boasting? Do our works bring God's acceptance? Not at all! It was not our works of keeping the law but our faith in his finished work that makes us right with God. So our conclusion is this: God's wonderful declaration that we are righteous in his eyes can only come when we put our faith in Christ, and not in keeping the law.

The God of All People

We are all invited into the family of God! The gospel is not for a favored few; it is for "whosoever will," for "everyone who calls on the name of the Lord will be saved" (Acts 2:21). Paul boldly declares the gospel is for both Jew and non-Jew, for he was called and appointed to do so: "For the same God who empowered Peter's apostolic ministry to the Jews also flowed through me as an apostle to those who are gentiles" (Galatians 2:8).

Verses 29–30

> After all, is God the God of the Jews only, or is he equally the God for all of humanity? Of course, he's the God of all people! Since there is only one God, he will treat us all the same—he eliminates our guilt and makes us right with him by faith no matter who we are.

"No Matter Who We Are"

How wondrous is God's boundless love! Salvation is from God and to all people who will receive Jesus as Savior. We are all, Jew or gentile, welcomed and wanted in God's household of faith. In the Old Testament, God promised a coming day when David's tabernacle of worship would be restored: "And the prophet's words are fulfilled: 'After these things I will return to you and raise up the tabernacle of David that has fallen into ruin. I will restore and rebuild what David experienced so that all of humanity will be able to encounter the Lord including the gentiles whom I have called to be my very own,' says the Lord. 'For I have made known my works from eternity!'" (Acts 15:15–18). We are now living in that day! Now, "all humanity" can encounter the Lord just as he promised.

Verse 31

> Does emphasizing our faith invalidate the law? Absolutely not. Instead, our faith establishes the role the law should rightfully have.

Faith Establishes the Role of the Law

Faith puts the law in its proper place by establishing its divine role, which is *to reveal sin*. An example of this in our daily lives would be traffic laws. The speed limit sign does not have the *power* to make us go a certain speed. However, it certainly justifies the punishment of a speeding ticket when we break that lawful requirement imposed through the sign. In the same way, the law of God itself cannot make someone do what is right. However, when we break God's laws, his righteous requirements, the law reveals it as utterly sinful. The law *exposes* sin but cannot *eliminate* sin. Only faith in Christ can do that.

Righteousness by Faith, Illustrated
(Romans 4:1–8)

In these next few verses, Paul uses the lives of two famous and faithful men to illustrate the righteousness that comes through faith—Abraham and David. Both of these heroes of faith give us great encouragement. Faith, not their goodness or good works, was the basis of their intimate relationship with God, and "this testimony of faith is what previous generations were commended for" (Hebrews 11:2).

Abraham Justified by Faith

Abraham is famously known as the father of faith. Here in Romans, Paul uses Abraham, the very "founder of Judaism" (4:1), as a clear example that righteousness before God was never achieved by any means other than faith in God.

Verses 1–3

> Let me use Abraham as an example. It is clear that humanly speaking, he was the founder of Judaism. What was his experience of being made right with God? Was it by his good works of keeping the law? No. For if it was by the things he did, he would have something to boast about, but no one boasts before God. Listen to what the Scriptures say:
>
> > Because Abraham believed God's words, his faith transferred God's righteousness into his account.

The Power of Faith

Faith is the "muscle" that pulls heaven's promises into our lives. Abraham received a full account before God because he believed. Abraham received the promise and entered into covenant with God *before* there was a Torah or circumcision. Entirely based upon hearing God's call and saying yes by faith, Abraham entered into the promises of God. He is our example of a life of faith, for his "faith fastened onto [his] promises and pulled [him] into reality!" (Hebrews 11:33).

From Hope to Faith

- Faith brings hope into reality.
- Faith is the realization of what we hope for.

- We see, with hope-filled vision, the promises of the heavenly realm, and then by faith, we pull the promises down, as it were, into the earthly realm.

- Faith is the channel through which the power of God will always flow.

- Heaven is waiting for your agreement and partnership of faith.

- "Living within you is the Christ who floods you with the expectation of glory! This mystery of Christ, embedded within us, becomes a heavenly treasure chest of hope filled with the riches of glory for his people, and God wants everyone to know it!" (Colossians 1:27).

- "For we continue to wait for the fulfillment of our hope in the dawning splendor of the glory of our great God and Savior, Jesus, the Anointed One" (Titus 2:13).

- "Now faith brings our hopes into reality and becomes the foundation needed to acquire the things we long for. It is all the evidence required to prove what is still unseen" (Hebrews 11:1).

Verses 4–5

When people work, they earn wages. It can't be considered a free gift, because they earned it. But no one earns God's righteousness. It can only be transferred when we no longer rely on our own works, but believe in the one who powerfully declares the ungodly to be righteous in his eyes. It is faith that transfers God's righteousness into your account!

Faith Is the "Currency" of Heaven

Abraham received a *divine transaction* when he exchanged faith for righteousness. Faith brings the unseen promises into the seen realm—into our lives—to have, to experience, and to enjoy. No, we don't earn wages with God. However, our faith *acquires so much*.

- Faith empowers us to see spiritually (Hebrews 11:3).

- Faith is rewarded by God (Hebrews 11:6).

- Faith pleases God (Hebrews 11:6).

- Faith turns our dreams into reality (Hebrews 11:1).

- Faith moves mountains (Matthew 21:21).

- Faith brings us God's righteousness (Galatians 2:16).

- Faith was birthed within us by Jesus (Hebrews 12:2).

- Faith, when tested, empowers us (James [Jacob] 1:3).

- Faith establishes the role of the law (Romans 3:31).

- Faith's power conquers kingdoms, establishes justice, and shuts the mouths of lions (Hebrews 11:33).

- Faith brings happiness, God's blessings, and the victor's crown (James [Jacob] 1:12).

- Faith extinguishes the fiery darts of the evil one (Ephesians 6:16).

- Faith abolishes fear (Hebrews 11:27).

- Faith releases the life of Christ deep within you (Ephesians 3:17).

- Faith (your faith) does the impossible (Luke 17:6).

- Faith pulled down Jericho's walls (Hebrews 11:30).

- Faith heals crippling diseases (Acts 3:16).

- Faith empowers us to conceive (Hebrews 11:11).

- Faith opens blind eyes (Matthew 9:29).

- Faith releases healing (Luke 8:48).

- Faith releases forgiveness (Luke 5:20).

David Confirms Faith Alone

As Romans 4 verse 5 says, God powerfully declares over you, "You are righteous in my eyes!" Oh, how God longs to do that for every person's soul! But only those who seek his forgiveness and turn from their rebellion can *receive* his "not guilty" verdict. David testifies to this truth.

Verses 6–8

> Even King David himself speaks to us regarding the complete wholeness that comes inside a person when God's powerful declaration of righteousness is heard over our life. Apart from our works, God's work is enough. Here's what David says:
>
>> What happy fulfillment is ahead for those
>> whose rebellion has been forgiven
>> and whose sins are covered by blood.
>> What happy progress comes to them
>> when they hear the Lord speak over them,
>> "I will never hold your sins against you!"

God's Powerful Declaration

God has made a decree of righteousness over the life of every believer. Over your life is an eternal declaration that remains: "I will never hold your sins against you!"

For whom is that declaration made? All believers. All of heaven and all hell know who you are in Christ. Do you? Before almighty God and all of his creation, seen and unseen, you are as righteous as the Lord Jesus Christ. Who he is, is who you are, and everything that is true of him will be true of you in every way. This declaration brings "complete wholeness" (v. 6) inside of you. Your faith, your simple trust in him, has made you complete *in him.* Are you living in the reality of that "powerful declaration" (v. 6) of God over your life? Friend, you can and should!

"Happy Fulfillment" and "Happy Progress"

Are you beginning to see the true picture? God has declared you righteous. You have nothing to *fear,* only something to *expect:* deeper communion with him. This is the heavenly transaction that took place when you trusted in Christ for salvation by grace through faith. Now, live like it!

Rest in the Reality of His Righteousness

Don't fall into the trap of believing that you have to finish the work he started. We are in the process of maturing in faith: "I pray with great faith for you, because I'm fully convinced that the One who began this gracious work in you will faithfully continue the process of maturing you until the unveiling of our Lord Jesus Christ!" (Philippians 1:6). Don't accept any type of religious bondage, no matter how holy it might sound, because you cannot get more righteous than Jesus' blood has already made you. You cannot achieve righteousness by your own power: "Your new life began when the Holy Spirit gave you a new birth. Why then would you so foolishly turn from living in the Spirit by trying to finish by your own works?" (Galatians 3:3). The same grace that saved you also keeps you, empowers you, and finishes you.

Abraham Justified by Grace, Not Law-Keeping (Romans 4:9–17)

The "Father of Faith"

Abraham's simple faith and humble obedience to God's voice brought a wondrous heavenly deposit in his life: God's own righteousness. He didn't earn it or strive for it; it came to him only by faith. As has always been God's intention from the garden and throughout time, love, not labor, is the basis of our relationship with our Creator.

Verses 9–12

Now, think about it. Does this happiness come only to the Jews, or is it available to all who believe? Our answer is this: faith was credited to Abraham as God's righteousness!

How did he receive this gift of righteousness? Was he circumcised at the time God accepted him, or was he still uncircumcised? Clearly, he was an uncircumcised gentile when God said this of him! It was later that he received the external sign of circumcision as a seal to confirm that God had already transferred his righteousness to him by faith, while he was still uncircumcised. So now this qualifies him to become the father of all who believe among the non-Jewish people. And like their "father of faith," Abraham, God also transfers his righteousness to them by faith. Yes, Abraham is obviously the true father of faith for the Jewish people who are not only circumcised but who walk in the way of faith that our father Abraham displayed before his circumcision.

Abraham, the True Father of Faith

God made two prophetic promises to Abraham:

- *Count the Stars*—"He took him outside and said, 'Look up at the sky and count the stars—if indeed you can count them.' Then he said to him, 'So shall your offspring be'" (Genesis 15:5 NIV).

- *Count the Sand*—"I will surely bless you and make your descendants as numerous as the stars in the sky and as the sand on the seashore. Your descendants will take possession of the cities of their enemies" (Genesis 22:17 NIV).

These two metaphors for the seed of Abraham—*sand* and *stars*—signify that his offspring were both *earthly* and *heavenly*.

All the Blessings of Abraham

Every promise in the Book is yours. As Paul says, "And so the blessing of Abraham's faith is now our blessing too!" (Galatians 3:9). Abraham received the promise *because of faith*. As his spiritual, heavenly offspring, we inherit every promise. If you're unsure of all that means for you, take a look at Genesis 12:1–3. Expect and live the blessed life that is yours *in Christ*. Natural Israel received an earthly inheritance, but we receive a kingdom that cannot be shaken along with all it entails:

> Every spiritual blessing in the heavenly realm has already been lavished upon us as a love gift from our wonderful heavenly Father, the Father of our Lord Jesus—all because he sees us wrapped into Christ. This is why we celebrate him with all our hearts! (Ephesians 1:3)

The Promise of Faith versus Keeping the Law

God never desired a transactional relationship with his children. Never. He created man and woman and placed them in a garden. That garden was called Eden, which means "bliss," "pleasure," or "delight," because that's God's desire for us: bliss. God didn't place the man and the woman in a factory and then demand their blood, sweat, and tears. However, that is sadly how many of us live out our Christianity. Let's thrill our Father's heart by stepping out of the works mentality and stepping into the faith-rest in which Abraham lived.

Verses 13–17

> God promised Abraham and his descendants that they would have an heir who would reign over the world. This royal promise was not fulfilled because Abraham kept all the law, but through the righteousness that was transferred by faith. For if keeping the law earns the inheritance, then faith is robbed of its power and the promise becomes useless. For the law provokes punishment, and where no law exists there cannot be a violation of the law.

The promise depends on faith so that it can be experienced as a grace-gift, and now it extends to all the descendants of Abraham. This promise is not only meant for those who obey the law, but also to those who enter into the faith of Abraham, the father of us all. That's what the Scripture means when it says:

"I have made you the father of many nations."

He is our example and father, for in God's presence he believed that God can raise the dead and call into being things that don't even exist yet.

Religious Duty versus Relational Love

We are devoted lovers and dedicated disciples of Jesus Christ. Therefore, we serve, study, fast, pray, worship, obey, sacrifice (our time, energy, talents, pleasures, and more), give, and minister, not out of a sense of duty but out of love. Because we are loved, we do for him whatever we can. We don't "do" in order to be loved. We operate from victory of the cross, not striving for victory.

Paul's Effective Historical Examples

How masterfully Paul dismantled the arguments for righteousness acquired by the law. No one can deny the blessing, friendship, and covenants enjoyed by both David and Abraham with God. They received blessing and promises fulfilled, as well as right-standing with a holy God, by faith...and so do we! Brick by brick, Paul is tearing down the excuses for self-righteousness and law-righteousness.

God's Love Language

What moves God's heart? What really grabs hold of his attention and moves him? Trust. Just as we earthly parents want the trust of our own children (exhibited by peace and rest in our love and care), how much more so does Father God! Your faith moves mountains, and your trust moves the mountain maker. Trust in the promises. Trust in his Word. Trust in his nature. Trust in him. He will never fail you. No never.

Let's Go Deeper!

Questions

1. In this lesson, there are several mentions of God's declaration over you. Read Romans 3:26 and 28 and 4:5, 6, and 8. What is this "powerful declaration"? What does it mean to you that the voice that formed galaxies has spoken this amazing truth over you?

2. As discussed, under grace there is no room for boasting. Why do you think mankind still boasts? What does this reveal about our faith and trust? Are there some aspects of your Christianity in which you boast (either privately or openly)? How can you ensure God gets all the glory and credit from your life?

3. Paul points out that Abraham was justified by faith *prior to circumcision*. Circumcision was an outward sign of an inward reality. Unfortunately, God's people came to trust in the outward show above the inward seal. Do Christians in our day tend to do this as well, not by circumcision but other outward signs? How so? What is God's solution for this incorrect mindset? Read 4:18. How are you also "[taking] God at his word" as Abraham did?

4. In 4:3 and 5, we see that because of Abraham's faith, God transferred righteousness into his "account." This is from the Greek word *logizomai,* which is used eleven times in this chapter. This concept teaches us that our faith is "considered or calculated" as righteousness before God. Interestingly, this word was used in secular transactional documents of the day. Therefore, we see God made a *transaction* with Abraham and put into Abraham's account—placed on deposit for him, credited to him—righteousness! Abraham possessed righteousness in the same manner as a person would possess a sum of money placed in his account in a bank. So, what is also in your heavenly bank account, and how did it get there?

5. What is the background of David's life when he said the words quoted in verses 4:7–8? (See Psalm 32.) Why do you think Paul used David as an example? If Abraham and David could not earn their forgiveness through works, do you have any hope of doing so? Since you have put your trust in Jesus, what is God's verdict over you?

Deeper Still!

Activations

Scandalous Grace!

Grace has to be a scandal, otherwise it has been diluted by works and by religion. The scandal of grace is not that we can do whatever we want but rather that we are so free that we don't want to do those sinful things anymore. Jesus wants us living in that kind of freedom and said, "So if the Son sets you free from sin, then become a true son and be unquestionably free!" (John 8:36).

Freedom is not about more information; it is about *transformation*. Transforming grace is at work inside of you *because you believe*. God has made a powerful declaration over you that you are righteous and that your sins will never be held against you. This means you have permission from God to be free. So free. Free indeed! This kind of scandalous freedom and grace will annoy religious folk. Those who are working hard at pleasing God and earning his favor will always be offended by *free* grace, but don't waver. Let your bold boast be in the scandalous grace of God that declares the sinner *not guilty!*

Let's Pray

> *Father, what is left to say but thank you! I am so grateful for your grace. I am so thankful that you chose me, that you "bother with puny mortal man" (Psalm 8:4). I praise you for providing the sacrifice for my many, many sins through Jesus in order to declare me unquestionably free, forgiven, and not guilty. Thank you that, like David, even after his great sin of adultery and murder, you are not holding my sin against me, and it's all because of your grace and mercy. Thank you for your scandalous grace. I don't deserve it and can never earn it, but Lord, I receive it. I receive your powerful declaration over my life of "not guilty!" Amen.*

The Blessings of Our New Life

(Romans 4:18–5:11)

Justification by Resurrection Power, Not Human Effort (Romans 4:18–25)

Overcome the Impossible

God turned an empty womb into a nation through Abraham and Sarah. Their impossible situation was actually a setup for the miraculous. We can also see our impossibilities in the same light by simply believing God will keep his promises. Nothing is impossible for God.

Verse 18

> Against all odds, when it looked hopeless, Abraham believed the promise and expected God to fulfill it. He took God at his word, and as a result he became the father of many nations. God's declaration over him came to pass:
>
>> "Your descendants will be so many
>> that they will be impossible to count!"

Faith's Reality

Abraham gives us the essence of faith. He is an example to us of how faith looks into the unseen realm and grasps the invisible promises of God, making them a reality. Faith sees the things that "don't even exist yet" (v. 17) and calls them into existence!

Faith Overrides Impossibilities

"When it looked hopeless" was the perfect timing for a miracle. The story of Abraham, Sarah, and Isaac is really an amazing showcase for the power of God through faith. It so wonderfully illustrates the miraculous power released through the partnership of people and God. When God wants to do something on the earth, he looks for a human to partner with. He wanted a family of faith on the earth, so he found Abraham and made a covenant with him. This is exactly what he wants to do with each one of us. Will you partner with heaven as Abraham and Sarah did?

Verses 19–21

> In spite of being nearly one hundred years old when the promise of having a son was made, his faith was so strong that it could not be undermined by the fact that he and Sarah were incapable of conceiving a child. He never stopped believing God's promise, for he was made strong in his faith to father a child. And because he was mighty in faith and convinced that God had all the power needed to fulfill his promises, Abraham glorified God!

Faith Always Glorifies God

Do you want to magnify and exalt the Lord? Of course you do! Here is the key: *believe him*. When you exhibit unwavering faith in God, he gets all the glory. When we, against all hope, continue to hope, we are lifting high the wonderful One. Can't you just picture that heavenly transaction! The God of the universe allows himself to be moved to action on your behalf simply because you have expected

Faith tested ds. 1: 3
Faith in God alone, with no wavering
THE BLESSINGS OF OUR NEW LIFE
ds. 1: 6-8

him to. Our childlike trust captivates God, moves God to act, and ultimately brings him fame and honor.

Verses 22–25

> So now you can see why Abraham's faith was credited to his account as righteousness before God. And this declaration was not just spoken over Abraham, but also over us. For when we believe and embrace the one who brought our Lord Jesus back to life, perfect righteousness will be credited to our account as well. Jesus was handed over to be crucified for the forgiveness of our sins and was raised back to life to prove that he had made us right with God!

Abraham's Blessing Is Ours

Abraham's faith experience is our experience. His four-thousand-year-old faith is our faith. The declaration of righteousness by faith didn't go to the grave with Abraham. In Christ, we are Abraham's spiritual children and inherit all his covenant blessings. Membership has its privileges, and you are a privileged member of the household of faith.

The Resurrection

If Jesus did not pay for every one of our sins, Jesus would still be in the grave. The resurrection of Jesus is the proof that all of our sin—past, present, and future—is paid for, guilt is fully removed, and righteousness is now given to us. We get resurrection life through faith in what Christ has accomplished. Our faith is now in his resurrection. If you ever doubt it, take a moment and meditate on the empty tomb.

Abundant Life (Romans 5:1–11)

The Blessings of New Life in Christ

In this chapter, Paul highlights all the blessings that come to us in Christ! "Oh, for a thousand tongues to sing!" There are just not enough ways or words or languages to describe the wondrous riches of blessings we have because of Jesus. We are so *grateful,* aren't we? Because he willingly laid his life down, we now live by his life... his abundant life! Faith transfers that abundant life to us now and forever.

Peace with God

Paul focuses on this blessing first. The Hebrew word is *shalom,* which means "lack of conflict," "physical strength," and "abundance and freedom from lack." There is not a one-word equivalent for *shalom* in the English language; it is just so multilayered. The Greek word for "peace" is *eirene,* which is actually the word for "dovetail." So the meaning conveyed is of a joining together perfectly, seamlessly, and harmoniously. What once was discordant and disjointed is made into peaceful unity in Christ. We have been made one with Jesus and now are fully reconciled to God. We have peace with God.

Verse 1

> Our faith in Jesus transfers God's righteousness to us and he now declares us flawless in his eyes. This means we can now enjoy true and lasting peace with God, all because of what our Lord Jesus, the Anointed One, has done for us.

Life-Union

The overall meaning to us when Paul says we have "peace with God" is *union.* We are in life-union with the Anointed One. We "dovetail" with the Trinity. We are enfolded into the triune glory. Jesus is in us, the Holy Spirit is in us, and Jesus said he and the Father will make their dwelling place in us (John 14). Therefore, you are wrapped around with God. What peace! What bliss! We match, we blend, we "dovetail" in oneness with him. It is a beautiful mystery well worth pondering for ages to come.

Access to God's Glorious Hope

Faith guarantees us permanent access to God. What do we have access to? The kindness of God. When you are fully convinced you deserve an angry rebuke, God surprises you with a merciful kiss. There is none so kind as Jesus Christ. How merciful, how gracious is he.

Verse 2

> Our faith guarantees us permanent access into this marvelous kindness that has given us a perfect relationship with God. What incredible joy bursts forth within us as we keep on celebrating our hope of experiencing God's glory!

Marvelous Kindness

The English word *kindness* comes from how we act among our own "kind." Jesus expands this to Samaritans and Roman soldiers. Paul expands this to God himself. We are made in the image of God—his kind—and are to love all of humankind. We could try—and it would be a wonderful goal!—but we will never plumb the depths of God's vast ocean of loving-kindness. He is good, and his love endures forever. When sin and sin's effects have bent us down in defeat, he will meet us there and lift us up. We have full access to his faithful love. We can always call to him and come to him, knowing that he listens and responds. Because of this love dynamic, our hearts blossom, opening up to him with great confidence like David's did when he said, "But I keep calling out to you, YAHWEH! I know you will bend down to listen to me, for now is the season of favor. Because of your faithful love for me, your answer to my prayer will be my sure salvation" (Psalm 69:13). Be receptive to the Holy Spirit.

Hope of Glory

True biblical hope points to glory. Our hope is in the truth that *glory* is our *future*. This is a cause for celebration! Are you living in this reality? I encourage you to do so, friend, because joy will fill you as you look forward to experiencing God's glory right now and for eternity. Gloom, doom, and dread are not your future…glory is! You're not "in trouble"; you're "in Christ." Therefore, you have a truly glorious hope.

Glory to Glory

Oh, friend! Get your hopes up! So much good awaits you as you go from glory to glory to glory. He is not only the author of every virtue in our life, but he is also the *completer*. He is going to finish what he started *unto your glorious unveiling*. That's why Paul said with such confidence, "I pray with great faith for you, because I'm fully convinced that the One who began this gracious work in you will faithfully continue the process of maturing you until the unveiling of our Lord Jesus Christ!" (Philippians 1:6).

Troubles Transform Us

We all have troubles. Relationship with Christ does not exempt us from life's troubles, but it does guarantee that our troubles will accomplish something priceless in our lives: *transformation*. Only believers have this precious promise.

Verses 3–4

> But that's not all! Even in times of trouble we have a joyful confidence, knowing that our pressures will develop in us patient endurance. And patient endurance will refine our character, and proven character leads us back to hope.

Pressures Develop Us

Heb 11:1-6 NKJV
faith is substance

Whatever difficulties we go through—sickness, job loss, accidents, relationship troubles, and more—we will never go through them alone or without the strong arm of the Lord supporting us. He will never fail us. Therefore, "We view our slight, short-lived troubles in the light of eternity. We see our difficulties as the substance that produces for us an eternal, weighty glory far beyond all comparison" (2 Corinthians 4:17). This is why our pressure is actually a

112

Kintsugi

- underlying reality
- Hebrew: that which is gathered together
- proof — until today we have all survived 100% of our trials & traumas
- physical existence
- foundation
- physical material from which something is made

prophecy. Paul encourages us with the hope of knowing that the pressures we endure in this life are prophesying our character transformation. Have you been in the "pressure cooker" of troubles? Then you can be sure that just as pressure turns coal into diamonds, your life is being transfigured into priceless beauty as well.

We Redeem Our Troubles by the Grace of God

God takes horrible situations and thoroughly redeems them. In the book of Genesis, starting in chapter 39, Joseph's life is a beautiful example of this principle. He will do the same for us as we continue in the grace of God at work in our lives.

- *The Pit, the Prison, the Palace*—Like it or not, this is the path we all take to Christlikeness. Let's be "Josephs" and not waste our betrayals, losses, persecutions, pains, rejections, false accusations, abandonments, or *pressures.* We can of course escape the pressure through various forms of escapism (sin, addictions, and entertainments), but if we instead choose to remain in that crucible, we will experience the refinement that causes us to come forth as gold.

- *Your Limitation Brings You into the Glory*—Who put Joseph in the palace finally? The very ones who sought his harm and betrayed him. The very ones who harm us are actually pushing us into our destiny. In the end, for Joseph, it was all revealed as a divine setup. His setback was a setup, and this is the "recipe" for a miracle *every time.* Think of Abraham and Sarah's dead womb, Paul's imprisonment, Joseph's pit, David's cave, and Jesus' tomb.

- *Embrace Your Troubles*—Though we could certainly fight the process or try to escape the process, it won't help. The only way out is *through.* And on the other side is *more glory!* Proven character will result, and promotion is always on the back end of every trouble.

Greek : "substance" (Heb. 11:1) (#5287) — "a placing or setting under, a substructure or foundation" (faith our foundation)
Luke 6:48-49 Christ is the rock on which we must build our foundation

113

God's Cascading Love

The Spirit of the Lord is inside of you, dispensing his love into you, causing it to cascade over you and into you continually. Every need inside you is remedied in the flow of his cascading love. It is relentless and continual, a 24/7 life source available to you because you are *in Christ.*

Verses 5–8

> And this hope is not a disappointing fantasy, because we can now experience the endless love of God cascading into our hearts through the Holy Spirit who lives in us!
>
> For when the time was right, the Anointed One came and died to demonstrate his love for sinners who were entirely helpless, weak, and powerless to save themselves.
>
> Now, would anyone dare to die for the sake of a wicked person? We can all understand if someone was willing to die for a truly noble person. But Christ proved God's passionate love for us by dying in our place while we were still lost and ungodly!

"The Endless Love of God"

You exist under the smile of heaven. You delight the heart of our heavenly Father simply because you are his. And each morning is a fresh beginning in him, full of mercy and even more love. God's love is a covering for us. His endless love covers our sin, and "because of the LORD's great love we are not consumed, for his compassions never fail. They are new every morning; great is your faithfulness" (Lamentations 3:22–23 NIV).

"When the Time Was Right"

We are *always* ready for God to come to our rescue and bring our "new day," but we can trust him to show up right when he should. His timing may not always be *our agenda,* but it is always *heaven's agenda,* and it is impeccable. There is an "appointed time" God has designated for your breakthrough, and you can trust him with the timetable.

- *His* Kairos *Is Worth the Wait—Kairos* means "the opportune moment." During the wait for God's *kairos,* the change you long for is taking place. Don't hijack the process; instead, embrace the wait. Just like the caterpillar in its chrysalis, you are going to have an awesome breakthrough.

  o *Qavah* is the Hebrew word for "wait." It also means "rope" and implies a sense of tension. Picture a rope. It's not a single strand; intertwined strands are pulled to form something strong and useful. This is what happens during the wait. You are being intertwined with the Trinity—with his heart—and growing into deeper unity and Christlikeness that makes you strong and useful.

  o *Qavah* implies that we wait actively with anticipation, hopefully watching for God to act. The most familiar passage in Scripture where we see *qavah* is Isaiah 40:31: "But those who wait [*qavah*] on the LORD shall renew their strength; they shall mount up with wings like eagles, they shall run and not be weary, they shall walk and not faint" (NKJV). Expect strength and renewal in your life as you endure the waiting.

- *Maturity Is the Result*—Jesus adores us in our immaturity, but he longs for a mature bride. Maturity is the absolutely *priceless* result of your waiting. In the end, your greater level of maturity will cause you to say, *Yes, Lord, it was right for me to wait. Thank you.* We will be able to agree with David, who said, "My life, my every moment, my destiny—it's all in your hands" (Psalm 31:15), and with the wise words of Solomon, who

said, "He has made everything beautiful in its time"
(Ecclesiastes 3:11 NIV).

"While We Were Still Lost and Ungodly"

What king is kind to his *enemy?* This is proof of Jesus' amazing love.
He himself said that there is no greater love than a someone who
lays his or her life down for *friends* (see John 15:13), but he went
even further. He died for his foes as well, in order to bring them
to his heart and make them his friends. Jesus Christ is a lover. He
is love itself. When we face difficult people or life's injustices, we
can look full into his wonderful face and see what love would do.
Love washed Judas' feet. Love said, "Father, forgive them." Love
died for the whole world in order to redeem a bride. Jesus is love
personified!

But We See Jesus

Never judge God's love by what you're going through. Instead, judge
by what he went through. It is the proof of his love. We will never
escape life's troubles and sorrows, but Jesus has gone before us and
borne our sorrows.

- *Trouble Is Inescapable*—"Yet man is born to trouble as
  surely as sparks fly upward" (Job 5:7 NIV).

- *Jesus Has Borne Our Trouble*—"Yet he was the one who
  carried our sicknesses and endured the torment of our
  sufferings. We viewed him as one who was being pun-
  ished for something he himself had done, as one who
  was struck down by God and brought low. But it was
  because of our rebellious deeds that he was pierced and
  because of our sins that he was crushed. He endured
  the punishment that made us completely whole, and in
  his wounding we found our healing" (Isaiah 53:4–5).

- *He Bore It for the Joy of Having You*—"We look away
  from the natural realm and we focus our attention and
  expectation onto Jesus who birthed faith within us and

116

who leads us forward into faith's perfection. His example is this: Because his heart was focused on the joy of knowing that you would be his, he endured the agony of the cross and conquered its humiliation, and now sits exalted at the right hand of the throne of God! So consider carefully how Jesus faced such intense opposition from sinners who opposed their own souls, so that you won't become worn down and cave in under life's pressures" (Hebrews 12:2–3).

Rescued from Sin and Wrath

You and I will never experience the convicting justice of God. We have been completely spared the judgment that comes against sin and sinful humans because of what Jesus has done for us. Through the death of his own Son, God has delivered us from sin and all its consequences. We have been rescued.

Verses 9–10

And there is still much more to say of his unfailing love for us! For through the blood of Jesus we have heard the powerful declaration, "You are now righteous in my sight." And because of the sacrifice of Jesus, you will never experience the wrath of God. So if while we were still enemies, God fully reconciled us to himself through the death of his Son, then something greater than friendship is ours. Now that we are at peace with God, and because we share in his resurrection life, how much more we will be rescued from sin's dominion!

"Fully Reconciled"

From enemies to friends…that is what we are. Because of the cross, we are no longer in opposition to God. While we were his *enemies*, he reconciled us to himself, so just imagine what will come from our *friendship!* Now that you have become his lover, his daily companion, and his bride, what joyous delight ensues.

Jesus Has Rescued Us

Jesus carries the burden for our sin and guilt. He has and will continually rescue us from sin's dominion. Sin surely has no hold on anyone who has laid hold of the wonder of such love and grace. Let's get "wrecked" by this heart-melting love. We have such a great salvation and *so much* to be grateful for. We were drowning and sinking in sin's dominion, but Jesus rescued us.

Reconciled to God

We can get our Holy Spirit hopes up because we have been brought eternally near to God through the shed blood of Christ. There was once an unscalable wall of separation between the holiness of God and our desperate hearts, but no more! Now, we are right where we belong, right next to God's heart, forever reconciled by love.

Verse 11

> And even more than that, we overflow with triumphant joy in our new relationship of living reconciled to God—all because of Jesus Christ!

All Because of Jesus

You and I could never ever bridge that chasm of sin's separation. No matter how good or well-intentioned our efforts, nothing could ever close that gap between us and God.

So he came.

There was only one way to reconcile the distance and restore us to God: the cross. And our precious Savior did not consider it too great a price. We are so very blessed. Yes, "We overflow with triumphant joy" (v. 11).

Let's Go Deeper!

Questions

1. As you went through this lesson, what did you see, experience, or realize for the very first time?

2. What specific questions do you have from this lesson? Ask God to reveal the answers to you over the days and weeks ahead. Be expectant!

3. Romans 5:5 says that our hope is not a fantasy. God has a perfect and trustworthy timing at work in our lives. What does waiting on God accomplish? See Matthew 5:4; Psalm 59:9; Psalm 27:14; and Isaiah 40:31.

4. In this lesson, we talked about how troubles transform us. Have you been in the "pressure cooker" of troubles? Then you can be sure that just as pressure turns coal into diamonds, your life is being transfigured into priceless beauty as well. What are your troubles doing for you? Who is in control of the temperature of your fiery trial? (See 1 Corinthians 10:13.)

5. Romans 5:9 says we will never experience the wrath of God, and he has declared us righteous in his sight. Do you live in this reality, or do you fear his wrath? Why or why not? Who *does* experience his wrath? (See Romans 2:8.) Read Galatians 5:24 and explain why you have escaped his wrath.

Deeper Still!

Activations

A One-Minute Challenge

- Take sixty seconds and journal the truths from this lesson that really affected you and why.

- From your journaling, pull out a sentence or two to tweet, post on other social media, or text to a friend in order to encourage someone else.

Let's Pray

How can I put into words, Lord, the depth of gratitude I feel when I think of all I receive because of Jesus. What can I say? Before I was even born, you planned this glorious life for me. My life record was written in your book. You knew my name and wove me together in my mother's womb. You gave me breath and life. You have been everything I need even before I knew you. And now that I do know you, I am your friend, fully reconciled! My heart is "dovetailed" into yours; we are entwined as one. All I can say is, I love you, I love you, I love you! If I had a thousand tongues, I'd make every one of them sing your praise. If I had a thousand lifetimes, I'd want every one of them yielded and given over to you. I thank you, Lord, for your cross and that I am justified, sanctified, and glorified in your eyes. Amen.

The Triumph of Grace

(Romans 5:12–6:10)

Reigning in Life (Romans 5:12–21)

Over the next several verses Paul begins to develop the theme of *reigning in life*. Doesn't that sound wonderful? What does it truly mean for you and me to *reign* in life? Reigning connotes *royalty*. We have a new identity *in Christ*, and that includes our adoption into the family of God. Let's dive in and discover what reigning with him looks like.

The Grace and Glory Message

We have been focusing on the very important grace and glory message of Romans. So far, we have really been highlighting God's astounding grace, and later on in this study, we will go more in-depth into the glory aspect of Romans. There is a key portion of Scripture that illuminates both concepts so well:

> We always have to thank God for you, brothers and sisters, for you are dearly loved by the Lord. He proved it by choosing you from the beginning for salvation through the Spirit, who set you apart for holiness, and through your belief in the truth. To this end he handpicked you for salvation

through the gospel so that you would have the glory of our Lord Jesus Christ. (2 Thessalonians 2:13–14)

In this power-packed passage, we see that we were "hand-picked" by God for salvation—that's grace—so that we would experience the glory of the Lord Jesus Christ. How tremendous! Grace will always bring us into the glory of God. This is his ultimate intention for each one of us "from the beginning."

Verses 12–14

When Adam sinned, the entire world was affected. Sin entered human experience, and death was the result. And so death followed this sin, casting its shadow over all humanity, because all have sinned. Sin was in the world before Moses gave the written law, but it was not charged against them where no law existed. Yet death reigned as king from Adam to Moses even though they hadn't broken a command the way Adam had. The first man, Adam, was a picture of the Messiah, who was to come.

"Death Reigned"

Death was a monarch. It reigned with absolute authority from Adam to Moses. No one escaped death during that entire period except one man: Enoch. Enoch walked in such intimacy with God that God took him: "Enoch walked faithfully with God; then he was no more, because God took him away" (Genesis 5:24 NIV). Death has no power over God's bride, the church of Jesus Christ.

Two Groups of People

From God's perspective, there are only two groups in the earth: those in Adam and those in Christ. We, as believers, are, of course, *in Christ*. In the eyes of the Father, we are everything that Jesus is, and all that he has, we have. As Paul taught in Corinthians, "Even as all who are in Adam die, so also all who are in Christ will be made alive" (1 Corinthians 15:22). "In Christ" is our new reality.

Therefore, when we pray, it is as if Jesus is asking the Father because we ask "in the name of Jesus."

Adam's Sin versus Christ's Gift

There really is no "apples to apples" comparison between our sin and God's gracious gift of salvation. It is just mind-blowing. Rather than trying to wrap our minds around such amazing grace, let's spend our energy simply marveling. Just think, where would you be—in your life right now—without the blood of Jesus?

Verse 15

> Now, there is no comparison between Adam's transgression and the gracious gift that we experience. For the magnitude of the gift far outweighs the crime. It's true that many died because of one man's transgression, but how much greater will God's grace and his gracious gift of acceptance overflow to many because of what one man, Jesus, the Messiah, did for us!

"No Comparison"

Well, there is no denying that Adam blew it, big time. However, let's really recognize and refocus on the truth that his transgression is nothing compared to the beautiful gift of sonship we experience because of God's grace. It is as though we have more in Christ than we even lost in Adam. No comparison!

Verse 16

> And this free-flowing gift imparts to us much more than what was given to us through the one who sinned. For because of one transgression, we are all facing a death sentence with a verdict of "Guilty!" But this gracious gift leaves us free from our many failures and brings us into the perfect righteousness of God—acquitted with the words "Not guilty!"

"Much More"

This particular phrase occurs three times in this chapter (vv. 10, 16, and 17). God is saying, with emphasis, we have so much already and have so much to look forward to *because of grace.*

"Not Guilty!"

In Adam, we were all under a death sentence. The verdict of "guilty" was stamped upon us, and we existed under that weight, awaiting the final punishment—*but God!* Now, because of the precious, sacred blood of our Lord Jesus, we have been freed from our many failures and have been given *his* perfect righteousness. We have been acquitted eternally with the words "Not guilty!"

The Reign of Two Kings—Death and Grace

Perhaps, you have never thought of your spiritual condition this way before, but the truth is we all bow to a "king." Either we bow to death because of our sin or we bow to Christ. Paul highlights the truth to us that we are fully "held in the grip of grace" and are forever free from death's stranglehold.

Verse 17

> Death once held us in its grip, and by the blunder of one man, death reigned as king over humanity. But now, how much more are we held in the grip of grace and continue reigning as kings in life, enjoying our regal freedom through the gift of perfect righteousness in the one and only Jesus, the Messiah!

Grace Has Dethroned Death

Death is no longer your master. It has been overthrown by God's amazing grace. Now, grace reigns in you, and you reign in life:

- Death has no hold on you.

- Sin has no hold on you.

- You enjoy "regal freedom."

- You enjoy the "gift of perfect righteousness."
- You are "in the one and only Jesus, the Messiah."

One Transgression versus One Righteous Act

The gift of salvation is so much greater than the penalty of sin. The victory of the cross is so much greater than the defeat of Adam's disobedience, and Jesus' "once and for all" (Romans 6:2) sacrifice victoriously swallows up the death that came through Adam's transgression. (See Hebrews 9:25–28.)

Verses 18–19

> In other words, just as condemnation came upon all people through one transgression, so through one righteous act of Jesus' sacrifice, the perfect righteousness that makes us right with God and leads us to a victorious life is now available to all. One man's disobedience opened the door for all humanity to become sinners. So also one man's obedience opened the door for many to be made perfectly right with God and acceptable to him.

One Righteous Act

How much we would benefit from taking time to simply rest in these foundational truths of our new life in Christ! One powerful act set us free eternally. One holy act of devotion and love delivered us from our captivity and instantly made us captives of God's heart. Now we are free to say, "I love you, God! I love you, Lord!" and fully realize his love...all because of "one righteous act."

A Victorious Life

Jesus' victory brings us and leads us into one victory after another. That is to be our life story. We go from glory to glory and from victory to victory; upward and onward is our new trajectory in Christ. Triumph is our destiny. Overcoming is our new life, which means we will have difficulties, obstacles, and, of course, our old "beast nature" we must overcome.

Law versus Grace

Law has done its work, making sin utterly sinful. But now grace reigns! Sin is dethroned and "sin-conquering grace" (5:21) now rules in us because of Jesus.

Verses 20–21

> So then, the law was introduced into God's plan to bring the reality of human sinfulness out of hiding. And yet, wherever sin increased, there was more than enough of God's grace to triumph all the more! And just as sin reigned through death, so also this sin-conquering grace will reign as king through righteousness, imparting eternal life through Jesus, our Lord and Messiah!

More Sin, More Grace

Let's celebrate God's greatness and goodness! There is more than enough grace to triumph. This is why the greatest sinners become the greatest lovers; they are overwhelmed by his goodness and his greatness. The truth is we should all love greatly, but many of us don't fully understand the debt of sin that was against us. We don't realize how sinful we were or where we would be without the blood of Jesus. *Lord, awaken our hearts to the wonder of your great grace.*

The Triumph of Grace over Sin (Romans 6:1–10)

Co-Buried and Co-Raised

Jesus did more than die for us. He was also buried and resurrected for us. We must identify with his death, burial, and resurrection and appropriate the fullness of life he died to give us.

Verses 1–3

> So what do we do, then? Do we persist in sin so that God's kindness and grace will increase? What a terrible thought! We have died to sin once and for all, as a dead man passes away from this life. So how could we live under sin's rule a moment longer? Or have you forgotten that all of us who were immersed into union with Jesus, the Anointed One, were immersed into union with his death?

Once and for All

We have died to sin, "once and for all." If we can truly get hold of that powerful truth, we will live in such freedom and faith. We are not staying in the old system of ritual sacrifice by "killing ourselves" trying to be holy. No, we are already dead *in Christ*. Through our union with him by grace through faith, we "were immersed into union with his death." If your current theology and mindset don't match this truth, then get your heavenly adjustment today, right now. Jesus died to give you new life through him.

How Can We Live in Sin?

This is a rhetorical question. The obvious answer is that we can't. We shouldn't. Why would we? Living in the awe of the price that was paid for our freedom will make us want to love him with the same fierce, fiery, and radical love he shows to us. How? How could we "play games" with God or "play with fire," so to speak, when sacred, holy blood was spilled to purchase our *total freedom* from the grip of sin?

Have You Forgotten? You Are Co-Buried

How do we overcome sin? By getting into the tomb with Jesus. He overcame for us! He already dismantled the hierarchy of sin that once reigned in us. We can't *add* to what he already did. To try to do so is to diminish the cross and the purity of his grace that saves us, and friends, that is *another gospel*. Paul described this reality by saying,

> My old identity has been co-crucified with Christ and no longer lives. And now the essence of this new life is no longer mine, for the Anointed One lives his life through me—we live in union as one! My new life is empowered by the faith of the Son of God who loves me so much that he gave himself for me, dispensing his life into mine! (Galatians 2:20)

Verses 4–5

> Sharing in his death by our baptism means that we were co-buried with him, so that when the Father's glory raised Christ from the dead, we were also raised with him. We have been co-resurrected with him so that we could be empowered to walk in the freshness of new life. For since we are permanently grafted into him to experience a death like his, then we are permanently grafted into him to experience a resurrection like his and the new life that it imparts.

Co-Resurrected

Hallelujah! We were co-crucified, co-buried, and co-raised *in Christ*. We are living by resurrection life and power, just like Jesus. He is seated at the right hand of God now...and so are we. Our destiny is to reign, not someday "somewhere over the rainbow" but now and forevermore. We reign in life with our beautiful Jesus—he in heaven and we on earth as his ambassadors, finishing the course he began two thousand years ago when he birthed the church. We, too, will finish well and then enter into his joy.

"Empowered to Walk"

The substitutionary life of Jesus is not just what he did on Calvary. It is fully operating in your life right now, empowering you, helping you, strengthening you as you go through all of life's many hills and valleys. His is "with me, with me, all the way" as the old hymn says, and praise him for it! He ever lives to intercede for us, and we live by his life in us.

"The Father's Glory Raised Christ"

If the Father's glory raised Jesus, what do you think will raise you? That's right. *Glory!* The Father's glory infuses you *daily* to live in the "freshness of new life." Are you getting this into your spirit? You are no longer living your old life. That is over. Your new life in Christ is fresh, clean, holy, and fully empowered by the Father's glory.

Co-Union, Sharing His Life

This is the climax of the love story of the ages! Jesus left heaven's glory to redeem a bride. The bride of Christ often symbolizes the church, illustrating the beautiful relationship God shares with his people. He did not die the horrible death of the cross just to create a new philosophy or start a new religion. Oh, no. He wanted you. He died for a bride, one to bring into his triune glory for all eternity. Our old life is buried, and we live "in the fullness of his life" (6:8).

Verses 6–10

Could it be any clearer that our former identity is now and forever deprived of its power? For we were co-crucified with him to dismantle the stronghold of sin within us, so that we would not continue to live one moment longer submitted to sin's power.

Obviously, a dead person is incapable of sinning. And if we were co-crucified with the Anointed One, we know that we will also share in the fullness of his life. And we know that since the Anointed One has been raised from the dead to die no more, his resurrection life has vanquished death and its power over him is finished. For by his sacrifice he died to sin's power once and for all, but he now lives continuously for the Father's pleasure.

The Fullness of His Life

This is what we have now because of Christ's sacrifice. We are living by his life—it's a *borrowed life*. Any good thing that is exhibited through us—gift, talent, beauty, ability, excellence, or virtue—is a result of his grace-life in us. We should certainly not boast in those things. Nor should we be overly impressed when they are displayed in the lives of others. Every expression of the marvelous grace of God has but *one purpose*: to glorify the Lord. It is all for the glory and exaltation of Jesus. Isn't that the song of heaven? All will proclaim his greatness for all he has done: "Then every living being joined the angelic choir. Every creature in heaven and on earth, under the earth, in the sea, and everything in them, were worshiping with one voice, saying: 'Praise, honor, glory, and dominion be to God-Enthroned and to Christ the Lamb forever and ever!'" (Revelation 5:13).

The Grace-Gifts

The words *grace* and *gift* both come from the same Greek word, *charis*. All the appointments and assignments given by God to humans are both *from* him and *for* him. After Jesus had accomplished the work of the cross and before ascending to heaven, he left behind these needed and precious "grace gifts" for the building, growing, and strengthening of his church:

> And he has generously given each one of us supernatural grace, according to the size of the gift of Christ. This is why he says:
>
> > "He ascends into the heavenly heights
> > taking his many captured ones with him,
> > and gifts were given to men"...
>
> And he has appointed some with grace to be apostles, and some with grace to be prophets, and some with grace to be evangelists, and some with grace to be pastors, and some with grace to be teachers. (Ephesians 4:7–8, 11)

They are his gifts of his grace for the building of his church for his glory!

Let's Go Deeper!

Questions

1. What did Adam bring into the world? What reigned from Adam to Moses (Romans 5:13–14)? What reigned through death? For those in Christ, what reigns now (v. 21)?

2. List the attributes of Adam and of Christ from this portion of Romans 5. How is Adam a type, or "picture," of Christ (v. 14)?

3. Romans 5:10, 16, and 17 each contain the phrase "much more." Study those verses and write down what grace has brought you "much more" of through Jesus.

4. Are you co-crucified, co-buried, co-raised, and co-seated with Christ? Take a moment to look back at Romans 6:1–10 and write down all that this truth means for you. How does this reality make it possible for you to live the "victorious life" (5:18) Jesus died to give you?

5. In this lesson, we see a very clear delineation: every person on the earth is either "in Adam" or "in Christ." Every born-again saint is in a whole new paradigm. You are not a sinner waiting for heaven. No, you are a saint bringing heaven to earth. Meditate on the foundational truth that you are no longer in Adam, and you are not under the reign and rule of sin and death. You are in Christ and under the dominion of grace. List the effects of this truth for you personally. How can you apply it by faith in practical ways in your daily life, family, relationships, and other areas?

Deeper Still!

Activations

Victorious Living!

Jesus died and was raised again. We died with him, and we rose with him. He was victorious, and we now share in his victory. We have learned in Romans 6 that "by his sacrifice he died to sin's power once and for all, but he now lives continuously for the Father's pleasure" (Romans 6:10).

This is now your reality and your inheritance in Christ as well. Your promised land is where sin has no power over you and you live continuously for the Father's pleasure. Have you settled for less? Have you been in a wrestling match with sin (bad habits, bad attitudes, bad behavior) instead of reckoning yourself dead to it? Our Lord Jesus has paved the path to freedom for us, and we walk it through sweet surrender. This is how we take up our cross and follow him.

Let's Pray

Father, thank you for such grace! Thank you that sin's power has been destroyed. How can I live in sin in light of the beautiful cross and my beautiful Savior? Today, I surrender, Lord. I want out of this battle with sin. I choose your life of victory, the borrowed life of Christ. At each crossroad of my day and each moment of surrender, help me to reckon myself dead to sin and alive in Christ. I am under the dominion of grace. That is my new reality, and I yield to it, in Jesus' name. Amen.

Living Our New Identity

(Romans 6:11–23)

We are so enriched and blessed because of Paul's letters in the New Testament. Of the twenty-seven New Testament books, at least thirteen of them were explicitly signed by the apostle Paul. What an assignment and stewardship from heaven he was given!

Notably, in all his letters, he always began with *encouragement*. First, he brought loving assurance before bringing loving rebuke, correction, or warning. This is a very good and practical example for us in our dealings with one another: first, encouragement. Building up and blessing others should be the first priority in our communication.

The pattern in Paul's letters over and over follows a basic two-part structure: doctrine and application. He spends the first half of his letters *teaching*. He lays the solid, doctrinal foundation of truth *first*. Only then does he exhort his readers to the practical application of those truths. This is key because understanding God's heart, mind, and will builds us up and empowers us to apply his Word to our daily living. First the blueprint, then the house; first the foundation, then the building. In Romans, chapters 1–5 are focused on laying a solid, doctrinal foundation. Chapters 6–8 and 12–14 give us practical applications of those doctrinal truths.

Yielding to God (Romans 6:11–20)

Living from a New Perspective

The victory is ours. The price is paid, and the reign of sin is over for those in union with Christ. We are eternally one with the Three-in-One, but in order to live that new life, we must do so from a new mindset, fully knowing the old has passed and our new life is one of abiding in Christ.

Verse 11

> So let it be the same way with you! Since you are now joined with him, you must continually view yourselves as dead and unresponsive to sin's appeal while living daily for God's pleasure in union with Jesus, the Anointed One.

"Continually View Yourselves"

This verse contains secrets for victorious living. View yourself as *dead* and *unresponsive* to sin's appeal. You are new in Christ! Make God's pleasure your driving motivation. Experience that pleasure in your constant union with Jesus. View yourself as the look-alike, radiant partner of the Lord Jesus Christ. That is who you really are. That is certainly how he sees you and how he wants you to see yourself.

Verses 12–13

> Sin is a dethroned monarch; so you must no longer give it an opportunity to rule over your life, controlling how you live and compelling you to obey its desires and cravings. So then, refuse to answer its call to surrender your body as a tool for wickedness. Instead, passionately answer God's call to keep yielding your body to him as one who has now experienced resurrection life! You live now for his pleasure, ready to be used for his noble purpose.

"Sin Is a Dethroned Monarch"

Listen, you have been delivered. Get excited about your new life gift from God! Sin was once your king, but now you have a new King, and his name is above all other names. Every other name—sickness, fear, addiction, anger, deception, pride, or bondage—bows to the name of Jesus. Everything in heaven and on earth is under his jurisdiction, and he is your champion defender and your reigning sovereign. Sin has no hold on you nor any claim to you. We must live from that powerful perspective, knowing we are victorious, free conquerors, who can say confidently, "So death, tell me, where is your victory? Tell me death, where is your sting? It is sin that gives death its sting and the law that gives sin its power. But we thank God for giving us the victory as conquerors through our Lord Jesus, the Anointed One" (1 Corinthians 15:55–57).

Keep Yielding

See yourself as one with Jesus. God's math says one plus one equals one…not two! Like a steeping tea bag in boiling water, you are a new creation. You're not a teabag plus hot water; you're tea, something new in Christ. As you continue yielding to him and remain in life-union with him, the transformation is becoming more and more your reality. So abide. Remain. "Keep yielding" as Paul says in Romans 6:13, and you will grow and go from glory to glory to glory!

Answer God's Call

How do we yield? We answer God's call. We "refuse to answer" sin's call, and we choose to "passionately answer God's call." When he calls, we come running, don't we? We are his bridal company, and we are attuned to his loving call.

Favor

In these next few verses, we are reminded of the power of God's grace—his unmerited favor—in our lives. He has chosen you in love. You will find that as you live from love, sin loses its allure, and you will step into a whole new realm that surpasses mere law, rules, and duty. In that realm of bridal devotion, where we live as one who has been conquered by God's love, the desire for intimacy with Jesus overrides all other desires. That is the power of favor.

Verses 14–15

Remember this: sin will not conquer you, for God already has! You are not governed by law but governed by the reign of the grace of God.

What are we to do, then? Should we sin to our hearts' content since there's no law to condemn us anymore? What a terrible thought!

A Conquered Life

You have been conquered by grace. His loving-kindness has melted your heart, and all the fight has gone out of you. You are captive to his eyes of fiery love, and you just can't look away. You are captivated, captured, and conquered by God. Sin has been dethroned, and now grace reigns supreme. Evil is always overcome by good. Darkness is always overcome by light. In the same way, sin is *always overcome* by Christ's life. This is how we overcome:

- *Know*—We are in life-union with Christ.

- *View*—We continually view ourselves as dead to sin.

- *Yield*—We yield our lives and bodies to him.

- *Obey*—We answer his call and obey.

Governed by Law or by Grace

Many Christians today are still governed by the law, thinking and behaving as if salvation is somehow earned and that right-standing with the Lord is based on a merit system. For example, many saints do what is right often out of a sense of duty and dread rather than love. This brings discouragement, stress, and fear of failure. This way of life, though it may seem good and wholesome, is not the life of Christ. Words carved in stone cannot change and liberate us, but grace transfers to us the borrowed life of the Anointed One—real life. His Spirit of life frees us from sin and death, "for the 'law' of the Spirit of life flowing through the anointing of Jesus has liberated us from the 'law' of sin and death" (Romans 8:2).

The new life we now live is Spirit-empowered. Striving and fear are over because "now every righteous requirement of the law can be fulfilled through the Anointed One living his life in us. And we are free to live, not according to our flesh, but by the dynamic power of the Holy Spirit!" (Romans 8:4).

His Grace in Us

Here is an amazing secret: every command of God carries within it the grace to fulfill it. Therefore, it has always been and always will be *grace alone* by which we live. If the new covenant commands that we must walk in love, which it does, then as we "know, view, yield, and obey," grace will empower us to love! God will never command us to do what he does not empower us to do. With God all things are possible. Therefore, if he requires it of us, it will happen through us…by the power of his grace. The "thou shalts" become for us a prophetic *promise* in Christ. He hasn't planned any defeats for us, only victories, and we *can*, *should*, and *must* live that way. You are now free and empowered to embrace every command.

Freedom

Thank God! Grace brings us into a *supernatural freedom* to choose what and whom we will obey. We are no longer slaves. At one time, we had *no choice* but to sin. But that is our life no more. Jesus has paid the necessary redemption price to free us from the bondage of our sin nature. Now we can choose him.

Verse 16

> Don't you realize that grace frees you to choose your own master? But choose carefully, for you surrender yourself to become a servant—bound to the one you choose to obey. If you choose to love sin, it will become your master,

and it will own you and reward you with death. But if you choose to love and obey God, he will lead you into perfect righteousness.

So Free

Personal freedom—free will—is a treasured gift from God. He didn't save us and then make us fear-led drudges or drones. No, he gave us our freedom so that we could choose to worship him and love him with our whole hearts and lives. Now, we choose our thought life, our physical life, our emotional life, and our spiritual life. And, since he commands us to love him with our heart, soul, mind, and strength, we are free to do so. Our freedom is complete, for "if the Son sets you free from sin, then become a true son and be unquestionably free!" (John 8:36). We are not just free *from something*, but we are also free *to do something*—to worship God with our whole lives.

Verses 17–18

> And thanks be to God, for in the past you were servants of sin, but now your obedience is heart deep, and your life is being molded by truth through the teaching you are devoted to. And now you celebrate your freedom from your former master—sin. You've left its bondage, and now God's perfect righteousness holds power over you as his loving servants.

"Heart Deep"

Now your obedience is *heart deep*. Oh, sing hallelujah! Aren't you so very glad for this truth? Our obedience is not outward, empty, ritualistic, or burdensome. Our obedience springs from the deep well of his love in us through the Holy Spirit! It bursts forth *naturally* supernaturally because we have been born again. Jesus spoke to us of the "well-spring living" that he came to give us, saying, "Believe in me so that rivers of living water will burst out from within you, flowing from your innermost being, just like the Scripture says!"

(John 7:38). And, "But if anyone drinks the living water I give them, they will never be thirsty again. For when you drink the water I give you, it becomes a gushing fountain of the Holy Spirit, flooding you with endless life!" (4:14). He is passionate about us living from the overflow of his life in us.

A New Master

Everything is new now because of Jesus! Now, in him, you have a new "boss," and he is kind, loving, humble, gentle, and oh-so-easy to please. Listen afresh to his sweet words of welcome: "Simply join your life with mine. Learn my ways and you'll discover that I'm gentle, humble, easy to please. You will find refreshment and rest in me" (Matthew 11:29).

Verses 19–20

> I've used the familiar terms of a "servant" and a "master" to compensate for your weakness to understand. For just as you surrendered your bodies and souls to impurity and lawlessness, which only brought more lawlessness into your lives, so now surrender yourselves as servants of righteousness, which brings you deeper into true holiness. For when you were bound as servants to sin, you lived your lives free from any obligation to righteousness.

"So Now Surrender"

It is time to surrender. It is time to let go and live as "servants of righteousness." That is true freedom! God is saying, *Let go of your death grip of control on your life and live the simple life of sweet surrender. My peace, real peace, will catch you and embrace you in the place of surrender.*

Living from Life Union (Romans 6:21–23)

Fruitfulness

You are the garden of the Lord. You are his fruitful vineyard. These metaphors from Scripture reveal God's heart for his family—you and me. He intends for our redeemed and resurrected lives to fill the earth with his bounty. Through our union with him, life springs forth. The earth is filled with his glory *through* his glorious bride.

Verses 21–23

So tell me, what benefit ensued from doing those things that you're now ashamed of? It left you with nothing but a legacy of shame and death. But now, as God's loving servants, you live in joyous freedom from the power of sin. So consider the benefits you now enjoy—you are brought deeper into the experience of true holiness that ends with eternal life! For sin's meager wages is death, but God's lavish gift is life eternal, found in your union with our Lord Jesus, the Anointed One.

"Joyous Freedom"

Sin is not a part of you anymore! Freedom is your new normal in Christ. In him, you are not living a depressing, religiously bound up life of "dos and don'ts." You have a joyous freedom. You aren't bound to sin or to the law; you are bound to Jesus' heart, to righteousness, to power, and to love. Your sins? Your past? They have all been canceled and deleted. Check it out:

He canceled out every legal violation we had on our record and the old arrest warrant that stood to indict us. He erased it all—our sins, our stained soul—he deleted it all and they cannot be retrieved! Everything we once were in Adam has been placed onto his cross and nailed permanently there as a public display of cancellation. (Colossians 2:14)

Sin's Meager Wages

The word for "wages" in Romans 6:23 is *opsonion,* which is taken from the word *opsarion,* meaning "dried fish." This was a day's wage for a Roman soldier—one piece of dried fish. That's the profit of sin. What a great illustration of the worthlessness, pointlessness, and futility of a life bound to sin. This is contrasted with God's amazing gift of eternal life—*no comparison!*

God's Lavish Gift

Sin is dethroned. We have been immersed into Christ's death, burial, resurrection, and his exaltation. We now share life-union— one life—with Jesus the Anointed One. This is our new reality: "The one who joins himself to the Lord is mingled into one spirit with him" (1 Corinthians 6:17). "One spirit" with Jesus is the garden restored—unbroken communion, unending bliss.

Fruitfulness Is Your Future

You are *one spirit* with Jesus. That is your new reality! The more you embrace that reality and continue in it through the abiding life of John 15, you will become more and more and even more *fruitful.* This is Jesus' description of his vision for you:

> I am the sprouting vine and you're my branches. As you live in union with me as your source, fruitfulness will stream from within you—but when you live separated from me you are powerless…But if you live in life-union with me and if my words live powerfully within you—then you can ask whatever you desire and it will be done. When your lives bear abundant fruit, you demonstrate that you are my mature disciples who glorify my Father! (John 15:5, 7–8)

Beloved, receive this true statement: your destiny is to bear much fruit. Through your beautiful, fruit-laden life in union with Christ, you will bring your heavenly Father much glory. Yes, indeed, your future in him is bright, even better than you've imagined. But you can be sure he has imagined it all, and he is faithfully bringing you into it, every moment.

This is our destiny and our legacy: life-union! We carry his fragrance, his life, his glory, and his love. This is the profound truth and power of Romans 6, and it is ours if we choose it. Let's choose life.

Let's Go Deeper!

Questions

1. According to 6:11–13, how must you view yourself? What has been dethroned? What call must you refuse? What call must you answer? (Write these answers out as complete sentences; they make excellent faith declarations to speak over yourself.)

2. Refer back to Romans 6:13–14 and fill in these blanks:

   - Refuse to _____ [sin's] call or _____ your body to it.
   - Keep _____ your body to God because you have experienced _____ life.
   - You are not _____ by the law, but are _____ by the reign of _____.

3. Once, you had no choice; you were sin's slave. Read 6:16–19 and describe the power you have now to choose or not choose sin. Whose dominion are you under now?

4. We are so free! Some would argue that we are free enough to continue in sin because of grace, but what are the consequences of any such poor choices (v. 23)? What will a sinful lifestyle keep us from according to verses 21–23?

5. In verse 21, Paul speaks of your legacy as a Christian. We can either leave a legacy of defeat and shame or of righteousness and holiness. Do you think this eternal perspective is beneficial in helping you surrender yourself to be a servant of righteousness? How so?

Deeper Still!

Activations

Sin's Reign Is Over

Hallelujah! Sin is no longer your king. Jesus is King, and he rules in righteousness, peace, and joy. That is the kingdom of God: "For the kingdom of God is not a matter of rules about food and drink, but is in the realm of the Holy Spirit, filled with righteousness, peace, and joy" (Romans 14:17).

No matter what your circumstances, the devil, or your own thoughts may be telling you, the truth is you have been translated out of one kingdom and into another. Now, your path forward is a simple one: simply yield to God.

Answer God's Call

How do we yield? *We answer God's call.* We "refuse to answer" sin's call, and we choose to "passionately answer God's call." When he calls, we come running because we are his bride, attuned to his loving call. We should respond to him with the same enthusiasm the Shepherd-King asks of his Shulamite:

> Can you not discern this new day of destiny
> breaking forth around you?
> The early signs of my purposes and plans
> are bursting forth.
> The budding vines of new life
> are now blooming everywhere.
> The fragrance of their flowers whispers,
> "There is change in the air."
> Arise, my love, my beautiful companion,
> and run with me to the higher place.
> For now is the time to arise and come away with me. (Song of Songs 2:13)

Let's Pray

Lord, I truly want to live a yielded life. In this moment right now, I lay everything down at your beautiful feet in full surrender. I am finished with striving and struggling. Instead, I choose to answer your call. How privileged I am, Lord, to be your bride who hears your voice! Help me to hear and to heed and to yield to your loving voice as you guide me from victory to victory and glory to glory. I believe and I know that you have not planned any defeat for me. I trust you to take me all the way over and into every single promise that is mine because of the death, burial, and resurrection of Jesus Christ. Yes, Lord, now and always. Amen.

No More Bondage

(Romans 7:1–25)

Dead to the Law of Moses (Romans 7:1–6)

More than Conquerors

Up to this point in Romans, we have covered the definitions of sin and the lostness of humanity in chapters 1–2. We have looked into the mercy and grace of God toward us in chapters 3–4. In chapter 5, Paul gave us a beautiful list of all the benefits that are ours in Christ and how we are to reign in life. Chapter 6 brought us to a personal application in our lives of how through grace we overcome sin and learn to live by our new nature, the co-resurrected, borrowed life of Christ. Through the cross, we overcome not only the guilt but also the power of our sin.

Now in chapter 7, Paul further develops the understanding that we are co-crucified, co-buried, co-raised, and co-seated with Christ. Sin cannot conquer us because God already has! In fact, the conquering love of God has made us *more than conquerors*. We are free in Christ to yield to the new life within us and walk this world in victory, not defeat.

Verses 1–3

> I write to you, dear brothers and sisters, who are familiar with the law. Don't you know that when a person dies, it ends his obligation to the law? For example, a married couple is bound by the law to remain together until separated by death. But when one spouse dies, the other is released from the law of the marriage. So then if a wife is joined to another man while still married, she commits adultery. But if her husband dies, she is obviously free from the marriage contract and may marry another man without being charged with adultery.

The Illustration of Marriage

As an object lesson of just how free we are from the law of sin and death, Paul uses marriage. How does the institution of marriage relate to the law and to grace? In the same way that the covenant of marriage lasts "until death do us part," the old covenant, based on the law, ends when we become co-crucified, co-buried, and co-raised in Christ. Truly, the former contract is null and void, and everything is new.

Verses 4–5

> So, my dear brothers and sisters, the same principle applies to your relationship with God. For you died to your first husband, the law, by being co-crucified with the body of the Messiah. So you are now free to "marry" another—the one who was raised from the dead so that you may now bear spiritual fruit for God.
>
> When we were merely living natural lives, the law, through defining sin, actually awakened sinful desires within us, which resulted in bearing the fruit of death.

Death Frees Us from the Law

Paul uses this very unique illustration to show us how completely free we are from the bondage of the law. Death is final. We have died with Christ to our former "spouse," the law. Now, we are "free to marry another," Jesus Christ. We are free to enjoy our union with him with no obligation to our former marriage partner. We have no obligation to the law. We are dead to it completely! In fact, to go back to it in any way would be adultery.

Your Marriage to the Law Is Over

What a harsh companion is the law. It is the haunting voice of "never enough, never enough, never enough." No matter how hard we strive with the best of intentions, the law cannot be satisfied by human effort. Jesus fulfilled the righteous requirements of the law for us that we would never be able to fulfill on our own. Now, through his death, we are co-crucified with him and dead to the law completely. *Completely.* We have been released from that contract and obligation. Therefore, we can no longer be accused by the law.

You Are Clean

Our conscience is clean before God. Sometimes our conscience can be "over-sensitive" and actually condemn us inordinately. We must reject this carnal tendency (fueled by sin consciousness) and stand our spiritual ground by faith. We are no longer bound to the law. The blood of Jesus has paid every debt and made us clean. *Completely.* There is absolutely nothing you can add to the grace of God that has set you free from the law of sin and death.

The Freshness of New Life in the Spirit

Like an old, cumbersome cloak covering us and keeping us from the sunlight of a fresh, spring day, we need to throw off the law and all its trappings. We need to run full speed, hand-in-hand with our Bridegroom-King, into the new life he purchased for us with his own blood. Let nothing deter you from the "freshness of a new life in the power of the Holy Spirit" (7:6).

Verse 6

> But now that we have been fully released from the power
> of the law, we are dead to what once controlled us. And our
> lives are no longer motivated by the obsolete way of follow-
> ing the written code, so that now we may serve God by living
> in the freshness of a new life in the power of the Holy Spirit.

"The Written Code"

We were once bound to a written code carved on stone, literally
set in stone. Cold, hard, dead. It ruled and controlled us. That way
of life has been eradicated through Christ. We are not motivated
by a code anymore; we are motivated by *love*. We must guard that
freedom and never again let ourselves come under that written code
that only produces death.

"The Freshness of a New Life"

What a contrast! This new life is nothing like the old order. Once
motivated by fear and guilt, we served God at the lowest level of
heart commitment—out of mere obligation. Not now! Through
Christ and the power of the Holy Spirit, we can worship and serve
God in new and dynamic ways. Is your commitment and service
flowing from your heart, empowered by the Holy Spirit? It can,
should, and must be.

Jesus Is All!

Listen, anything that calls to your heart, luring you to think you
have to add anything to the cross, is a hellish lie. Don't receive it or
come under it. It may sound holy, but it is not. Your new life is in
Jesus Christ. That is it. That is all. He is your righteousness. He is
your victory. He is your wedding garment. He is your beauty and
your crown and your strength and your... You get the idea. Jesus
is above all, before all, our all in all. That is the grace gospel. Don't
settle for a mere written code. You have the living Christ!

The Purpose of the Law (Romans 7:7–14)

The Law Defines and Awakens Sin

In the next few verses, Paul explains the role of the law. Does the law have a place at all in the work of God in the hearts of people? Is the law evil? Obviously, the law is not sinful; in fact, the opposite is true. We see that the law is both holy and helpful in its God-ordained role.

Verse 7

> So, what shall we say about all this? Am I suggesting that the law is sinful? Of course not! In fact, it was the law that gave us the clear definition of sin. For example, when the law said, "Do not covet," it became the catalyst to see how wrong it was for me to crave what belongs to someone else.

The Law Is a Catalyst

In itself, the law is not sinful; it is holy. However, the law can only diagnose the sin problem. *It cannot cure it.* The law serves the purpose of clearly and powerfully identifying what sin is. The law helps us recognize sin and our need to be freed from the power and penalty of sin.

Verse 8

> It was through God's commandment that sin was awakened in me and built its base of operation within me to stir up every kind of wrong desire. For in the absence of the law, sin hides dormant.

The Commandment Awakens Sin

The more law you put on yourself and others, the more sin is awakened in you. Rebellion is actually a response to commandments. When our self-rule and self-will are confronted by the law, the carnal response is defiance, insubordination, and "every wrong desire." If we will hold up the life of Jesus (his voice, his nature) before ourselves and others as the goal and focus, *not the law*, then righteousness and righteous longings will be awakened in us.

Verses 9–11

> I once lived without a clear understanding of the law, but when I heard God's commandments, sin sprang to life and brought with it a death sentence. The commandment that was intended to bring life brought me death instead. Sin, by means of the commandment, built a base of operation within me, to overpower me and put me to death.

The Law Brings Death

The law serves its purpose by shining law on the darkened ways within us. Once sin is defined and exposed by the law, it is effectively empowered to set up rulership in us. In this way, the law kills. Sin is exposed, yes, but not dethroned and therefore works death in us. Only grace can dethrone sin.

Verses 12–13

> So then, we have to conclude that the problem is not with the law itself, for the law is holy and its commandments are correct and for our good.
>
> So, did something meant to be good become death to me? Certainly not! It was not the law but sin unmasked that produced my spiritual death. The sacred commandment merely uncovered the evil of sin so it could be seen for what it is.

The Law Shows Sin "for What It Is"

We can be clear on this fact: the law is holy and good. It is God's law and therefore cannot be anything less than good. It is sin "unmasked" by the law that produces spiritual death. Through the law, sin is made utterly sinful and our need for grace, utterly clear. The law drives us to the cross where sin is finally broken.

The Law Cannot Change You

This is the conclusion we finally come to concerning the law. It is good for diagnosing our sin problem but completely incapable of bringing the spiritual healing we long for. This holy longing is what ultimately brings every saint of God to their knees at the foot of the cross.

Verse 14

> For we know that the law is divinely inspired and comes from the spiritual realm, but I am a human being made of flesh and trafficked as a slave under sin's authority.

Trafficked as a Slave

When you try to live under the law, your reality becomes *slavery*. In the flesh, our human nature, we cannot fulfill the law. Our nature is under the rule of sin, and there is no way out…except the cross, death. The law was a means to an end, bringing us to God for saving grace. At the cross of Calvary, we find relief from the burden of the law.

> For God achieved what the law was unable to accomplish, because the law was limited by the weakness of human nature.
>
> Yet God sent us his Son in human form to identify with human weakness. Clothed with humanity, God's Son gave his body to be the sin-offering so that God could once and for all condemn the guilt and power of sin. So now every righteous requirement of the law can be fulfilled through the Anointed One living his life in us. And we are free to live, not according to our flesh, but by the dynamic power of the Holy Spirit! (Romans 8:3–4)

Sin, the Unwelcome Intruder (Romans 7:15–25)

Sin Is No Longer a Part of Our Identity

This is the beauty of our new birth! This is the power of grace and what distinguishes Christianity from mere self-help religions and humanistic philosophies. You have a new identity, and it is not a "sinner saved by grace." No, you are brand new. The true you has been freed from sin's dominion, and every day you are growing into becoming more like Jesus. You no longer need to have a fearful, sin-focused mindset. It is time to be Christ-focused, for glory is your destiny.

Verses 15–20

> I'm a mystery to myself, for I want to do what is right, but end up doing what my moral instincts condemn. And if my behavior is not in line with my desire, my conscience still confirms the excellence of the law. And now I realize that it is no longer my true self doing it, but the unwelcome intruder of sin in my humanity. For I know that nothing good lives within the flesh of my fallen humanity. The longings to do what is right are within me, but willpower is not enough to accomplish it. My lofty desires to do what is good are dashed when I do the things I want to avoid. So if my behavior contradicts my desires to do good, I must conclude that it's not my true identity doing it, but the unwelcome intruder of sin hindering me from being who I really am.

"My True Identity"

Sin is the unwelcome intruder hindering us from being who we really are. Jesus came to give us a new identity. In him, we are freed from low-level living, freed from the Adamic nature. You don't have to suppress your sin nature, push it down, or bind it. You can't make yourself "good" or convert the flesh. It must be reckoned as dead.

You simply surrender to God and yield to the Christ-life in you. We are released from the slavery of sin's dominion, and we are brought into a new kingdom of great grace. Grace is completely other! It is not human. It is of God. It is supernatural. The law says, "Do this and live," but grace says, "It is finished! You are alive in Christ!"

So, what is your true identity? You are a son or daughter of God. You are freed from the domain of sin because Christ has won the battle against sin for you already. The war is over! You have all the benefits of the family without earning a single thing. That, my friend, is called inheritance, and it is yours *in Christ.*

The Old and the New Cannot Coexist

The old self, enslaved to sin, has indeed died (Romans 6:6), and the new self, righteous in Christ, has indeed been generated by the Holy Spirit (Colossians 3:10). But, unfortunately, the pervasive position taken by most Christian leaders is that the old self is still "alive and well" within the believer and that our sinful performance gives daily testimony to this as "fact."

From this viewpoint, the old self apparently leaps in and out of the tomb many times during the typical day. However, one seldom hears a teacher claim that the new self leaps in and out of the womb. Most never see that the very existence of either precludes the existence of its opposite. The two can't coexist any more than the two kings can rule. It was the death of the old self that enabled the new self to be born. It is impossible for the new self to exist until the old self has died, and the old self cannot resurrect itself. There is but one life that has such resurrection power…the life of Christ!

When Sin Intrudes

This isn't to say we will not be tempted to sin and give into this temptation. As expressed in 1 John 1:8–9,

> If we boast that we have no sin, we're only fooling our-
> selves and are strangers to the truth. But if we freely admit
> our sins when his light uncovers them, he will be faithful
> to forgive us every time. God is just to forgive us our sins

because of Christ, and he will continue to cleanse us from all unrighteousness.

Paul himself says, "My lofty desires to do what is good are dashed when I do the things I want to avoid" (Romans 7:19). What the truth of verse 20 tells us is that sin is the unwelcome intruder, not our old nature coming through. Christians still sin, but we are not defined by that sin.

You Are Free to Choose

This truth does not release us from full responsibility for our sin. In reality, when we accept as fact that Christians no longer have a sin nature, it places each of us even more squarely "on the hook" and totally responsible to choose, moment-by-moment, against the wooings, deceptions, and accusations of indwelling sin working through the flesh. Freedom from sin doesn't mean we will never sin again; it means we are now free to resist when temptation comes. The old self, enslaved to sin, was powerless and had no choice but to cave when sin attacked. The new self has resources to fight back. That means we are without excuse when we sin because we know we possess the life ("Christ in me"), which overcomes on a moment-by-moment basis.

Jesus achieved victory over sin and death on the cross so that we have the choice to live the "borrowed life" of being in Christ and "continually share in the death of Jesus in our own bodies so that the resurrection life of Jesus will be revealed through our humanity" (2 Corinthians 4:10). It is not by our will that we can achieve victory over sin but rather by Jesus' victory on the cross.

Our Former Identity Is Powerless

Note: This isn't just our sins that Christ paid for on the cross—although praise the Lord for that blessed truth—but the old "you" died there with him so that your body (which is the instrument of sin) might be made ineffective and inactive for evil and we might no longer be slaves of sin. Now you are dead to sin! The true you is empowered by grace to live victoriously in Jesus' victory. This glorious reality caused Paul to say with such emphasis, "Could it be any clearer that our former identity is now and forever deprived of its power? For we were co-crucified with him to dismantle the stronghold of sin within us, so that we would not continue to live one moment longer submitted to sin's power" (Romans 6:6).

Law-Keeping Cannot Set You Free

Paul expertly leads us to this pride-shattering conclusion: you can't do it on your own. He was very qualified to make this important argument in his case for grace. Paul was an expert in the law, flawless even. But his experience with law-keeping only made clear to him that he needed much more than mere rules to obey—he needed a heart transplant! And the good news is that a new heart is what Jesus died to give us.

Verses 21–23

> Through my experience of this principle, I discover that even when I want to do good, evil is ready to sabotage me. Truly, deep within my true identity, I love to do what pleases God. But I discern another power operating in my humanity, waging a war against the moral principles of my conscience and bringing me into captivity as a prisoner to the "law" of sin—this unwelcome intruder in my humanity.

The Battle Within

Galatians 5:17 says that the flesh "craves the things that offend the Holy Spirit" and vice versa, and there is obviously a war going on inside of every Christian, but it's not the old self versus the new self doing battle. Those cannot exist simultaneously. The Greek word often interpreted as "flesh" in all pertinent New Testament verses refers to the body...the physical body with its frailties and vulnerability to sin. Romans 7:20 speaks of the power of indwelling sin (not the sin nature) working in people to produce undesirable (sinful) behavior. The power of sin simply deceives the Christian, suggesting to the will that a choice be made to perform according to the old, self-serving patterns programmed in previously. This is referred to as "walking after the flesh."

Perception Is Not Reality

Satan could never deceive a Christian with a direct approach as a "man with horns in a red suit." He must disguise himself if he is to have any hope of defeating us. There is only one way to accomplish this deception, and that is to masquerade in the thought life of Christians, posing as their unique versions of the old self. Some naive Christians believe they are generating the unchristian suggestion and therefore focus defensive efforts against the wrong foe—what they perceive to be a darker side of themselves. They fire all their bullets at a shadow. This is the explanation for the frustration depicted in Romans 7:15: "I'm a mystery to myself, for I want to do what is right, but end up doing what my moral instincts condemn."

Verses 24–25

> What an agonizing situation I am in! So who has the power to rescue this miserable man from the unwelcome intruder of sin and death? I give all my thanks to God, for his mighty power has finally provided a way out through our Lord Jesus, the Anointed One! So if left to myself, the flesh is aligned with the law of sin, but now my renewed mind is fixed on and submitted to God's righteous principles.

"Fixed on and Submitted"

As a result of Adam's sin, we were all born sinners, and we received a sinful nature. Our sinful nature was entirely hostile to him, and we were his actual enemy. The only possible cure for your old sinful life was death. The good news is that God has already provided the solution for us in Christ. When you were born again, you were crucified with Christ, and you were buried with him. Your old sinful nature died, and you received God's divine nature to replace it. You have received his all-sufficient life in exchange for your old sinful nature and have been forever "mingled into one spirit with him" (1 Corinthians 6:17).

Your old sinful self died, and you became a new creation. Even though you will still have temptation to sin, you have the choice to say no. You were resurrected with Christ and have a brand-new life with a brand-new nature. Your old sinful life wasn't changed; *it was exchanged* with real life, the very life of Jesus! You now have a nature of righteousness, holiness, blamelessness. You have no need to work to become a better person because God has already made you into a new person. In Christ, we have become partakers of the divine nature. Peter described this divine partnership this way:

> As a result of this, he has given you magnificent promises that are beyond all price, so that through the power of these tremendous promises we can experience partnership with the divine nature, by which you have escaped the corrupt desires that are of the world. (2 Peter 1:4)

Dear beloved, even when you do say yes to sin, remember that God has forgiven you. Confess your sin; do not dwell in shame. In Christ, you have a new identity: not guilty. Dwell instead in this.

"I Give All My Thanks to God"

Look what the Lord has done. All sin is broken through Christ, and we have the victory in him. Amen! So, thanks, thanks, and even more thanks be to God who has "provided a way out through our Lord Jesus Christ, the Anointed One!" Sin is defeated. Death is defeated. We have the victory because of the Lamb who was slain.

Let's Go Deeper!

Questions

1. What affected you most from this lesson? What did you learn about the heart of God that perhaps you didn't see as clearly before?

2. As put forth by Paul in verses 1–6, how does the illustration of marriage accurately describe our relationship to the law?

3. Do you have an obligation to the law? Why or why not?

4. How is the law beneficial? (See vv. 7, 12, and 13.) What is the law powerless to do? (See v. 14 and 8:3–4.)

5. What is the "unwelcome intruder," and how do we overcome it? (See vv. 17, 20, and 23–25.)

Deeper Still!

Activations

Are You Living Grace-Based?

We live from our belief system, not mere information stored in our brain. In other words, we live out what we believe to be true in our heart. For example, I may know intellectually that God has removed my sin as far as the east is from the west, but if my heart still condemns me, I will bear a guilty conscience unnecessarily. We always operate in line with our highest values. We have to get our highest values in order and focus them on Christ. Our behavior will follow.

Examine your own life. Are you living, acting, or thinking as if you are still married to the law and bound to it?

Some symptoms of this would be:

- Difficulty receiving God's forgiveness
- Difficulty forgiving yourself and others
- Self-hatred, self-centeredness, self-abasement
- Judgmental and "holier-than-thou" attitudes
- Getting your peace, identity, and worth from your behavior
- People pleasing
- Holding yourself and others to impossible standards
- Feeling guilty for needing help from God and others

If you see any of these faulty mindsets at work in your life, then you are likely living under a false obligation to the law. It is time to break up with that old system of dos and don'ts and the "two-nature" belief system. You are truly, actually, entirely free in Christ. All sin and sin's results were dealt with at Calvary. You can't get freer, holier, or more acceptable to God than you are right now through the blood of Christ. Dear friend, it is time to live that way!

Let's Pray

Father, I confess my trust in you and in the blood of Jesus. You're my salvation and my song. I renounce trusting in my own works, strength, or goodness to earn right-standing with you. I renounce self-righteousness and confess that all my hope is in you and you alone. Help me to live grace-based, not law- or fear-based. Help me to proclaim through my life, my words, and my actions the pure grace gospel. In Jesus' mighty name, I pray. Amen.

The Goal of Grace and Glory

(Romans 8:1–16)

Romans 8 is the climax of the message Paul has been building. It isn't as though Romans diminishes in any way after chapter 8, but rather, this chapter is just truly sublime! So, as you enter into this study of Romans 8, I pray you will be forever amazed by its magnificence and that the Holy Spirit will write its truths upon your heart and drive all discouragement from you, amen.

No Condemnation (Romans 8:1–4)

We have seen verse by verse and chapter by chapter that Paul has been systematically dismantling every argument against the grace gospel and every excuse of human reasoning. Now he begins this amazing chapter with the words: "So now the case is closed." Get ready, saint! Receive the "gospel truth" of Romans 8 into your heart of hearts. You are free, clear, and dearly loved.

Verse 1

> So now the case is closed. There remains no accusing voice of condemnation against those who are joined in life-union with Jesus, the Anointed One.

"No Accusing Voice"

Every accusing voice has been silenced by the cross. This is the critical message Paul unfolds throughout the chapter. Those who are in Christ will not face condemnation in any way. Do you live that way? Do you live under a shadow of impending doom? Paul is urging every believer: This is who you really are. You are in Christ.

Verse 2

> For the "law" of the Spirit of life flowing through the anointing of Jesus has liberated us from the "law" of sin and death.

"The Law of the Spirit of Life"

This is really a fascinating phrase and worth our deep reflection. We normally do not group "law" and "spirit" together in the same context, but Paul does. He does so in the course of making a comparison between two laws:

- *The Law of Sin and Death*—This law is irrefutable, isn't it? All have sinned. All are under sin's dominion. The only thing capable of breaking this law is a greater law.

- *The Law of the Spirit of Life*—This is the greater or higher law. It is capable of overriding the law of sin and death. It is constant and predictable, so Paul refers to it as a law. It is *sure*—as sure as the sun in its course and the force of gravity keeping every heavenly body in its position. The law of the Spirit of Life is constant and irrevocable. This is the law that now governs and determines your new life in Christ.

The Spirit Life

The *spirit life* is the only thing that can liberate you from the *sin life*. Through the Spirit, we soar above the power of sin. Faith brings us and keeps us in this higher life—by grace alone, through faith alone, in Christ alone.

Verse 3

> For God achieved what the law was unable to accomplish, because the law was limited by the weakness of human nature.
>
> Yet God sent us his Son in human form to identify with human weakness. Clothed with humanity, God's Son gave his body to be the sin-offering so that God could once and for all condemn the guilt and power of sin.

The Law Failed

The law of Moses was holy and good, but it failed. It could not make humans holy: "For the law has never made anyone perfect, but in its place is a far better hope which gives us confidence to experience intimacy with God!" (Hebrews 7:19).

The law was limited because its success depended on human strength. Jesus had to come and meet the requirements of the law on our behalf, and he did! Once and for all, it is finished. Through Jesus' sacrifice on the cross, God judged our sin forever. The law failed, but God did not. Jesus conquered sin for us.

Jesus Identifies with Human Weakness

We need to soak in this amazing truth. God put skin on so that he could identify with us. He, therefore, is able to be the compassionate High Priest on our behalf. Before Christ, "The law appointed flawed men as high priests, but God's promise, sealed with his oath, which succeeded the law, appoints a perfect Son who is complete forever!" (Hebrews 7:28). And Jesus was tested in every way, as we are, but prevailed and was sinless. There is nothing we will ever go through, experience, or feel that Jesus does not understand. He gets it—he gets us—because he selflessly and lovingly became one of us.

Not a Manual—Emmanuel

The law couldn't do it, so God came—in the flesh. Isaiah foretold the Messiah would be known as "Emmanuel," which means "God became one of us," "God with us," or "God among us" (Matthew

1:23). He didn't have to come, but he refused to have an eternity without you. He can do anything, but he would not do that. The passionate love of Christ for you moved him to do the inconceivable: "He emptied himself of his outward glory by reducing himself to the form of a lowly servant. He became human! He humbled himself and became vulnerable, choosing to be revealed as a man and was obedient. He was a perfect example, even in his death—a criminal's death by crucifixion!" (Philippians 2:7–8).

Jesus came and lowered himself in order to lift you up. This is why he is forever exalted and has been given the name above every name. Jesus accomplished our salvation by coming and being our substitutionary sacrifice. He locked himself eternally into human form. We deserved death, so he died for us. We deserved punishment, so he took our punishment for us. Beware the lie that says there is more you must add to his beautiful work. Remember, grace plus anything else is no longer grace.

Verse 4

> So now every righteous requirement of the law can be fulfilled through the Anointed One living his life in us. And we are free to live, not according to our flesh, but by the dynamic power of the Holy Spirit!

"We Are Free"

Now, through the perfect and powerful life of Jesus Christ, the requirements of the law are met, and we are free to live by the power of the Holy Spirit. The law no longer controls us in any way. It has been fulfilled already for us because we are *in Christ*. Paul reiterates this truth continually because it is the center of everything. The cross is the hinge of humanity. We each have a personal before Christ and after Christ. We had an old life before we were in Christ and a new life in Christ. That glorious position—in Christ—is the basis of everything in the new covenant. If you have your hope in any other thing (like works, ministry, intellect, or approval), it is entirely misplaced. Place your hope *fully* in "the Anointed One living his life in [you]"!

"The Dynamic Power of the Holy Spirit"

Gone are dead rituals and empty religion. We live by the power of the Holy Spirit. We are his Zion people, born from above. When people or systems try to put us under the old order of the law, it doesn't work because it can't bring life. We live by an entirely new life of Christ in us—the dynamic, effervescent power of the Holy Spirit. It always trumps every evil and surpasses what the law can do. There is no comparison. Life in the Spirit is an entirely new paradigm of total victory *through Christ.* The law cannot control or dictate that life. Law and grace cannot be mingled.

No Domination (Romans 8:5–13)

No sin, no darkness, no habit, no attitude, nor any written code will dominate us as we live by the dynamic power of the Holy Spirit in Christ.

Verses 5–6

🍃   Those who are motivated by the flesh only pursue what benefits themselves. But those who live by the impulses of the Holy Spirit are motivated to pursue spiritual realities. For the sense and reason of the flesh is death, but the mind-set controlled by the Spirit finds life and peace.

"Life and Peace"

Life and peace are what the human heart longs for. The only way to this bliss of life and peace is to live controlled by the Spirit. Jesus is the Way! Only through him can we have eternal life. As Paul says in 1 Timothy, "So fight with faith for the winner's prize! Lay your hands upon eternal life, to which you were called and about which you made the good confession before the multitude of witnesses!" (6:12). Take the promises of God—virtue, power, peace, life—and pull them into the now by faith. Don't put them off into the future;

Christ paid for you to have life and peace today. He is "the key of David" that unlocks heaven on earth. Dear friend, you can claim the promises of eternal life because, as a believer in Jesus, eternal life is already yours.

Verses 7–8

> In fact, the mind-set focused on the flesh fights God's plan and refuses to submit to his direction, because it cannot! For no matter how hard they try, God finds no pleasure with those who are controlled by the flesh.

"The Flesh"

The Greek word here for "the flesh" is *sarx,* which is basically our human nature, unregenerate humanity. Here Paul instructs us: the mindset of the flesh is *in opposition to God.*

- It *fights* God's plan.
- It *refuses* to *submit* to God's direction.
- It *cannot submit* to God.
- It *cannot please* God.

Pleasing God

So then, how does one please God? This is a simple and profound truth: only in Christ. You are now hidden in Christ and clothed with Christ. When God looks at you, he sees his Son. And he looks good on you! In fact, the very words that the Father proclaimed from heaven over Jesus—"You are my Son, my cherished one, and my greatest delight is in you!" (Mark 1:11)—are over you *eternally* as well because you are *eternally in Christ.* God does not look upon you in judgment, anger, or wrath but with a holy and relentless love: "He looked upon me with his unrelenting love divine" (Song of Songs 2:4).

Your Sabbath Rest

This is your resting place: being found in Christ. We must make this our foundational reality. You are not in a mess, in a struggle, or in a place of defeat—you are in Christ. You thrill the Lord, and you are simply his delight. This is your new reality in Jesus: "Now I know that I am for my beloved and all his desires are fulfilled in me" (Song of Songs 7:10).

Dominated by the Holy Spirit

Now, you have an entirely new source of power. The flesh has been dealt with on Calvary, and you now live dominated by the Holy Spirit of God. Someone else is on the throne of your heart these days, and he is all good all the time.

Verse 9

> But when the Spirit of Christ empowers your life, you are not dominated by the flesh but by the Spirit. And if you are not joined to the Spirit of the Anointed One, you are not of him.

"Empowers Your Life"

This can also be translated as "makes his home in you." You are empowered because the Lord makes his "home in you." His Spirit dwells in you, and he can't be separated from his *power*. You will never be alone again. You are his home, and he is yours—you are in Christ, and Christ is in you. This is your power, your strength, and your position *eternally*. You are "plugged in" to the power source, and he is plugged into you, hallelujah!

- "Don't you realize that together you have become God's inner sanctuary and that the Spirit of God makes his permanent home in you?" (1 Corinthians 3:16).

- "Jesus replied, 'Loving me empowers you to obey my word. And my Father will love you so deeply that we will come to you and make you our dwelling place'" (John 14:23).

- "When that day comes, you will know that I am living in the Father and that you are one with me, for I will be living in you" (John 14:20).

- "The One who is living in you is far greater than the one who is in the world" (1 John 4:4).

Verses 10–11

Now Christ lives his life in you! And even though your body may be dead because of the effects of sin, his life-giving Spirit imparts life to you because you are fully accepted by God. Yes, God raised Jesus to life! And since God's Spirit of Resurrection lives in you, he will also raise your dying body to life by the same Spirit that breathes life into you!

"The Spirit of Resurrection"

We have the hope of resurrection life in this world and in the world to come. He "will raise your dying body." Praise God! The Greek word for "Spirit" is *pneuma*, which is "breath" or "wind." God breathes his Spirit wind into you. Present tense. You walk this world in God's power, carried by his wind, filled with his breath of life. You are "raised" above the flesh life.

Verses 12–13

So then, beloved ones, the flesh has no claims on us at all, and we have no further obligation to live in obedience to it. For when you live controlled by the flesh, you are about to die. But if the life of the Spirit puts to death the corrupt ways of the flesh, we then taste his abundant life.

"No Claim" and "No Obligation"

Resurrection life "puts to death the corrupt ways of the flesh." You are raised above that corruption, and it no longer has a claim or hold on you. You are unbound from those old grave clothes, and you are walking in the power of the Spirit of life. You are in a new realm, like one who has awakened from a bad dream, and now you actually "taste his abundant life" and see his wonderful face. You are freed from the shadow and live in the reality and light of the very life of God.

No Desperation (Romans 8:14–16)

In this portion of verses, Paul describes the wonderful reality of the believer's *place in the family of God.* We do not operate in God's household as slaves or servants, begging for blessing and desperate for acceptance. Rather, we are fully accepted and have all the benefits and blessings of being a cherished member of God's holy family.

Sons and Daughters Destined for Glory

What a glorious future you have now that you have been brought into the family of God! You will never be abandoned, rejected, left helpless, or shamed. Grace has placed you eternally in the very arms of God, so be encouraged to focus your full attention on that realm of love and glory, not on sin or the devil. Let's determine to be glory-minded believers.

Verses 14–16

> The mature children of God are those who are moved by the impulses of the Holy Spirit. And you did not receive the "spirit of religious duty," leading you back into the fear of never being good enough. But you have received the "Spirit of full acceptance," enfolding you into the family of God. And you will never feel orphaned, for as he rises up within us, our spirits join him in saying the words of tender affection, "Beloved Father!" For the Holy Spirit makes God's fatherhood real to us as he whispers into our innermost being, "You are God's beloved child!"

"The Spirit of Full Acceptance"

This has been translated by others as "the spirit of adoption." The beautiful truth conveyed is that we have been brought fully into God's family and thus into his heart. This is so peace-filled and love-driven—so utterly different from the "spirit of religious duty." *Full acceptance* is what you have been given because of the precious blood of Christ. We must never yield to the spirit of slavery after all that Jesus suffered in order to give us the full rights, full acceptance, and the full benefits of being one of the family.

"The Fear of Never Being Good Enough"

What a terrible state of being to live in the fear of rejection from God based on your own goodness. What a trap! After all, how good is good enough? Compared to God's goodness, our goodness is anemic at best. We could never measure up in our own effort or virtue. This is just the type of fruitless cycles of fear that the flesh and the devil will keep us in if we don't become rooted and grounded in God's Word and God's love.

"The Family of God"

This is not just the family of fellow believers worldwide and throughout history. The family of God is first and foremost Father, Son, and Holy Spirit. This is what the blood of Christ has brought you into...with full acceptance. God is not ambivalent about your place in his family; he wants you there—passionately!

"Enfolded"

Just get this picture of true sonship branded upon your heart: you are enfolded, surrounded, covered, encircled, held, and cherished by God. Nothing and no one can remove you from that place that Jesus died to give you. In order that we would live from that place of security, Jesus spoke to us these words of deep assurance: "I give to them the gift of eternal life and they will never be lost and no one has the power to snatch them out of my hands" (John 10:28).

"Beloved Father"

This is *Abba,* the Aramaic word for "beloved father," "daddy," or "papa." Jesus spoke Aramaic, and this was how he referred to Father God. Romans 8:15 tells us that now, by the spirit of full acceptance, we are able to join in with our brother Jesus and call the Most High God *Abba.* Through the Holy Spirit, the fatherhood of God is made real to us. Hallelujah!

"Beloved Child"

He whispers into our heart, into the very depths of our soul, *Beloved Child, you are mine!* This is not a small nor an insignificant manifestation of God's great love because an incredible price has been paid to make it possible. We have the indwelling Spirit of God, who fills us with the overflowing love of God. Now, because of Jesus, we are born again into the family of God. This was his great plan from the beginning.

The Whispers of God

What healing, help, and hope are ours because we now hear his whispers. His love words over us are a banner of unrelenting divine love that declares, *You are mine!* Everything you need you will find in your Father, and your Father welcomes you joyfully as his very own.

Sonship (including Daughters)

This is your new reality. The Sonship of Jesus is now yours because you are in Christ. When we don't see ourselves correctly as fully accepted sons and daughters of God Almighty, we fear, we strive, we sweat, and we work for our inheritance in God. The enemy and the carnal mind will really try to convince us of a slave mentality of duty and dos and don'ts, but we must soak in this truth: we can't get more loved, cleaner, or more accepted than the cross has made us.

Many Sons and Daughters

You have been brought into the triune glory *by grace.* Jesus came to bring "many sons to glory":

For now he towers above all creation, for all things exist through him and for him. And that God made him, pioneer of our salvation, perfect through his sufferings, for this is how he brings many sons and daughters to share in his glory. (Hebrews 2:10)

We share in his glory! As you enter into life-union with Jesus Christ, you enjoy all the benefits, and this is his desire for you. Jesus came to bring you into the very heart of God—no veils, no limits, no condemnation, no fear, no desperation…only grace and glory.

Let's Go Deeper!

Questions

1. What truth from this lesson from the "pinnacle of Romans" affected you the most and why?

2. Romans 8 begins with this mind-blowing, religion-crushing, devil-defeating truth: "So now the case is closed. There remains no accusing voice of condemnation against those who are joined in life-union with Jesus, the Anointed One." Think back on your past (your "BC" life). How does it affect you to hear God say over your guilty past that the case is closed and that you are now declared free and clear? What about your future; is it also free and clear? Read Ephesians 1:7; 1 John 2:12; Colossians 2:13–14; and Hebrews 10:11–14. Just how "not guilty" and forgiven are you?

3. Below are possible definitions of *condemn* from *Merriam-Webster Dictionary*:

   1: to declare to be reprehensible, wrong, or evil usually after weighing evidence and without reservation

   2a: to pronounce guilty: convict

   2b: sentence, doom[14]

   Once you were those things: reprehensible, guilty, doomed, and wrong. But now you are holy, innocent, elevated, and right *because you are in Christ.* Are you living that way? Begin to use your sanctified imagination to see yourself as God does and make your constant self-declaration this powerful truth: "I am in Christ!" List some of the benefits of being "in Christ" that you have learned so far in this study.

4. Verse 9 says, "And if you are not joined to the Spirit of the Anointed One, you are not of him." This is an unusual Greek clause that can be translated as, "If anyone is not joined to the Spirit of Christ, *he cannot be himself.*" A similar construction is used in Luke 15:17: "[The prodigal son] came to himself" (NKJV). What conclusion can you make about the necessity of union with Christ in order to discover your true self, your true identity?

---

14 *Merriam-Webster.com Dictionary*, s.v. "condemn," accessed November 24, 2021, https://www.merriam-webster.com/dictionary/condemn.

5. This lesson highlights the distinction between being a slave or servant in God's house versus being a son (or daughter). Create a chart and list the differences. Examine your own heart and identify any "slave thinking" that you need to replace with the truth of who you really are in Christ.

Deeper Still!

Activations

"Beloved Father"

God is your "Beloved Father" (Romans 8:15). *Abba* is not a Greek word but an Aramaic word transliterated into Greek letters. *Abba* is the Aramaic word for "father." It is also found in Mark and Galatians.

- "He prayed, 'Abba, my Father, all things are possible for you. Please—remove this cup of suffering! Yet what I want is not important, for I only desire to fulfill your plan for me'" (Mark 14:36).

- "So that we would know that we are his true children, God released the Spirit of Sonship into our hearts—moving us to cry out intimately, 'My Father! My true Father!'" (Galatians 4:6).

Abba is also a word used for devotion, a term of endearment. This is why some have concluded that *Abba* could be translated as "Daddy" or "Papa." It is hard to imagine a closer relationship to have with God than to call him "Abba, our Beloved Father."

"Beloved Child"

Do you experience God as *your Abba,* your daddy, dad, papa? Your older brother Jesus does, and therefore, so can you! Because you have received the Spirit of full acceptance (adoption), you can't get any closer to your Abba God than you are at this moment because of Jesus' glorious work of Calvary. Beloved child of God, it is time to walk in your full sonship. Allow the Holy Spirit to lovingly lead you in that walk, "For the Holy Spirit makes God's fatherhood real to us as he whispers into our innermost being, 'You are God's beloved child!'" (Romans 8:16).

Make This Faith Declaration:

I am God's beloved child. With me, he is well pleased!

Let's Pray

> *Lord, I believe you that I am fully accepted in the Beloved. But I confess that I don't fully enjoy that reality like I should and like I want to. Please tear down any wall of fear and shame in my heart. Lord, I ask you to remove those lies in my soul and free me to walk in this amazing truth that I am accepted, wanted, and intimately entwined with you through Christ. I thank you for doing this beautiful work in me. In Jesus' name. Amen.*

A Glorious Unveiling

(Romans 8:17–22)

The Spirit of Full Acceptance (Romans 8:17)

This is the Spirit that is working deep within every child of God. You have been fully received into the triune glory. This reality is not dependent on your behavior, good or bad. The Spirit of full acceptance brings you completely into your identity of a dearly loved child of God and enables you to know him as Abba, or Daddy, just like Jesus does. Your history is under the blood, and your destiny is secure in Christ.

Glorified with Christ

Can you believe it? What privileged ones are we that we should be called the sons and daughters of God! We are those who can proclaim this truth: I am glorified with Jesus Christ. We are called, justified, sanctified, and, yes, *glorified* with him.

Verse 17

> And since we are his true children, we qualify to share all his treasures, for indeed, we are heirs of God himself. And since we are joined to Christ, we also inherit all that he is and all that he has. We will experience being co-glorified with him provided that we accept his sufferings as our own.

Qualified

You are fully qualified to share in Christ's inheritance.

> Your hearts can soar with joyful gratitude when you think
> of how God made you worthy [qualified] to receive the
> glorious inheritance freely given to us by living in the light.
> (Colossians 1:12)

All that God can give a human being, he has already given
to you. If he gave you any *more*, it would threaten the Trinity, and
we would have to call it a quartet. This is my attempt at humor, but
friend, this is an important truth that every believer must step into
by faith. If you are still striving or trying to attain a higher standing
with God, then you have missed the point of the death, burial, and
resurrection of Jesus Christ. You have already reached the pinnacle
of love divine: you are in Christ. Few places in Scripture so clearly
articulate this truth as what we see in Ephesians 1.

> In love he chose us before he laid the foundation of the
> universe! Because of his great love, he ordained us, so that
> we would be seen as holy in his eyes with an unstained
> innocence. For it was always in his perfect plan to adopt us
> as his delightful children, through our union with Jesus, the
> Anointed One, so that his tremendous love that cascades
> over us would glorify his grace—for the same love he has
> for the Beloved, Jesus, he has for us. And this unfolding
> plan brings him great pleasure! (vv. 4–6)

You "Share in All His Treasures"

The riches of heaven are yours now in Christ. You are fully blessed.
You are an heir of God. Maybe you have grown familiar, perhaps
too familiar, with this Christian terminology, so stop and rest in
this profound reality. God Almighty has heirs…and you are one of
them. In the kingdom of God, you don't have to wait for the death
of the parent in order to inherit, but rather you mature into your
full inheritance.

Co-Glorified

You will experience being co-glorified as you see his sufferings as your own. His cross is yours. What he endured, you identify with and benefit from. You don't go through the sufferings. You don't suffer for your sins. He bore them *for you*; it was a substitutionary death. But we mustn't stop there! It was also a substitutionary resurrection. Because he lives, we also live. We live by his life. We fully identify with the victory of the cross, and consequently, we fully identify with the victory of his resurrection. He conquered and made us more than conquerors because we pass over the death into the life—in Christ. He took the scourging, the nails, the thorns, the spear—he took it all so that we can be co-glorified with him. What amazing grace! This grace is for the purpose of bringing you into glory.

Glory!

The next stage of God's dealings with the church is the glorification of his bride. You have already been called, justified, sanctified, and glorified. This glorification is not yet fully realized, but it is *your destiny*. Friend, Jesus paid for your glorification...so step into your inheritance. It is time!

The Glorious Bride

Jesus is coming again for a radiant, glorious bride. Before he appears to us, he will appear through us. A glorified bride will walk the earth and bring Jesus back. Oh, let's get excited about that, thrilled even! Jesus, our Bridegroom-King is helping us prepare for his appearing: "All that he does in us is designed to make us a mature church for his pleasure, until we become a source of praise to him—glorious and radiant, beautiful and holy, without fault or flaw" (Ephesians 5:27).

The Greek word for "radiant" in this verse is *endoxos,* and it means "glorified." This is your destiny! Do you believe that way, talk that way, act that way, and respond to him that way? We live out of our belief system, and that means as our thinking becomes holy and right, so will our behavior. Glory is your destiny—let that be a guiding truth within your heart.

Co-Equal Heirs

You are the change agent that God wants to use to change the world around you. The Father loves the Son so much that he is filling the earth with Jesus' look-alike partners, his glorious bride. His glorified ones will populate this earth and fill it with his glory-light.

> You are the light of the world. A town built on a hill cannot be hidden. Neither do people light a lamp and put it under a bowl. Instead they put it on its stand, and it gives light to everyone in the house. In the same way, let your light shine before others, that they may see your good deeds and glorify your Father in heaven. (Matthew 5:14–16 NIV)

No Intimidation (Romans 8:18–22)

Thus far, we have examined the truth that, because we are in Christ, we experience no condemnation, no domination, and no desperation. Now, let's lay hold of a vision of our future with *no intimidation!*

Verse 18

> I am convinced that any suffering we endure is less than nothing compared to the magnitude of glory that is about to be unveiled within us.

"Any Suffering We Endure"

What a power-packed verse this is! Paul, who arguably suffered more than any of us is ever likely to suffer, announces his deep conviction that nothing we endure in this life can even be compared to the glory to be unveiled in us. Paul understood suffering. (See also 2 Corinthians 11:24–28.) Because of the life of service and reckless abandon he lived, Paul had a qualified and deep perspective we are privileged to glean from in portions of Scripture, where he describes his "less than nothing" sufferings.

> We are like common clay jars that carry this glorious treasure within, so that this immeasurable power will be seen as God's, not ours. Though we experience every kind of pressure, we're not crushed. At times we don't know what to do, but quitting is not an option. We are persecuted by others, but God has not forsaken us. We may be knocked down, but not out. We continually share in the death of Jesus in our own bodies so that the resurrection life of Jesus will be revealed through our humanity. (2 Corinthians 4:7–10)

As Paul teaches us how to view our earthly struggles in the light of eternity, he is not speaking out of theories or principles; he is speaking out of the depths of his own experience, his own history with God. He endured great hardship, and through it all, he learned the deep truths of Romans 8. Jesus is worth it all. Nothing compares to Jesus and the glory we share in him.

Portals To Glory

Paul saw his sufferings as *portals* into glory…and so can we! He saw all wounding and suffering as a way to partake more fully of the Christ-life within. When you endure hardship, when you are misunderstood and abused, when you walk through dark valleys, when family members mock you and call you names, when coworkers despise and slander, may it be Jesus who spills from your lips and his precious, costly praises that pour from your heart. Paul viewed this suffering as a privilege, an honor from the King.

"Unveiled within Us"

We can discern old covenant doctrine from new covenant doctrine in this way:

- Old covenant was always from the outside→ in.
- New covenant is always from the inside→ out.

Any teaching that is focused on suppressing sinful tendencies and achieving righteousness through doing outward works is not in line with the New Testament grace gospel. Jesus came and brought a *new order*. Ritual was replaced with reality. Form was replaced with fire. Moses prayed, "Now show me your glory" (Exodus 33:18 NIV), but we are those who carry his glory *within us!* This inside-out living is beautifully detailed in this portion of Scripture in which the glory of the law, called the "ministry of condemnation," is compared with the ministry of the Spirit of grace that brings a "permanent impartation of glory."

> Even the ministry that was characterized by chiseled letters on stone tablets came with a dazzling measure of glory, though it produced death. The Israelites couldn't bear to gaze on the glowing face of Moses because of the radiant splendor shining from his countenance—a glory destined to fade away.
>
> Yet how much more radiant is this new and glorious ministry of the Spirit that shines from us! For if the former ministry of condemnation was ushered in with a measure of glory, how much more does the ministry that imparts righteousness far excel in glory. What once was glorious no longer holds any glory because of the increasingly greater glory that has replaced it. The fading ministry came with a portion of glory, but now we embrace the unfading ministry of a permanent impartation of glory. (2 Corinthians 3:7–11)

Now, God is unveiling his glory within us to those who are bound, blinded, and lost. He is releasing his fullness from within you from the inside out. This is the new-covenant reality.

Creation Groans

Creation is yearning for your unveiling. The universe has been subjected to the consequences of human sin, but the death that came into creation at the fall will be vanquished forever as God's glorious sons and daughters arise. Who will silence creation's groan? Jesus Christ unveiled in us.

Verse 19

> The entire universe is standing on tiptoe, yearning to see the unveiling of God's glorious sons and daughters!

The Glorious Unveiling

The entire universe is longing to see "the unveiling of God's glorious sons and daughters!" Creation is groaning in expectation. The Greek word used here means "intense anticipation," or "anxiously anticipating what is about to happen" (with an outstretched neck). The glorious unveiling of the bride of Christ will silence the cry of creation. An unveiling is coming! Your destiny is unveiled glory, so lift your expectation out of the shrubbery of "fake it till you make it" thinking and begin to think God's thoughts. He has planned a wedding celebration that defies anything you have conceived so far, and *it will be glorious.* You are the look-alike partner of Jesus, and when he is unveiled, so will you be. Make that the horizon line of your focus—your glorious unveiling is imminent. He has a plan for this glorious unveiling.

> And through the revelation of the Anointed One, he unveiled his secret desires to us—the hidden mystery of his long-range plan, which he was delighted to implement from the very beginning of time. And because of God's unfailing purpose, this detailed plan will reign supreme through every period of time until the fulfillment of all the ages finally reaches its climax—when God makes all things new in all of heaven and earth through Jesus Christ.
>
> Through our union with Christ we too have been claimed by God as his own inheritance. Before we were even born, he gave us our destiny; that we would fulfill the plan of God who always accomplishes every purpose and plan in his heart. (Ephesians 1:9–11)

Apokalypsis

Interestingly, this Greek word for "unveiling" is the same word for
the full title of the last book of the Bible, "The Revelation [Unveiling]
of Jesus Christ." The created universe is but the backdrop for the
dramatic appearing of God's sons and daughters unveiled with
the glory of Jesus Christ upon them. The verb tense in the Greek
text is clear that this "unveiling" is imminent, soon to happen and
destined to take place. Christ's glory will come to us, enter us, fill
us, envelop us, and then be revealed through us as partakers of the
glory. Although God will not share his glory with another, we are
no longer "another," for we are one with the Father, the Son, and the
Holy Spirit through faith in Christ. (See John 17:21–23.)

Who You Truly Are

Dear saint, God sees the true you. He saw you with the eyes of his
heart and birthed you forth into creation (Psalm 139). He has a
beautiful dream with your name on it. You delight his heart, and
his dream of you, in all his glory, will come true. Every veil is being
removed. Oh yes, the anticipation is building. The full completion
of God's long-range plan is at hand. Believe it, see it with your eyes
of faith, and walk in it! Knowing our sin is gone, our condemnation
is removed, and our guilt is carried away, "We can all draw close to
him with the veil removed from our faces. And with no veil we all
become like mirrors who brightly reflect the glory of the Lord Jesus.
We are being transfigured into his very image as we move from one
brighter level of glory to another. And this glorious transfiguration
comes from the Lord, who is the Spirit" (2 Corinthians 3:18).

Living Stones

Naos is the Greek word for "dwelling place" or "the sanctuary of
God." It is no longer a stone cold building that God indwells. No, it
is a living temple made up of many lively stones. Each one of us is
his individual as well as his corporate sanctuary. Your body is his
dwelling! So, "Come and be his 'living stones' who are continually
being assembled into a sanctuary for God" (1 Peter 2:5).

Sealed by God

We talk quite a lot in Christendom about the mark of the beast, but why don't we focus on the mark of God, the seal of God? We are the marked ones! We are filled and sealed with his glory and his fire.

> The Holy Spirit of God has sealed you in Jesus Christ until you experience your full salvation. So never grieve the Spirit of God or take for granted his holy influence in your life. (Ephesians 4:30)

Beloved, don't let "The Unveiling of Jesus Christ," the book of Revelation, produce any fear in you. Never! Rather, let it stir your heart to the passionate, bridal pursuit of your glorious destiny: the mystery of your marriage union with Christ for all eternity.

Focus on Glory

There is an opportune (*kairos*) time or season in which full salvation will be unveiled to the universe. Peter speaks of this "full salvation" that is ready to be unveiled: "Through our faith, the mighty power of God constantly guards us until our full salvation is ready to be revealed in the last time" (1 Peter 1:5).

A new revelation of our salvation is yet to be unveiled and revealed to us. Isn't that interesting? Amazing even? It is "ready to be revealed." What is God up to? Is he wringing his hands over an antichrist or four apocalyptic horsemen? No, we must shift out of the doomsday mindset and get into the glorious unveiling mindset. Stop focusing on gloom and start focusing on glory. Glory is your destiny.

Verses 20–22

> For against its will the universe itself has had to endure the empty futility resulting from the consequences of human sin. But now, with eager expectation, all creation longs for freedom from its slavery to decay and to experience with us the wonderful freedom coming to God's children. To this day we are aware of the universal agony and groaning

of creation, as if it were in the contractions of labor for childbirth.

The Result of Sin Is Being Reversed

Because of man's sin, all creation has been subjected to the results of the fall. Sin, our sin, brought "hell on earth," literally. God will undo the curse of sin and deliver creation through the glory of his sons and daughters. Shining ones are coming. Radiant ones are coming. "Infused ones" (Greek *endoxos*) with God's glory shining brightly through their lives will lead the way to God in these last days.

> Those who are wise will shine like the brightness of the heavens, and those who lead many to righteousness, like the stars for ever and ever. (Daniel 12:3 NIV)

It Is Time for a Re-presentation

The bride of Christ, all-glorious within, will correctly *re*-present Christ to this world that is trapped in decay and darkness. Religion has muddied the waters and misrepresented him for long enough. It is time for the real Jesus to be seen and heard. And he shall be… *through you, his glorious, shining bride.*

"Wonderful Freedom"

Ponder this: The freer you get, the freer the universe gets. The "slavery to decay" for all of God's creation is being overturned as God's children go from glory to glory. The journey of ever-increasing glory is where you are right now, for "we can all draw close to him with the veil removed from our faces. And with no veil we all become like mirrors who brightly reflect the glory of the Lord Jesus. We are being transfigured into his very image as we move from one brighter level of glory to another. And this glorious transfiguration comes from the Lord, who is the Spirit" (2 Corinthians 3:18).

God has done his part. Jesus paid it all. He loudly proclaimed at Calvary, "It is finished, my bride!" (John 19:30). He has given us all we need (every blessing, every weapon, every promise), and now he is calling us onward and upward. He is saying, *Arise! Arise, my daughter, my son. Be unveiled. Let the fullness of your true identity and who you are divinely designed to be come forth. Shine! Release my glory. All nations will come to the brightness of my glory within you.*

The Agony and Groaning of Creation

When earthquakes, hurricanes, tempests, and any earthly shakings take place, the church's default explanation is often "God is judging," but that's not the full story. The shakings are a manifestation of the agony of God's creation. It is the universe itself experiencing birth pangs. Out of our "cocoon" of this natural order, something magnificent is waiting to be unveiled. This is how we should be praying. Let's not be problem-oriented or judgment/sin-focused. Rather, let's be Jesus-centered. What is *his* focus? His bride is his focus. Let the bride arise and gather more souls into that bridal company of loving saints. The Spirit and the bride say, "Come!" (Revelation 22:17).

Let's Go Deeper!

Questions

1. According to Romans 8:14, the mature sons and daughters of God are those who are "moved by the impulses of the Spirit." In the Greek, it is emphatic: *those, and only those, who are moved by the impulses of the Spirit.* Is this similar to or perhaps different from your personal definition of spiritual maturity? How so? What does it mean to be moved by his impulses? (Think of specific examples in your own life.)

2. Take a closer look at 8:17. The benefits of being "his true children" from this verse are listed below. For each benefit, describe what it means to you personally. Be specific.

   1. We qualify.

187

2. We share all his treasures.

3. We are God's heirs.

4. We inherit all he has and all he is.

5. We experience co-glorification with Jesus.

3. In reference again to verse 17, all those wonderful benefits come "provided that we accept his sufferings as our own." This does not mean that we must suffer what he suffered but rather that we accept his substitutionary sufferings. In other words, we were co-crucified with him and now live by his resurrection life. How is this mindset different from the common religious mindset that there is more we must add to the finished work of the cross? Did Jesus truly pay it all? If so, what does accepting his sufferings as your own mean in your own life as you face difficulties, temptations, and testings of your faith?

4. In verse 18, Paul speaks of the glory about to be revealed in us. The Aramaic can be translated, "with the glory which is

to be perfected in us." The Greek participle *eis* can be translated, "into us," "upon us," or "to us." His glory, at this very moment, is being perfected into you, upon you, and to you. Glory is your imminent future. God's plan for you is not to slide through the pearly gates by the skin of your teeth. Your destiny is glory! Read Isaiah 60:1–3; Exodus 33:14–33; Psalm 50:2; Luke 9:29; 2 Corinthians 3:18; and Colossians 1:27. What do these glory verses reveal to you about your future?

5. What will eventually release all of creation from its bondage to decay? What does this truth reveal to you about your identity as a mature son or daughter of God, the true you? (See 8:19–22.)

Deeper Still!

Activations

Dear beloved saint of God, have you been sin-focused rather than glory-focused? It is time to continually fix your hope on the glory that is about to be unveiled within you. Sin is no longer the issue. The cross took care of sin along with all its terrible consequences, "once and for all." Remember, the next event on God's timetable is the glorification of his bride. It is time to focus on that, on your Bridegroom-King, and on the day of his great gladness. So, put your rejoicing on, and rise up, for we are destined for glory, and Jesus is preparing us for his wedding day:

> Rise up, Zion maidens, brides-to-be!
> Come and feast your eyes on this king
> as he passes in procession on his way to his wedding.
> This is the day filled with overwhelming joy—
> the day of his great gladness. (Song of Songs 3:11)

Let's Pray

Lord, I feel you shifting my entire being to a new mindset, a new center of focus: you! I choose to let go of all self-centered and fear-centered thinking that elevates my issues above your cross. I repent and I thank you, Lord, that your suffering was mine, and now I am free to soar with you. Sin cannot conquer me because you already have. Death has no hold on me because I am held in the grip of love. Lord, baptize me afresh in your love and fire. Moses prayed, "Show me your glory." But I pray, "Lord, endoxos me! Make me radiant." I praise you that you have brought me into your triune glory and that glory is my inheritance in you, not by anything I could ever do to earn it but simply by your grace. I receive your grace and your glory, for Jesus' sake. Amen.

The Goal of Grace Is Glory

(Romans 8:23–29)

Grace Is Taking Us to Glory! (Romans 8:23–27)

Grace is not just taking you to heaven—it is taking you to glory! The hope of glory, Christ unveiled in you, is the deepest and purest longing of your heart. Your destiny is to be transformed into Jesus' likeness, bearing his image and displaying his beautiful nature to all in your sphere of influence. Dear saint, glory is your destiny, so lift your sights higher than the goal of merely surviving until you die. God's plan is to unveil Christ in you. Your future is truly glorious.

Believers Groan

Along with all creation, every lover of God is also groaning, yearning to come into our fullness. Like a butterfly emerging from its chrysalis, believers in Christ are in a beautiful process of transformation. Yes, we groan with longing, but we do not fear, for we are safe in God's grace, held by divine love.

Verse 23

> And it's not just creation. We who have already experienced the firstfruits of the Spirit also inwardly groan as we passionately long to experience our full status as God's

sons and daughters—including our physical bodies being transformed.

The Firstfruits of the Spirit

We have experienced the *firstfruits,* so what will the *harvest* be like? If all the gifts, fruit, wisdom, and power of the Holy Spirit that are available and working in us now are only the firstfruits, then it's time to buckle up our seat belts and get ready. The harvest and fullness that is coming will be mind-blowing. Think of your most amazing encounter thus far with God…That is only the *firstfruits,* friend.

"Our Full Status"

In Ephesians, Paul explains that the Holy Spirit is the sign that, as God's children, we will be receive all the blessings God has promised us.

> Now we have been stamped with the seal of the promised Holy Spirit.
> He is given to us like an engagement ring, as the first installment of what's coming! He is our hope-promise of a future inheritance which seals us until we have all of redemption's promises and experience complete freedom— all for the supreme glory and honor of God! (Ephesians 1:13–14)

Arrabon is the Greek word often translated as "down payment," "guarantee," and "earnest," but it is essentially the Greek word for "engagement ring." The Holy Spirit is God's engagement ring. He has marked you and set you apart as his own. He is going to come for you and take you as his bride, and his promise to do so is the deposit of his Spirit within you. So just imagine what the wedding will be like!

"We Passionately Long"

Let's be careful that we don't put every promise off into a future "someday" scenario. This verse teaches that we as God's people inwardly groan in passionate longing to experience our full status as sons and daughters—a status that includes physical transformation. Let's believe for that glory now. We have eternal life *now*. Eternal life filled us the moment we received Jesus as Lord and Savior. Therefore, there is a logical "leap" that we can make: whatever we are to have "in eternity," we can believe for *now*. Believe now for God to come through for you.

Verses 24–25

> For this is the hope of our salvation.
> But hope means that we must trust and wait for what is still unseen. For why would we need to hope for something we already have? So because our hope is set on what is yet to be seen, we patiently keep on waiting for its fulfillment.

"We Patiently Keep on Waiting"

We have so much to look forward to. This "hope of our salvation" fills our hearts as we yearn for Christ's appearing. His unveiling is also our unveiling, and so we keep our eyes focused on that which is above and not on earthly distractions. This waiting is not passive. It is an active waiting during which we entwine our hearts with the Lord in loving expectation. The Greek word for *wait* here is *apek-dechomai*, and it means "to wait eagerly." The connotation is that of a purposeful waiting. The prefix *apo-* means "away from," and the root means "to welcome." So we receive from these encouraging verses the call to wait eagerly with our focus fully removed from the world and its allurements and fully fixed on the glorious future before us in Jesus. Are you waiting well? We can wait with hearts that are welcoming the Lord's imminent appearing—and we should.

The Holy Spirit Groans

Ah, we are not alone in our longing and groaning. Our divine encourager, the precious Holy Spirit, will "super-intercede on our behalf" (8:26). Still your soul before him even now, and you will sense his loving presence all around you, loving you and lifting you. He is with you always, preparing you for your wedding and making you magnificent. (See Matthew 22:4.)

Verse 26

> And in a similar way, the Holy Spirit takes hold of us in our human frailty to empower us in our weakness. For example, at times we don't even know how to pray, or know the best things to ask for. But the Holy Spirit rises up within us to super-intercede on our behalf, pleading to God with emotional sighs too deep for words.

Your Human Frailty

What comfort we receive from this amazing verse! Are you in the grip of fear, anxiety, or trauma? No, you are in the grip of grace. The Holy Spirit "takes hold of us" and "empowers us in our weakness." Never fear your frailty—God doesn't.

A Specific Weakness: Prayer

Paul, under divine inspiration, highlights one area of "frailty" in particular: prayer. We have all experienced times when we struggle in prayer, not knowing how or what to pray. Praise God that in our weakness, the Holy Spirit takes over. The Greek word *hupererentugkhano* is best translated as "super- [or hyper-] intercession for us." We can only imagine how many blessings have poured into our lives because of the hyper-intercession of the Holy Spirit for us.

Have you entered into "warp-drive prayer"? You can! The Holy Spirit is ready at all times to meet you in your place of frailty and "super-intercede on [your] behalf." Allow him to break out through you in prayer.

Recognize that the Holy Spirit is highlighting your prayer life.

- The Holy Spirit can intercede for you 24/7.
- You have an intercessor living in you.
- He empowers you in your weakness.

- "He answered me, 'My grace is always more than enough for you, and my power finds its full expression through your weakness.' So I will celebrate my weaknesses, for when I'm weak I sense more deeply the mighty power of Christ living in me" (2 Corinthians 12:9).

Release him to do his powerful work of intercession in and through you!

- Your "prayer language," or speaking in tongues, is one way he does this.

- "They were all filled and equipped with the Holy Spirit and were inspired to speak in tongues—empowered by the Spirit to speak in languages they had never learned!" (Acts 2:4).

- This is a powerful tool and should not be minimized or ignored.

- Paul even said he was glad he spoke in tongues more than the entire church of Corinth…and look how the Holy Spirit "empowered" him.

- Speaking in tongues increases your spiritual sensitivity.

- "The one who speaks in tongues advances his own spiritual progress,…I give thanks to God that I speak in tongues more than all of you" (1 Corinthians 14:4, 18).

Receive the power of the Spirit.

- This blessing comes to you through the experience of the baptism of the Holy Spirit.

- It is available right now for the asking. Receive his fullness with all his gifts, fruit, and blessings.

- Once again, don't fear your frailty. Your weakness is actually the "on-ramp" to the power-filled Spirit life you were born for.

The Spirit's Groaning

Words cannot contain the deep, emotional sighs of the Holy Spirit's intercession within you. This is *divine* intercession, friend, not earthly. You can be sure that Father God, your *Abba*, hears the cry of the Holy Spirit's intercession within you. He will answer!

Jesus, Our Intercessor

Not only do we have this powerful Holy Spirit intercession going on inside of us here on earth, but Jesus, our King and Savior, is also interceding on our behalf in heaven. "So he is able to save fully from now throughout eternity, everyone who comes to God through him, because he lives to pray continually for them" (Hebrews 7:25).

The Trinity, Our Prayer Support

So get this picture into your heart: two-thirds of the Trinity is continually praying for you. The other third? Well, he is answering those prayers. You are captured, covered, and captivated by love—so fear not! The Trinity is your "prayer support." This is pictured in the Old Testament story of Moses being supported on each side by Aaron and Hur.

> Joshua fought the Amalekites as Moses had ordered, and Moses, Aaron and Hur went to the top of the hill. As long as Moses held up his hands, the Israelites were winning, but whenever he lowered his hands, the Amalekites were winning. When Moses' hands grew tired, they took a stone and put it under him and he sat on it. Aaron and Hur held his hands up—one on one side, one on the other—so that his hands remained steady till sunset. So Joshua overcame the Amalekite army with the sword. (Exodus 17:10–13 NIV)

In this story Joshua (same name as *Jesus*) represents Christ. *Hur* means "light" and represents the Spirit of light, the Holy Spirit. Aaron was the high priest and represents Jesus, our eternal High Priest. So, the picture is powerful! We are supported completely, upheld, and strengthened by the intercession of the Holy Spirit and Jesus. While we stand in that place, Jesus conquers for us. Our heavenly Joshua has defeated every enemy we face. Through Christ, we have already won every battle we will ever face.

Verse 27

> God, the searcher of the heart, knows fully our longings, yet he also understands the desires of the Spirit, because the Holy Spirit passionately pleads before God for us, his holy ones, in perfect harmony with God's plan and our destiny.

"The Searcher of the Heart"

This is an endearment, not a fearful label placed upon God. We never need to fear his searching gaze, but rather, we should welcome it. In this verse, we see God searches our hearts and "knows fully our *longings.*" Longings for what? Not for evil, but longings for more of him and his righteousness. He knows how we long for righteousness. The Holy Spirit prays ("passionately pleads") before the Father for us to bring us fully into our destiny. And this destiny is our glorious unveiling as Christlike and mature sons and daughters.

His Precious Pleadings

Oh, how we love, welcome, and *need* the workings and pleadings of the Holy Spirit on our behalf! Friend, you have a helper. Jesus promised him to us, saying, "I will send you the Divine Encourager from the very presence of my Father. He will come to you, the Spirit of Truth, emanating from the Father, and he will speak to you about me" (John 15:26). You are not an orphan, and you are not pressing through this life journey all on your own. The Holy Spirit is your intercessor who will ensure your final victory. Rest your heart in this astounding truth: God will not abandon you in your journey. He is faithful, and he will faithfully walk you all the way across the finish line, hand in hand and heart in heart.

No Miscalculation (Romans 8:28–29)

Every Detail Is Woven Together for Our Good

We now come to what is considered one of the most beloved verses in Scripture. Our hearts cling to this precious promise as we navigate by faith through life's journey. For, as much as we would wish it differently, that journey is sometimes painful, difficult, and confusing. We have an eternal hope in our hearts that carries us through, though, knowing God is weaving every detail (the good and not so good) into a beautiful tapestry. He has a plan…and it's good.

Verse 28

> So we are convinced that every detail of our lives is continually woven together for good, for we are his lovers who have been called to fulfill his designed purpose.

"Woven Together"

We don't judge our life (nor anyone else's life) based on one bad day, one failure, or one difficult season. We may live "one day at a time," but we certainly don't view our lives in a short-sighted, day-by-day way. Rather, we view our lives decade by decade, knowing that God has a wondrous, grand plan that he is working. Think of Joseph's life, for example. Betrayed, lied about, falsely accused, and imprisoned—not for days, not even for months, but for *many* years. It was a *journey*, not an event. And so it is for you and me. Some of the most beautiful words in the Bible are seen in the account of Joseph's heart-rending process. "The Lord was with Joseph" (Genesis 39:2 NIV).

This is repeated several times in his story. In other words, his story, his history, was formed through intimacy by the faithful love of God. God never failed or forsook Joseph…but that was not how it may have seemed during the process. During those desolate prison years, it appeared as if God had changed his mind about Joseph's destiny, but he hadn't. He was actually faithfully bringing Joseph into his full destiny. It is the same for you and me. Don't lose hope in the desolate moments. Don't despair because the truth is that your journey is not finished. He promised to finish what he started in you, and he surely will.

Growing into Your Answer from God

For Joseph, the day came when his dream was fulfilled. All his brothers were at his feet, and in that beautiful moment, he had no desire to "rub their faces" in their failure. Instead he said these gracious words: "God sent me ahead of you to preserve for you a remnant on earth and to save your lives by a great deliverance. So then, it was not you who sent me here, but God...You intended to harm me, but God intended it for good to accomplish what is now being done, the saving of many lives" (Genesis 45:7–8; 50:20 NIV).

How could Joseph respond in such a way? Because he fully realized what we must also realize: the powerful truth of Romans 8:28. Everything—the good, the bad, and, yes, even the ugly—will all fit together into God's wonderful, redemptive tapestry of our lives...not just for our good but also for the good of many others.

The Timing of God versus the Will of God

Often, because we know the will of God, we think we know the timing of God. We mustn't confuse these two realities. God's timing and his will are two different issues entirely. You can know the will and promises of God over your life, but that does not mean you know his timetable for bringing his purposes and his promises to pass. Maturity is revealed in us when we trust God with the timing. Again, like with Joseph, God is with us all the way through to the fulfilled promise. Even when his timing seems to be faulty, it is not. God is simply doing what he does—working every detail of our lives into his perfect plan. We can always trust him to do this. He is our Romans 8:28 and Jeremiah 29:11 God. During the turbulent, "wind and waves" moments of our life, we have this promise: "'For I know the plans I have for you,' declares the LORD, 'plans to prosper you and not to harm you, plans to give you hope and a future'"

(Jeremiah 29:11 NIV). Rest assured, he has a plan, and it is a good one. Guaranteed.

Purpose in "the Waiting Room"

This may not be a popular or pleasant encouragement, but it is needful and truthful nonetheless. The *purpose* of God's "waiting room" is *justified* by your impatience. This means your inability to wait in patient hope reveals your need for spiritual growth. In fact, the more you "stew" in angry frustration in the waiting of God, the more you delay the will of God. Waiting produces growth and maturity. Don't worry; the wait is never wasted. You will be thankful in the end that God did not stop the process when you whined, worried, or "wheeled and dealed" with him in the waiting. In the end (but not necessarily in the difficult moment), you will appreciate the timing of God. We can be like Job, who understood and spoke this truth in the midst of all his suffering: "I know that my redeemer lives, and that in the end he will stand on the earth" (Job 19:25 NIV).

The Final Picture

We talk about "the big picture," but we often don't like to endure well until it is revealed. You see, each strand, each (seemingly) mismatched detail of our lives is being woven like embroidery thread, bit by bit, into a beautiful masterpiece tapestry. Beloved, even the dark threads, God will use. Even the crimson, sinful, bloody-mess threads, God will use. Even the twisted and knotted threads you haven't been able to make sense of, God will use. Saint of God, even the shameful and hidden threads, God will use. Somehow, he will redeem it all, and in the end, you will see Jesus standing over all of it—your earth, your dust, your waste places—triumphant and glorified. Believe me, it will be worth the wait.

Therefore, as we wait, let's wait well. Let's focus on what truly matters. Let's fix our gaze above the storm, above the cloudy confusion. So many distractions and difficulties will pull for our attention,

> We see Jesus, who as a man, lived for a short time lower
> than the angels and has now been crowned with glorious

honor because of what he suffered in his death. For it was
by God's grace that he experienced death's bitterness on
behalf of everyone!...

[F]or this is how he brings many sons and daughters
to share in his glory...

He suffered and endured every test and temptation, so
that he can help us every time we pass through the ordeals
of life. (Hebrews 2:9, 10, 18)

Redeeming Love

Love has the power to make evil into good. Remember, Joseph said
to his traitorous brothers, "You meant it for evil, but God meant
it for good." You see, if you don't yield to bitterness, God will use
your difficulties, even the *evil* difficulties, for good. Love (yours and
God's) redeems! God's plan required Joseph's cooperation. We, too,
must cooperate with the Holy Spirit and be a conduit of his love in
order to redeem bad situations. Perhaps God will do a miracle when
you forgive and come into agreement with his redemptive plan. As
you wait, it is wise to ask, "Is God waiting on me?"

Redeeming Praise

If we know for sure (and we do!) that God will make everything
beautiful in his time, then why not praise him now? Why wait until
you get your breakthrough? Think about it. We see this illustrated
in the struggle of the unwanted wife of Jacob, Leah. She had a bitter
beginning, didn't she? We see her bitterness leaking out into the
names she gave her children. It was her way of getting back and
saying "nanny-nanny-boo-boo" to those responsible for her pain.
However, she did not remain in the place of bitter, unrectified pain.
God redeemed her situation and her legacy. Eventually, she gave
birth to Judah, whose name means "praise." She finally gave up her
fight in the "bride war" and just simply decided, "This time I will
praise the Lord" (Genesis 29:35 NIV). And Judah was Jesus' tribe.
Jesus came through Leah's lineage—what a redemption! For all eternity, she will have this wondrous pleasure: the Lord of Glory is in

her human lineage. Only God can take such a messed-up beginning and turn it into a beautiful ending. He does that. He likes to do that. He will do that in every "messed up" part of your life as well. So go ahead and surrender and praise him now. Like Leah, say, "This time I will praise the Lord," and you, too, will witness the redeeming power of your praise.

Verse 29

> For he knew all about us before we were born and he destined us from the beginning to share the likeness of his Son. This means the Son is the oldest among a vast family of brothers and sisters who will become just like him.

Sharing "the Likeness of His Son"

Your calling is not to build a big ministry (though you may), or be apostle "so and so," or prophet "this and such." No, your calling is to be like Jesus. Out of your secret place of intimacy with the Lord, people around you will sense God's presence in your life and recognize that you have been with Jesus. This was the case with the early apostles.

> The council members were astonished as they witnessed the bold courage of Peter and John, especially when they discovered that they were just ordinary men who had never had religious training. Then they began to understand the effect Jesus had on them simply by spending time with him. (Acts 4:13)

Ministry will always pursue you when you pursue Christ and Christlikeness. The overflow of our relationship with Jesus is called ministry. It's all an overflow from your intimate pursuit of him. If you are overflowing with the bliss of communion, you don't have to strive to produce. Fruitfulness comes from intimacy.

Let's Go Deeper!

Questions

1. What is something new you learned in this lesson about the heart of God?

2. Describe the three "groanings" discussed in this lesson. What is the desire behind each groaning?

3. The Greek word *doxa,* translated "glory" in 8:18, can also be translated as "radiant beauty," "splendor," "perfection." Look at that verse in light of its fuller meaning: "I am convinced that any suffering we endure is less than nothing compared to the magnitude of glory [radiant beauty, splendor, and perfection] that is about to be unveiled within us." This is your destiny! How does that affect you and strengthen your heart?

4. Living in this fallen world and having a sinful past can keep us "sin focused" instead of "glory focused." How would you describe the difference between those two orientations? Is God focused on your sin? Is Satan focused on your sin? Describe how your life would change for the better if you left the past behind and focused on your future glory with Jesus.

5. Verse 29 says, "For he knew all about us before we were born and he destined us from the beginning to share the likeness of his Son." The words "destined us" can also be translated as "sealed us." This means God has set his mark upon his children, his own treasured possession. As a master craftsman, it is as if he has put his "hallmark" upon his masterpiece—you—and he will bring you through to your destiny, which is Christlikeness. Read Colossians 3:4; Hebrews 2:11; Ephesians 2:10; and Philippians 1:6. Describe your destiny in your own words according to these verses. How does God see you, and how committed is he to the work he started? How secure should you feel, knowing you are "destined," "sealed" and "marked" by God?

Deeper Still!

Activations

As the saying goes, hindsight is 20/20. I've also heard it said that we live life forward but only understand it backward. If you have lived very long at all, you can probably add an "amen" to that. Perhaps, you are in one of those confusing and difficult moments of life right now, or perhaps you are "stuck" emotionally in a past trauma you haven't been able to figure out and lay to rest. Dear friend, take courage from the Romans 8:28 promise of God. God is working it all out. He has a beautiful plan, customized just for you. The enemy, along with dire circumstances may be shouting a different "truth," but the reality is that God cares. Deeply. You can be sure that if it isn't good yet, then he isn't done yet.

In a moment of quiet reflection, picture yourself with the Lord, even right up in his lap if you like. Prayerfully give to him each worry, each fear, each question, and even your anger. See yourself handing them over one by one, and ask, "Lord, in place of these burdens, what do you want me to have?" Let him speak to you and show you what he has to give you.

Let's Pray

Lord, help me to be content in my circumstances, whatever they may be. You have blessed me abundantly in so many ways, and besides all the blessings, you are the greatest blessing of all. Just you, Jesus. It is always only you. No matter what I may have to wade through or wait through in this life, it is all okay because I have you. It is all about you, Lord Jesus! I praise you in all things. I praise you in advance even before my miracle comes, and even if my miracle doesn't come in my timing, Lord, I will praise you anyway. You are worthy of that, worthy of my highest praise even in my lowest valleys. I will groan with all creation to simply have more of you and to be more like you. Amen.

The Case Is Closed

(Romans 8:30–39)

Complete in Christ (Romans 8:30)

From heaven's perspective, you are complete in Christ. In God's omnipotent and omniscient wisdom, it is as if he has placed a crown upon you and is helping you grow into it. You are absolutely treasured and adored in the heart of God just as you are, but he is not leaving you where you are. He is growing you up into your completion—from known, to called, to justified, to sanctified, and, yes, to *glorified*.

Called

We have a beautiful, expensive, and exquisite invitation from God handwritten with the blood of Christ. He has pulled you, called you, wooed you. The God of all creation has tugged on your heart individually, persistently, and personally. He wanted you and still does, and so he called you by name.

Verse 30

> Having determined our destiny ahead of time, he called us to himself and transferred his perfect righteousness to everyone he called. And those who possess his perfect righteousness he co-glorified with his Son!

Drawn to His Heart

Sometimes we fear our ability, or lack thereof, to hear God. We fear missing him due to our inability to hear him well. However, we can let go of that fear and fully put our trust in his ability to be heard. He knows how to call to his children. "The only way people come to me is by the Father who sent me—he pulls on their hearts to embrace me. And those who are drawn to me, I will certainly raise them up in the last day" (John 6:44). You are where you are right now because God Almighty called you into his embrace. Listen for his voice.

Proorizo

This is the Greek word for "horizon" or "toward the horizon." Your destiny is actually toward the horizon—known by God and marked out by him—predetermined. That place of destiny is *Christlikeness,* to be entirely and completely transformed into his image. Bet your life on that fact; he did. Get excited about your *proorizo!* Your predetermined destiny is not merely about going to heaven. Predestination is God's sovereign plan to move you toward your horizon of having the nature of Jesus and abiding in life-union with him. You have been positioned to succeed (see 1 John 3:2). Paul described the wondrous reality of God's preordained plan for you in his letter to the Ephesians, even saying his "plan will reign supreme." In other words, you can trust in it.

> Because of God's unfailing purpose, this detailed plan will reign supreme through every period of time until the fulfillment of all the ages finally reaches its climax—when God makes all things new in all of heaven and earth through Jesus Christ.
>
> Through our union with Christ we too have been claimed by God as his own inheritance. Before we were even born, he gave us our destiny; that we would fulfill the plan of God who always accomplishes every purpose and plan in his heart. (Ephesians 1:10–11)

Justified: He Has Transferred His Righteousness to You

This is the essence of what it means to be justified. You are now in Christ, and therefore, it is just as if you had never sinned. God has put all his righteousness upon you. You are as righteous as Christ before the Father. Get a little holy disdain toward all forms of accusation, intimidation, condemnation, and the fear of not being good enough. Don't even give those types of thoughts or words the least bit of your attention. Jesus' blood has lifted you above all condemnation. You cannot ever be condemned; he took your condemnation, your due punishment, at Calvary. You are absolutely hidden in God's beautiful Son, so never let any voice convince you otherwise.

Co-glorified with His Son

You have been co-glorified with Jesus, your beloved. This is your eternal status! Remember, he loved you so much that he chose, called, justified, sanctified and, yes, *glorified* you. In his heart, it really is "finished, my bride" (John 19:30). He put his seal upon you, his Spirit, as an engagement ring. It is a done deal. You are only awaiting the full unveiling of what is already settled in heaven. Live in this reality! Jesus and the Holy Spirit are both interceding for your glorious unveiling, and their intercession will culminate in the fullness of the hope of your calling: *Christ in you.*

> Living within you is the Christ who floods you with the expectation of glory! This mystery of Christ, embedded within us, becomes a heavenly treasure chest of hope filled with the riches of glory for his people, and God wants everyone to know it! (Colossians 1:27)

Grace Is Bringing You into Glory

Grace is not merely mercy but also much more. It is the power of God working within you right now to cause you to become the dream of God's heart. Glory is your destiny, for you "are being transfigured into his very image as [you] move from one brighter level of glory to another. And this glorious transfiguration comes from the Lord, who is the Spirit" (2 Corinthians 3:18). What is beyond your horizon line? Glory! Glory! Glory!

You Are Eternally in Christ

This really cannot be overemphasized. We must let go of sin-focused thinking and striving. Our new reality is glory. You are already fully blessed, fully loved, fully accepted, and fully glorified. We need to live, think, talk, and dream with God from that place of grace and glory. There will always be the fearful, accusing, and religious voices trying to convince you that you are just "a sinner saved by grace," but that is (at best) shortsighted. Lift your focus out of that low-level, sin-focused realm into the heavenly glory-realm. That's where you really are—seated in heavenly places with your beloved. (See Ephesians 2:6.)

No Separation (Romans 8:31–39)

The Triumph of God's Love

Ultimately, every detail of your life will have a banner of victory flying high above it. You are victorious because of Christ's victory. It isn't your power but his. It is the triumph of his unfailing love in your life. Like the Shulamite bride, you can confidently say, "I am truly his rose, the very theme of his song. I'm overshadowed by his love, like a lily growing in the valley!" (Song of Songs 2:1). Are you living like you are loved? Are you living in the knowledge that you are overshadowed, covered by God's omnipotent love? Paul knew this necessity for the life of every believer, and so he spends these next few verses emphasizing the truth that there is no force in the universe more powerful than the amazing love of God.

Verse 31

> So, what does all this mean? If God has determined to stand with us, tell me, who then could ever stand against us?

God Is for You!

There is so much comfort in this truth. Intimidation is powerless against the children of God who know how treasured they truly are within the heart of God. Listen, he is your champion defender. He gave everything in order to redeem you, and he's serious about his commitment to loving you and keeping you. He has indeed "determined to stand with us." Hallelujah! He is a good Father, and therefore, everything he is doing in your life is to bless you and bring you into your best moments and your *proorizo*. You are his beautiful poetry, and line-by-line, he is making his beautiful poetic song *sing* through the pages of your very life. Ah, yes, he is for you!

Verse 32

> For God has proved his love by giving us his greatest treasure, the gift of his Son. And since God freely offered him up as the sacrifice for us all, he certainly won't withhold from us anything else he has to give.

God Gave His Treasure to Gain You

If God gave the beautiful Christ in order to redeem you, what more wouldn't he give? He is not withholding anything. That is gospel truth. He is certainly not withholding his love, his attention, his help, his presence, his whispers, his wisdom, his fullness, his grace…you get the idea. You have everything heaven has to give.

Jesus Is Your Redeemer

Let's just keep this straight: Jesus is not the accuser. He is our champion defender. Jesus silenced the accuser with three nails and a hammer. Are you feeling crushed with accusations? Then shake it off! Jesus was crucified on your behalf so that you never would be. So many times, we come into agreement with hell about our destiny instead of being in agreement with heaven. Satan is the accuser, and everything that comes from him is fear-filled and hate-driven. Everything that comes from Jesus is hope-filled and love-driven. Let's become experts at discerning between these two opposing voices. Remember: "So now the case is closed. There remains no accusing voice of condemnation against those who are joined in life-union with Jesus, the Anointed One" (Romans 8:1).

God Has Declared Us Righteous

No doubt there are many accusing and condemning voices around us, but God's truth overrides them all. He has already made up his mind about you and has declared you forever innocent, righteous, clean, holy, lovely, wanted, cherished, and "not guilty."

Verse 33

> Who then would dare to accuse those whom God has chosen in love to be his? God himself is the judge who has issued his final verdict over them—"Not guilty!"

"Not Guilty!"

This is the eternal verdict over your life: *not guilty!* This is a legal decree. Please know that the devil and all of hell are very well aware of the verdict over your life, and they can never change it. However, all their efforts are focused on keeping you from knowing it. Beloved of God, give Jesus the satisfaction of his heart and the recompense of his glorious labor on Calvary by soaking in this heavenly truth until it is your reality. You are forever "not guilty!"

Christ Intercedes for Us

The only one worthy or qualified to condemn us has chosen to die for us. Jesus, our champion defender, now is ever praying for our full triumph. We cannot fail.

Verse 34

> Who then is left to condemn us? Certainly not Jesus, the Anointed One! For he gave his life for us, and even more than that, he has conquered death and is now risen, exalted, and enthroned by God at his right hand. So how could he

possibly condemn us since he is continually praying for our triumph?

Jesus Is Praying for You

Have you been at one of life's low points and felt all alone, perhaps forsaken, thinking no one really cares if you rise or fall? I believe we all have moments like that. Here in this verse, we find a truth that can encourage us even in the darkest of life's valleys: Jesus is praying for you. You are so valuable to him, and he wants you to know it. That is why he said, "What is the value of your soul to God? Could your worth be defined by an amount of money? God doesn't abandon or forget even the small sparrow he has made. How then could he forget or abandon you? What about the seemingly minor issues of your life? Do they matter to God? Of course they do! So you never need to worry, for you are more valuable to God than anything else in this world" (Luke 12:6–7). He is not aloof, somewhere out there in the cosmos working on more important matters. No, to him, you are what matters.

Christ Deeply Loves Us

The Bible is God's message to humanity, but it isn't mere dogma or rules. The Bible is a love letter. Within its pages is found the love story of the ages: God and you. Don't take my word for it, though. Take his: "For you reach into my heart. With one flash of your eyes I am undone by your love, my beloved, my equal, my bride. You leave me breathless—I am overcome by merely a glance from your worshiping eyes, for you have stolen my heart. I am held hostage by your love and by the graces of righteousness shining upon you" (Song of Songs 4:9). To search the Scriptures for any truth other than God's passionate love for us is to miss the point entirely. He has set his holy affection upon you, and his love is fiery and tenacious. It reaches past all your faults and pulls you into his triumph.

Verses 35–37

Who could ever divorce us from the endless love of God's
Anointed One? Absolutely no one! For nothing in the
universe has the power to diminish his love toward us.
Troubles, pressures, and problems are unable to come
between us and heaven's love. What about persecutions,
deprivations, dangers, and death threats? No, for they are
all impotent to hinder omnipotent love, even though it is
written:

> All day long we face death threats for your sake, God.
> We are considered to be nothing more
> than sheep to be slaughtered!

Yet even in the midst of all these things, we triumph
over them all, for God has made us to be more than conquerors, and his demonstrated love is our glorious victory
over everything!

God Has Made Us More than Conquerors in Four Ways

1. No situation in life can defeat us or dilute God's love.
2. Divine love and power are working for us.
3. We share in the victory spoils of every enemy and battle we
   face. Every enemy we face is going to let go of everything
   they have taken from us. We will rejoice in those spoils
   because Jesus is our champion defender.
4. We have conquered the Conqueror with one glance of our
   worshiping eyes. Your love conquers him. If you conquer
   the Conqueror, that makes you "more than a conqueror."
   This is the language he uses to describe how your sincere
   devotion touches him. "Turn your eyes from me; I can't
   take it anymore! I can't resist the passion of these eyes that
   I adore. Overpowered by a glance, my ravished heart—
   undone. Held captive by your love, I am truly overcome!

For your undying devotion to me is the most yielded sacrifice" (Song of Songs 6:5).

Love Brings the Triumph

The love God demonstrates toward us brings the victory. The way that we fight is to love Jesus all the more. When the enemy squeezes you by various trials and hardships, may Jesus' worship be what flows out.

Nothing Can Ever Separate Us from Eternal Love

Here is the powerful and heart-melting conclusion: love will triumph over every enemy. Jesus described this unquenchable, unconquerable love like this:

> This living, consuming flame
> will seal you as my prisoner of love.
> My passion is stronger
> than the chains of death and the grave,
> all consuming as the very flashes of fire
> from the burning heart of God.
> Place this fierce, unrelenting fire over your entire being.
> Rivers of pain and persecution
> will never extinguish this flame.
> Endless floods will be unable
> to quench this raging fire that burns within you.
> Everything will be consumed.
> It will stop at nothing
> as you yield everything to this furious fire
> until it won't even seem to you like a sacrifice anymore.
> (Song of Songs 8:6–7)

This is the quality of God's love that gives us deep security we need in life: God's love never fails.

Verse 38–39

> So now I live with the confidence that there is nothing in the universe with the power to separate us from God's love. I'm convinced that his love will triumph over death, life's troubles, fallen angels, or dark rulers in the heavens. There is nothing in our present or future circumstances that can weaken his love. There is no power above us or beneath us—no power that could ever be found in the universe that can distance us from God's passionate love, which is lavished upon us through our Lord Jesus, the Anointed One!

There Is No Separation

We never have reason to doubt or fear because

- God is for us.
- Christ died for us.
- God has declared us righteous.
- Christ ever lives to intercede for us.
- Christ deeply loves us.
- Christ's love makes us more than conquerors.
- Nothing will ever separate us from the eternal love of God.

Let's Go Deeper!

Questions

1. Within these verses (30–39), Paul completes his "case" that he has been building throughout Romans. He includes seven key questions, which he also answers. List those questions with their answers adding your own conclusions as well.

1.

2.

3.

4.

5.

6.

7.

2. The amazing truth that God has foreknown you, chosen you, and called you is brought out in verse 30. He has called you, and you have answered. Read John 15:16; Song of Songs 6:8–10; Psalm 71:6–7; Romans 1:6; and 1 Peter 2:9. Think back on the working and wooing of God in your life. Can you see how you didn't choose him, but he chose you? Briefly describe the moment when you finally surrendered to his call and said "yes."

3. One of the profound questions in this portion of Scripture is, "If God has determined to stand with us, tell me, who

then could ever stand against us?" What does it mean to you, personally, to know God is standing with you?

4. Your security as God's dear child is solely based in his love. *His love*—not your love, your goodness, your own righteousness (filthy rags, right?), or your own merit. List the things that can never separate you from God's great love (vv. 38–39).

5. God's glory is his goodness, his loving-kindness…his *great love*. God's plan for you is glorification! He wants his love to be your reality, your atmosphere, your source, and your nature. Describe how having a "glory-focus" versus a fear-based "sin-focus" helps you go from glory to glory. (See 8:30, 38–39, and 2 Corinthians 3:18.)

Deeper Still!

Activations

No Separation
Many of us deal with a fear of rejection or abandonment. Life circumstances and experiences may have taught us to expect the ones

we love to walk away. God knows, and he understands. No one has been more rejected than Jesus: "He was despised and rejected by men, a man of deep sorrows who was no stranger to suffering and grief. We hid our faces from him in disgust and considered him a nobody, not worthy of respect" (Isaiah 53:3).

Jesus bore your pain and rejection so that you could be enveloped eternally in the steadfast love of God. Now, because of Jesus, *nothing* can ever separate you from God's love.

Let's Pray

Lord, I desire to become as secure in your love as you want me to be. You really make it clear in these verses from Romans that you want me to be "rock-solid" in your love. So Lord, please come and heal my heart. I invite you, Holy Spirit, to search me and remove fear and heal all wounds of rejection. Lord, I choose to forgive every person who has knowingly or unknowingly rejected or abandoned me. I forgive, bless, and release them, in Jesus' name. Lord, please pull out any bitter root of rejection in my heart and replace it with love. Baptize me in your love, I pray. Make me to be more deeply rooted and grounded in your love, nourished by your love so that I am secure and able to love you and others well. Thank you, Lord. Amen.

God's Heart for Israel

(Romans 9:1–11:15)

Paul has now made his case, and it is complete. These next few chapters of Romans are somewhat of a parenthetical insert. Paul spends some time in Romans 9–11 discussing the subject of Israel, including his heart and God's heart for this beloved nation.

This section is no less important than other themes Paul has covered but rather addresses unique concerns likely to have been stirred within the hearts of his fellow Jews concerning God's plan for them. *Do they still matter? Are they still his covenant people? Has God abandoned them because of their rejection (as a whole) of their Messiah?*

Therefore, this portion of Romans is dear. In it, we not only see God's heart toward Israel but also his nature of covenant love. He is a faithful, promise-keeping God. He remains faithful even when his people are faithless. Perhaps the greatest miracle that you and I have witnessed in our day is the actual existence of the nation of Israel. For many years, Israel was but a historical footnote, but God literally resurrected it. Its language, culture, economy, and even its global presence have been brought back from the dead. Israel is a sign and wonder to the whole world that God is real and that he does not forsake his own.

The Jewish People (Romans 9:1–13)

Paul's Devotion to His Jewish Family

In these next few verses, we get a unique insight into Paul's heart for his people. His remarkable and self-sacrificing love for them could only be Holy Spirit inspired. We must take his example to heart and seek God for such love for the lost.

Verses 1–5

> O Israel, my Jewish family, I feel such great sorrow and heartache for you that never leaves me! God knows these deep feelings within me as I long for you to come to faith in the Anointed One. My conscience will not let me speak anything but the truth. For my grief is so intense that I wish that I would be accursed, cut off from the Messiah, if it would mean that you, my people, would come to faith in him!
>
> You are Israelites, my fellow citizens, and God's chosen people. To you belong God's glorious presence, the covenants, the Torah, the temple with its required sacrifices, and the promises of God. We trace our beginnings back to the patriarchs, and through their bloodline is the genealogy of the Messiah, who is God over everything. May he be praised through endless ages! Amen!

"My Grief Is So Intense"

Paul was such an intercessor, and here we see him display a love so great for his people, the Jewish nation, that he is willing to give up his eternal salvation (if possible) in exchange for their salvation. This is similar to Moses' intercession for God's people. Paul, therefore, becomes a Moses-type figure in the New Testament—a leader who is utterly selfless and willing to lay down everything for the sake of the people of God. Indeed, both Moses and Paul made it their life mission to bring God's people out of bondage and into their full inheritance.

God's Faithfulness to Israel

Is the nation of Israel a "failed experiment"? Certainly not. Your own salvation is a result of God's promise to Abraham. As Galatians 3:8 says, "The Scripture prophesied that on the basis of faith God would declare gentiles to be righteous. God announced the good news ahead of time to Abraham: 'Through your example of faith, all the nations will be blessed!'" Every day, as more and more souls experience the saving grace of God, the true Israel is expanding and filling the earth with God's glory.

Verses 6–13

Clearly, God has not failed to fulfill his promises to Israel, for that will never happen! But not everyone who has descended from Israel belongs to Israel. Physical descent from Abraham doesn't guarantee the inheritance, because God has said:

"Through Isaac your descendants will be counted as part of your lineage."

This confirms that it is not merely the natural offspring of Abraham who are considered the children of God; rather, the children born because of God's promise are counted as descendants. For God promised Abraham:

"Now is the time! For in nine months your wife, Sarah, will have a son!"

Now, this son was our ancestor, Isaac, who, with his wife, Rebekah, conceived twins. And before her twin sons were born, God spoke to Rebekah and said:

"The oldest will serve the youngest."

God spoke these words before the sons had done anything good or bad, which proves that God calls people not on the basis of their good or bad works, but according to his divine purpose. For in the words of Scripture:

"Jacob I have chosen, but Esau I have rejected."

True Sons of Abraham

God's Word is clear: the true sons of Abraham are those born of the promise, born from above. Isaac was a picture for us of the miracle of being born again because his birth was supernatural. We received divine life in our new birth that qualifies us to receive the blessings of Abraham, our inheritance of fullness of life in Christ. Isaac, we well know, was not the only child of Abraham, but he was the only one who was a promise from God. We inherit every blessing of Abraham because we, too, are spiritual sons and daughters, born from above, born of the Spirit.

God's Sovereignty Prevails (Romans 9:14–33)

God's Righteousness

God's ways are higher than ours, his ways are always right, and he is always good. These are basic truths about God's nature, and they perfectly complement one another even when our finite minds can't quite fathom it. We have to embrace the mystery of God, knowing that if things don't seem good yet or righteous yet or just yet, then it simply means God is not finished yet.

Verses 14–18

So, what does all this mean? Are we saying that God is unfair? Of course not! He had every right to say to Moses:

"I will be merciful to whomever I choose and I will show compassion to whomever I wish."

Again, this proves that God's choice doesn't depend on how badly someone wants it or tries to earn it, but it depends on God's kindness and mercy. For just as God said to Pharaoh:

"I raised you up as ruler of Egypt for this reason, that I might make you an example of how I demonstrate my miracle power. For by the example of how I deal with you, my powerful name will be a message proclaimed throughout the earth!"

So again we see that it is entirely up to God to show mercy or to harden the hearts of whomever he chooses.

God Has the Right to Choose Those to Whom He Will Show Mercy

Justice and righteousness are the foundation of God's throne, the basis of his kingdom rule and reign. The psalmist described his seat of authority with these words: "Your glorious throne rests on a foundation of righteousness and just verdicts. Grace and truth are the attendants who go before you" (Psalm 89:14)

All the activities of God's kingdom operate in those heavenly parameters. He is right, good, just, gracious, and merciful. Therefore, the way he deals with the nation of Israel will definitely and continually reveal his righteousness and justice.

God's Justice

God is just. God is right. God is just right! Life is not always fair, but God is fair. He operates in justice. We can trust him that he truly does make all things perfect and beautiful in his time.

Verses 19–29

Well then, one might ask, "If God is in complete control, how could he blame us? For who can resist whatever he wants done?"

But who do you think you are to second-guess God? How could a human being molded out of clay say to the one who molded him, "Why in the world did you make me this way?" Or are you denying the right of the potter to make out of clay whatever he wants? Doesn't the potter have the right to make from the same lump of clay an elegant vase or an ordinary pot?

And in the same way, although God has every right to unleash his anger and demonstrate his power, yet he is extremely patient with those who deserve wrath—vessels prepared for destruction. And doesn't he also have the right to release the revelation of the wealth of his glory to his vessels of mercy, whom God prepared beforehand to receive his glory? Even for us, whether we are Jews or non-Jews, we are those he has called to experience his glory. Remember the prophecy God gave in Hosea:

> "To those who were rejected and not my people,
> I will say to them: 'You are mine.'
> And to those who were unloved I will say:
> 'You are my darling.'"

And:

> "In the place where they were told, 'You are nobody,'
> this will be the very place where they will be renamed
> 'Children of the living God.'"

And the prophet Isaiah cries out to Israel:

> Though the children of Israel
> are as many as the sands of the seashore,
> only a remnant will be saved.
> For the Lord will act
> and carry out his word on the earth,
> and waste no time to accomplish it!

Just as Isaiah saw it coming and prophesied:

> If the Lord God had not left us a remnant,
> we would have been destroyed like Sodom
> and left desolate like Gomorrah!

God Chooses Those Whom He Glorifies

If God acted with justice alone, everyone would be destroyed. Even the people of Israel would merit the same fate as Sodom and

Gomorrah. Often the cry for "justice" or "fairness" comes from a misguided, deeply held belief that we can merit or earn acquittal in the courts of heaven. Romans points out this fallacy and reveals over and over the truth that it is only in Christ that we are "not guilty." In Christ alone, we are co-glorified.

If anyone is to be saved, Jew or non-Jew, it can only be as the result of God's action and choice, which is defined as mercy (9:15–18). To accuse God of injustice, to believe that he condemns some unfairly, means that we fail to see that apart from his choice of some of us, none of us would be his people. Let us then focus on his *mercy* and his amazing grace that saves us.

God's Grace

Simple faith in God transfers to us his perfect righteousness. That is grace. And like it or not (and many don't) grace is not "fair." It is supernatural, holy, heavenly, and divine. It is God's grace, not ours or any religion's. It can't be attained but only received.

Verses 30–33

> So then, what does all this mean? Here's the irony: The non-Jewish people, who weren't even pursuing righteousness, were the ones who seized it—a perfect righteousness that is transferred by faith. Yet Israel, even though pursuing a legal righteousness, did not attain to it. And why was that? Because they did not pursue the path of faith but insisted on <u>pursuing righteousness by works, as if it could be seized another way</u>. They were offended by the means of obtaining it and stumbled over the stumbling stone, just as it is written:
>
> > "Be careful! I am setting in Zion a stone
> > that will cause people to stumble,
> > a rock of offense that will make them fall,
> > but believers in him will not experience shame."

"They Were Offended...and Stumbled"

Grace is unearned and lavished on us by God in love. In this way and for this reason, grace is the great "leveler" of the "field" of life. We are all equally loved by God, and not one of God's children is above another in rank or belovedness. This is good news...for some. Others find it offensive because of pride. Which will you be? Will you be offended at the grace of God or humbly grateful for it?

God's Faithful Love for Israel (Romans 10:1–21)

The Reason for Israel's (Temporary) Rejection

The day will come, never doubt it, when God will restore Israel to himself. The eyes of the spiritually blind will open. They will "gaze on the one they have pierced" and see the glory of Jesus (John 19:37). Israel will be saved. But as of yet, some Jews are experiencing an apparent rejection. Paul addresses this temporary condition in Romans 10.

Verses 1–13

> My beloved brothers and sisters, the passionate desire of my heart and constant prayer to God is for my fellow Israelites to experience salvation. For I know that although they are deeply devoted to God, they are unenlightened. And since they've ignored the righteousness God gives, wanting instead to be acceptable to God because of their own works, they've refused to submit to God's faith-righteousness. For Christ is the end of the law. And because of him, God has transferred his perfect righteousness to all who believe.
>
> Moses wrote long ago about the need to obey every part of the law in order to be declared right with God:
>
> > "The one who obeys these things must always live by them."

But we receive the faith-righteousness that speaks an entirely different message:

> "Don't for a moment think you need to climb into the heavens to find the Messiah and bring him down, or to descend into the underworld to bring him up from the dead."

But the faith-righteousness we receive speaks to us in these words of Moses:

> "God's living message is very close to you, as close as your own heart beating in your chest and as near as the tongue in your mouth."

And what is God's "living message"? It is the revelation of faith for salvation, which is the message that we preach. For if you publicly declare with your mouth that Jesus is Lord and believe in your heart that God raised him from the dead, you will experience salvation. The heart that believes in him receives the gift of the righteousness of God—and then the mouth confesses, resulting in salvation. For the Scriptures encourage us with these words:

> "Everyone who believes in him will never be disappointed."

So then faith eliminates the distinction between Jew and non-Jew, for he is the same Lord for all people. And he has enough treasures to lavish generously upon all who call on him. And it's true:

> "Everyone who calls on the Lord's name
> will experience new life."

Jews Must Be Saved

There is not a separate path for Jews. No, Jews must be saved by grace through faith in Jesus Christ. Jesus is the way, the truth, and the life for all mankind. As "Jesus explained, 'I am the Way, I am the Truth, and I am the Life. No one comes next to the Father except through union with me. To know me is to know my Father too'" (John 14:6).

When Jesus spoke those words, he was speaking to a Jewish audience. It was true then, and it is true now. They must be enlightened. As Paul says here in Romans 10:2, they are devoted yet unenlightened.

Jesus Is the Fulfillment of the Law

Jesus is the end of the law. The law was meant to point people to Christ. He fulfilled the law…for you! If you have placed your trust in Jesus Christ, then "God has transferred his perfect righteousness" to you. Doesn't that make the gospel "good news"? Yes, indeed. Judaism for centuries said, "Do!" but Jesus Christ has once and for all said, "Done!" Any teaching that says you must add to what Jesus fulfilled is not in line with the gospel of grace.

"The Heart That Believes"

In these verses, Paul describes the temporary rejection of Israel— many have hardened their hearts. They have held onto their religion of trying to please God with works of righteousness and in doing so have actually rejected his gift of righteousness. To this day, the Jewish concept of righteousness is to be full of good works and to be a good person. This is absolutely contrary to the gospel of grace that says we have borrowed our righteousness from the Righteous One because *we have none.* How is this miracle of righteousness accomplished? Faith alone. Faith is heaven's currency, and by faith alone is righteousness transferred to your account. Your faith pleases God and conveys your total trust in his total love (Hebrews 11:6).

The Remedy for Their Rejection

Are the Jewish people without hope? Of course not. Their hope is the same hope of all mankind: the gospel. Whenever anyone, Jew or non-Jew, hears and receives the good news, faith will be "birthed in [his or her] heart" (v. 17) unto salvation.

Verses 14–17

> But how can people call on him for help if they've not yet
> believed? And how can they believe in one they've not yet
> heard of? And how can they hear the message of life if there
> is no one there to proclaim it? And how can the message
> be proclaimed if messengers have yet to be sent? That's why
> the Scriptures say:
>
>> How welcome is the arrival
>> of those proclaiming the joyful news of peace
>> and of good things to come!
>
> But not everyone welcomes the good news, as Isaiah
> said:
>
>> Lord, is there anyone who hears
>> and believes our message?
>
> Faith, then, is birthed in a heart that responds to God's
> anointed utterance of the Anointed One.

Messengers of Good News

The "joyful news" of salvation must be proclaimed by God's messengers. These sent ones take the "message of life" to those who have not yet heard it, both to Jew and non-Jew. Paul quotes from Isaiah 52:7 and Nahum 1:15, which describe these bearers of glad tidings as being welcomed, also translated as having beautiful feet. (See also Song of Songs 7:1.)

Their life-giving message is wanted and received…by some but not by all. We who know and have received the gospel message are called to spread it, but we are not responsible for how it is received. Messengers must be sent, have been sent, and will be sent. However, the hearers of that message must still respond rightly. To all those who receive and believe the message of Christ, both Jew and non-Jew, faith "is birthed in [their] heart" (v. 17). So again, salvation is by faith alone: "For by grace you have been saved by faith.

Nothing you did could ever earn this salvation, for it was the love gift from God that brought us to Christ!" (Ephesians 2:8).

The Results of Their Rejection

In these next verses, Paul describes the amazing wisdom of God at work in the earth through in his dealings with natural Israel. The true message of salvation "has gone to the ends of the earth!" (v. 18).

Verses 18–21

> Can it be that Israel hasn't heard the message? No, they have heard it, for:
>
> > The voice has been heard throughout the world,
> > and its message has gone to the ends of the earth!
>
> So again I ask, didn't Israel already understand that God's message was for others as well as for themselves? Yes, they certainly did understand, for Moses was the first to state it:
>
> > "I will make you jealous of a people who are 'nobodies.'
> > And I will use people with no understanding
> > to provoke you to anger."
>
> And Isaiah the fearless prophet dared to declare:
>
> > "Those who found me weren't even seeking me.
> > I manifested myself before those
> > who weren't even asking to know me!"
>
> Yet regarding Israel Isaiah says:
>
> > "With love I have held out my hands day after day,
> > offering myself to this unbelieving
> > and stubborn people!"

Israel Is Doubly Blinded

All humans are blinded through the fall, Adam's fateful sin in the garden. Israel is also experiencing a secondary condition of blindness—a judicial blindness—until the salvation of the gentiles is complete.

- *The Blindness of Fallen Humanity*—"Their minds have been blinded by the god of this age, leaving them in unbelief. Their blindness keeps them from seeing the dayspring light of the gospel of the glory of Christ, who is the divine image of God" (2 Corinthians 4:4).

- *The Blindness by God's Judicial Determination*—"My beloved brothers and sisters, I want to share with you a mystery concerning Israel's future. For understanding this mystery will keep you from thinking you already know everything. A partial and temporary hardening to the gospel has come over Israel, which will last until the full number of non-Jews has come into God's family" (Romans 11:25).

Natural and Spiritual Israel

God's faithfulness and covenant love with each of these two entities (the church and Israel) are not in opposition to his Word or his will. He will fulfill every promise to both. He deals with the church, and he deals with Israel according to his promises and his great love and wisdom. Aren't you so glad that this is who he is? He is love, and love never, ever, ever fails. Therefore, rest assured, God will complete every plan in his heart for his people.

True Worship

There is nothing in Scripture that teaches that observing Jewish religious activities brings you closer to God. The old has passed, and the new has come! The need for animal sacrifices is gone (Hebrews 10:1–9). God is not going to rebuild the temple in Jerusalem; we are the temple he is building. Jesus pointed to that coming reality, which is now here, when he said, "From now on, worshiping the Father will not be a matter of the right place but with a right heart. For God is a Spirit, and he longs to have sincere worshipers who adore him in the realm of the Spirit and in truth" (John 4:23–24). We are those who worship God in spirit and in truth. One day, one *glorious* day, the nation of Israel will receive their new sight and worship God in spirit and truth.

Grace and Legalism Cannot Be Mingled

We honor Israel, pray for its peace, and love it as God does; however, we cannot Judaize the church, teaching believers to keep the laws and rituals of Judaism. Remember, the powerful theme of Romans is *grace alone.* We cannot mix the law and grace. Grace plus *anything* is no longer grace. That grace is taking us somewhere. Grace is taking us onward to glory. God is not taking us back to the shadow of symbolic rituals and feasts. No, he is taking us into the substance of the reality that those former things actually pointed to—Jesus!

God's Remnant (Romans 11:1–15)

Paul

God has not abandoned or rejected his people. His character would never allow that. Paul highlights this fact by using his own salvation of proof that Jews are being saved.

Verse 1

> So then I ask you this question: did God really push aside and reject his people? Absolutely not! For I myself am a Jew, a descendant of Abraham, from the tribe of Benjamin.

"I Myself Am a Jew"

Paul uses his own salvation and faith in Jesus Christ as an example of the fact that there indeed is hope for the Jew. The gospel is for all, Jew and non-Jew. Even though, as a whole, Jews have experienced blindness through their rejection of Jesus, there is a remnant of loving Jewish followers of the Messiah. There has always been a faithful remnant of Messianic Jews from the day of Pentecost in Acts 2 and still today.

Elijah

In the next few verses, Paul references the prophet Elijah as another example of God's remnant saints. Through every dark time in Israel's history, God always had his people, his faithful ones.

Verses 2–10

God has not rejected his chosen, destined people! Haven't you heard Elijah's testimony in the Scriptures, and how he prays to God, agonizing over Israel?

"Lord, they've murdered your prophets; they've demolished your altars. Now I'm the only one left and they want to kill me!"

But what was the revelation God spoke to him in response?

"You are not alone. For I have preserved a remnant for myself—seven thousand others who are faithful and have refused to worship Baal."

And that is but one example of what God is doing in this age of fulfillment, for God's grace empowers his chosen remnant. And since it is by God's grace, it can't be a matter of their good works; otherwise, it wouldn't be a gift of grace, but earned by human effort.

So then, Israel failed to achieve what it had strived for, but the divinely chosen remnant receives it by grace, while the rest were hardened and unable to receive the truth. Just as it is written:

God granted them a spirit of deep slumber.
He closed their eyes to the truth
and prevented their ears from hearing
up to this very day.

And King David also prophesied this:

May their table prove to be a snare
and a trap to cause their ruin.

Bring them the retribution they deserve.
Blindfold their eyes and don't let them see.
Let them be stooped over continually.

The "Chosen Remnant"

This is a biblical concept that is seen throughout Scripture. God has his remnant—through every dark age of deception, every season of spiritual drought, and every hopeless time of persecution when it seems all is lost. All is never lost with God because he has a remnant. This remnant will inherit the promises of God.

God's grace is with his devoted ones and empowers them to be his light in the world. This light is his glory, and it will eventually cover the whole earth (Isaiah 60:1–3).

The Gentiles

Finally, Paul points to the hope that is ever before Israel. Yes, as a whole, they missed their Messiah's coming. However, their stumbling has brought a great salvation throughout the world. Paul describes how this great harvest of gentile souls is now actually being used by God to move Jewish hearts to "jealousy and desire" for God's amazing grace.

Verses 11–15

So, am I saying that Israel stumbled so badly that they will never get back up? Certainly not! Rather, it was because of their stumble that salvation now extends to all the non-Jewish people, in order to make Israel jealous and desire the very things that God has freely given them. So if all the world is being greatly enriched through their failure, and through their fall great spiritual wealth is given to the non-Jewish people, imagine how much more will Israel's awakening bring to us all!

Now, I speak to you who are not Jewish, since I am an apostle to reach the non-Jewish people. And I draw attention to this ministry as much as I can when I am among the Jews, hoping to make them jealous of what God has given to those who are not Jews, winning some of my people to salvation.

For if their temporary rejection released the reconciling power of grace into the world, what will happen when Israel is reinstated and reconciled to God? It will unleash resurrection power throughout the whole earth!

The Reconciliation of Israel

How jealous are *you* making Israel? Is the gospel that is being preached through your life a message that would inspire desperation for salvation, freedom, and a personal intimate relationship with God? It is God's desire that it does. Our faith lived out loud is sending the gospel light throughout the nations, including Israel, and speeding the return of the Lord. May we be so full of genuine worship and the miracle working power of God that we incite a jealous fire within the hearts of the Jewish people. Amen.

Let's Go Deeper!

Questions

1. What was Paul's purpose in these three chapters? Why do you think this was an important inclusion in Romans' message of grace and glory?

2. In Romans 3:1 Paul posed the question: "What advantage is there of being a Jew?" Here in Romans 9:4–5, he answers that question and gives eight advantages. List them and describe why they are beneficial.

-
-
-
-
-
-
-
-

3. What did the Jews "stumbled over" (9:32–33)? How have they tried to attain righteousness instead? Is their hope and path to true righteousness and salvation any different from the path you have had to take?

4. According to 10:14–21, is the message of the gospel being broadcasted to Jews? How (or through whom) is it sent? Describe how the display of salvation by grace that you have received will drive Jews to jealousy.

5. What will be unleashed throughout the whole earth when Israel is reconciled to God? See 11:13–15.

Deeper Still!

Activations

Mercy and Grace

The existence of the nation of Israel in our day, the mere fact that they are a nation on the earth despite all that has attempted to wipe them out, is a sign and wonder to all mankind that God is faithful, powerful, merciful, and true.

God's sovereign choice of Abraham in Genesis 12 to be the father of a people for God's own pleasure and purpose was and always will be solely based on his *mercy*—not Israel's *merit*. He chose them and called them just as he chose and called you. His love and mercy made them his own, and so he declared, "I have loved you with an everlasting love; I have drawn you with unfailing kindness" (Jeremiah 31:3 NIV). (See also Ezekiel 16:3–6.)

Salvation has always been by grace. This portion from Romans 9–11, though seemingly off-topic, is actually very relevant to the entire message of Romans: God has not altered his agenda nor his salvation plan…therefore, we must not alter it either.

If we are to correctly reflect God's heart—lighting up the darkness for the non-Jew and eliciting jealousy in the Jew—then we must display and herald the true grace gospel of Romans: the just shall live by faith.

Let's Pray

Father, purify my heart of any trust or reliance on my own goodness, ability, or merit. I have not been brought to your heart because I was wise, good, or strong enough to get there. It is only by your grace. Lord, make me a pure, undefiled message of the grace gospel so that no one would look at me and think I am saved by my own goodness. May my life broadcast your true message of salvation to all the world. In Jesus' name, I pray. Amen.

Right Relationships

(Romans 11:16–12:21)

In this lesson, we will finish Paul's teaching regarding God's dealings and plans for the future of Israel. Then we will move into the next section of Romans, which concerns the practical implementation of Christian doctrine.

Chapter 12 is a "hinge" in the book of Romans. Starting with chapter 12 and then on through chapter 16, Paul begins to bring personal applications of the important truths of the gospel. This is the model for all of Paul's letters: first exhortation, then application. We need the sound doctrinal foundations, and we need the practical application of those doctrines.

The Patriarchs and the "Olive Tree" (Romans 11:16–24)

Israel and the Church (Continued)

As Paul concludes this portion of Romans that addresses God's heart and plan for Israel, he uses the symbol of an olive tree to describe how the church and natural Israel are related and connected. This metaphor aptly depicts the church's placement into the family of God by grace alone and how we should remain humble in our heart attitude toward Israel, remembering we were once "nothing more than a wild olive branch" (v. 17). How grateful we should be! From Israel we have received the Torah, our Messiah and Savior, the New Testament Scriptures, and so much more.

Verses 16–18

> Since Abraham and the patriarchs are consecrated and set apart for God, so also will their descendants be set apart. If the roots of a tree are holy and set apart for God, so too will be the branches.
>
> However, some of the branches have been pruned away. And you, who were once nothing more than a wild olive branch, God has grafted in—inserting you among the remaining branches as a joint partner to share in the wonderful richness of the cultivated olive stem. So don't be so arrogant as to believe that you are superior to the natural branches. There's no reason to boast, for the new branches don't support the root, but you owe your life to the root that supports you!

Grafted In

Non-Jewish believers in Yeshua (the Hebrew name for Jesus) are all "grafted in" to the "root" of Abraham and his seed, thereby receiving all of Abraham's promises and blessings from God. The Jewish root has presented to us gentiles a Messiah, Jesus Christ, and we have been brought into an everlasting covenant with the living God. What wondrous blessing and grace are now ours in Christ. We were once so lost and ignorant of God: "For at one time you were not God's people, but now you are. At one time you knew nothing of God's mercy, because you hadn't received it yet, but now you are drenched with it!" (1 Peter 2:10).

Jesus, the Branch

Jesus our Savior was and is the offspring of the root of David. Zechariah foretold the coming Messiah, calling him "the Branch": "Tell him this is what the LORD Almighty says: 'Here is the man whose name is the Branch, and he will branch out from his place and build the temple of the LORD'" (Zechariah 6:12 NIV). This Lion of the Jewish tribe of Judah has come to save and deliver all who call upon his name, and his love for the Jewish people burns within his beautiful heart to this very day. He has not changed his mind.

Verses 19–24

You might begin to think that some branches were pruned or broken off just to make room for you. Yes, that's true. They were removed because of their unbelief. But remember this: you are only attached by your faith. So don't be presumptuous, but stand in awe and reverence. Since God didn't spare the natural branches that fell into unbelief, perhaps he won't spare you either!

So fix your gaze on the simultaneous kindness and strict justice of God. How severely he treated those who fell into unbelief! Yet how tender and kind is his relationship with you. So keep on trusting in his kindness; otherwise, you also will be cut off.

God is more than ready to graft back in the natural branches when they turn from clinging to their unbelief to embracing faith. For if God grafted you in, even though you were taken from what is by nature a wild olive tree, how much more can he reconnect the natural branches by inserting them back into their own cultivated olive tree!

"God Is More than Ready"

God is willing and wanting to restore natural Israel to himself. This is his heart and intention. What a glorious day that will be when Israel recognizes the Messiah! They will not become gentile believers; they will be messianic Jews grafted "back into their own cultivated olive tree!" (Romans 11:15).

The Mystery of Israel's Restoration
(Romans 11:25–36)

God Himself Will Bring All of Israel to Salvation

It will take a miracle for Israel to be saved, won't it? It also took a miracle for you to be saved as well as every other believer in Jesus. Our God is a miracle-working God. He is a saving God. In fact, the Bible says that salvation actually belongs to God (Revelation 7:10 and 19:1). Our God saves! And he will certainly save Israel.

Verses 25–26

> My beloved brothers and sisters, I want to share with you a mystery concerning Israel's future. For understanding this mystery will keep you from thinking you already know everything.
>
> A partial and temporary hardening to the gospel has come over Israel, which will last until the full number of non-Jews has come into God's family. And then God will bring all of Israel to salvation! The prophecy will be fulfilled that says:
>
> > "Coming from Zion will be the Savior,
> > and he will turn Jacob away from evil.
> > For this is my covenant promise with them
> > when I forgive their sins."

"A Mystery"

This is the Greek word *mysterion* found twenty-seven times in the New Testament. One of the mysteries of the New Testament is the mystery of Israel's future. For a long period of human history, it was the age of the Jew, in which God's dealings centered upon the Jewish people. Now, we are in the age of the church (which encompasses both Jew and gentile), and we will be so until the full number of gentiles has been saved. This does not negate the promises God made to Israel. Israel will recognize their Messiah and "turn…away from evil" (v. 26).

Verses 28–36

> Now, many of the Jews are opposed to the gospel, but their opposition has opened the door of the gospel to you who are not Jewish. Yet they are still greatly loved by God because their ancestors were divinely chosen to be his. And when God chooses someone and graciously imparts gifts to him, they are never rescinded.
>
> You who are not Jews were once rebels against God, but now, because of their disobedience, you have experienced God's tender mercies. And now they are the rebels, and because of God's tender mercies to you, you can open the door to them to share in and enjoy what God has given to us!
>
> Actually, God considers all of humanity to be prisoners of their unbelief, so that he can unlock our hearts and show his tender mercies to all who come to him.
>
> Who could ever wrap their minds around the riches of God, the depth of his wisdom, and the marvel of his perfect knowledge? Who could ever explain the wonder of his decisions or search out the mysterious way he carries out his plans?
>
>> For who has discovered how the Lord thinks
>> or is wise enough to be the one
>> to advise him in his plans?
>
> Or:
>
>> "Who has ever first given something to God
>> that obligates God to owe him something in return?"
>
> For out of him, the sustainer of everything, came everything, and now everything finds fulfillment in him. May all praise and honor be given to him forever! Amen!

The Land of Israel

Our God is Alpha and Omega. This means that when he starts
something, he already has the end in mind. Through the prophet
Jeremiah, God revealed his commitment to the ultimate victory of
his people by saying, "For I know the thoughts that I think toward
you, saith the LORD, thoughts of peace, and not of evil, to give you
an expected end" (Jeremiah 29:11 KJV). This means you have an
expected end, the church has an expected end, and so does Israel.
God promised a specific portion of land to Abraham and reiterated his promises when Joshua took the children of Israel over
the Jordan River, telling him that even every place his foot landed
belonged to him. God will keep every promise he makes.

In Conclusion of this Topic of Israel's Future

- God has set aside Israel *temporarily* so that we gentiles
  can be "grafted in" to the root and become recipients—
  heirs—of the promises of God for Abraham and his
  descendants.

- This temporary condition does not negate God's ultimate intention for his beloved Israel.

- God will keep every promise, and he indeed has a plan
  (mysterious as it may presently be to us) for the Jewish
  people.

- Natural Israel is not perfect nor are they more beloved
  than the church, but God has chosen to be merciful to
  them just as he has chosen to be merciful to you and me.

- Israel will be restored, God's plan for them will be
  fulfilled, and God's plan for the Middle East is much
  greater than what we see from a contemporary
  viewpoint.

Right Relationship with God (Romans 12:1–2)

Paul has used his gift in previous chapters to lay an excellent bedrock for his readers to build their lives upon. So now, knowing the power and magnitude of the grace at work in us to bring us from glory to glory, we are exhorted in practical keys for victorious Christian living, keys to "live a beautiful life" (Romans 12:2).

Genuine Worship

In these first few verses, Paul raises the standard of living in complete surrender—body, mind, and will—to God. It all starts with complete surrender. Everything else in our lives will be blessed as we prioritize first honoring God with our whole being.

Verses 1–2

> Beloved friends, what should be our proper response to God's marvelous mercies? To surrender yourselves to God to be his sacred, living sacrifices. And live in holiness, experiencing all that delights his heart. For this becomes your genuine expression of worship.
>
> Stop imitating the ideals and opinions of the culture around you, but be inwardly transformed by the Holy Spirit through a total reformation of how you think. This will empower you to discern God's will as you live a beautiful life, satisfying and perfect in his eyes.

"Living Sacrifices"

In the Greek, this phrase is "living martyr." How profound! We live our lives as those already surrendered completely to God's will. Isaac's sacrifice of Genesis 22 is a wonderful picture of what it means to be a living sacrifice. He allowed himself to be bound and then willingly laid himself down on the altar. No doubt he could have easily escaped or overpowered his elderly father, but he didn't. This is actually an Old Testament foreshadowing of Jesus' willing sacrifice on Calvary. Nails did not keep Jesus on the cross—love did.

Love kept him there for six long, painful hours. Love for Abraham kept Isaac on the altar as he watched his father raise a knife to sacrifice him. It is the same for you and me. Love will keep us in the place that Paul speaks of in these verses, a place of sacrificial love.

"Genuine Expression of Worship"

The truest expression of worship is always giving sacrificially. In fact, the very first mention of worship in the Bible is actually this very passage in Genesis 22:5

When God required Isaac of Abraham, Abraham willingly surrendered his Isaac, his dream, his promise. When we do the same—giving our all and our best to God—that is true worship. You cannot worship God without bringing a sacrifice. There is no such thing as worship without an offering. Likewise, there is no such thing as true Christianity without a cross to bear. The New Testament cross is the Old Testament wooden altar. It is a symbol of suffering, yes, but it is also the emblem of love.

Sacrifices

The old-covenant sacrifices were animals. What are the "sacrifices" of the new covenant? The first mention of "worship" in the New Testament is in Matthew: "[The wise men] inquired of the people, 'Where is the child who is born king of the Jewish people? We observed his star rising in the sky and we've come to bow before him in worship'" (Matthew 2:2).

And what did those wise men bring? Offerings. Gifts. Worship, therefore, is giving—giving sacrificially of your praise, gifts, offerings, time, money, and more.

Don't Be Conformed

This is a hallmark of the Christian life: we are different! We are pilgrims in this world—in it but not of it. Paul's powerful exhortation overarches every era of time and every cultural distinction. We must not conform to the "world" with its carnal philosophies and ungodly value system.

We have a kingdom culture. We are called to bring that culture here "on earth as it is in heaven." Our culture of the supernatural life of heavenly values will always offend the culture of this world. The cross itself is an offense. Jesus was and is a stone of stumbling. But we are not to be squeezed into the mold of what the world says is acceptable. We must not cave to the pressure of being palatable to sinful people. Instead, we have to determine that we will live in awe of God and be his living sacrifices, already martyrs within our hearts and dead to the opinions of those who don't obey God.

Be Reformed

We all came into our walk with God carrying loads of ideology and values that need to be reformed! Nobody gets saved already holy; it just doesn't work that way. Therefore, we must do the work of putting truth, God's Holy Word, into our minds.

We can't change our own hearts, try as we might. Heart transformation is supernatural. We can, however, do our part of immersing our minds into the water of the Word of God. We do our part, and God will do his part.

We all want the "beautiful life" that Paul mentions here, but it really begins with beautiful choices and beautiful thoughts. If you change your thoughts, God will change your life. He will indeed make it "satisfying and perfect in his eyes."

Living a Philippians 4:8 Life

You may wish it were different, but it is really this practical. No ritual, no prayer line, no fire tunnel, no prophetic word will replace the discipline of controlling your thought life. God does give us powerful and practical guidelines for our thoughts: "Keep your thoughts continually fixed on all that is authentic and real, honorable and admirable, beautiful and respectful, pure and holy, merciful and kind. And fasten your thoughts on every glorious work of God, praising him always" (Philippians 4:8).

So, as you think about your spouse, children, coworkers, neighbors, in-laws, government officials, leaders, and others, think

Philippians 4:8 kinds of thoughts! Your life will always reflect your thoughts. Beautiful thoughts will produce a beautiful life, guaranteed.

The Good and Perfect Will of God

As we align our will with God's will, the supernatural is released in us. Mountains get moved and long-standing character issues become resolved. We experience deep transformation—the change we long for—as we surrender our will to his. Jesus, our pattern, lived this way. His life of humble surrender to the Father is revealed in the simple yet profound prayer: "Father, if you are willing, take this cup of agony away from me. But no matter what, your will must be mine" (Luke 22:42).

His "secret" to success was his life lived from the secret place. He simply listened and obeyed. These are his own words describing this powerful dynamic: "The Son is unable to do anything from himself or through his own initiative. I only do the works that I see the Father doing, for the Son does the same works as his Father" (John 5:19). Jesus is our example. As we live yielded, we will also experience the supernatural works of the Father in us and through us.

Right Relationships with Other Believers (Romans 12:3-16)

In these next few verses, we enter into a biblical discussion on relationships and the relational victories that grace and glory will bring us into. First and foremost, of course, is our relationship with God. Our deep intimacy with the Lord is paramount to our success in all other relationships as well as every other area of our life. We must be living martyrs (12:1), wholly surrendered to God's will and ways. Secondly, is our relationship with others. Paul gives us powerful guidelines for right relationships with our fellow humans.

Honest Evaluation

Buckle up now as Paul pulls out all the stops, going deep into hidden places of the heart. There is no place in Christianity for play-acting. Jesus paid much too high a price for us to dip our toes into the River of Life whenever or only if we feel like it. The call is clear, the standard is high, and Jesus Christ is most worthy of our humility, honesty, and sincerity.

Verse 3

> God has given me grace to speak a warning about pride. I would ask each of you to be emptied of self-promotion and not create a false image of your importance. Instead, honestly assess your worth by using your God-given faith as the standard of measurement, and then you will see your true value with an appropriate self-esteem.

Faith Is "the Standard of Measurement"

God counsels us to let faith be the standard of measurement by which we assess our worth. Our faith is God-given. We are warned against pride and self-promotion because we need a warning. We are all tempted to assess our worth by worldly measures and then become puffed up with pride. Instead, we must look honestly at our faith and evaluate whether we are living in and by faith, knowing that "without faith living within us it would be impossible to please God. For we come to God in faith knowing that he is real and that he rewards the faith of those who passionately seek him" (Hebrews 11:6). And, because faith is the standard of measurement of our worth, no one is less or more worthy than any other believer.

Vital Cooperation

Next, Paul makes the point that we need a vital cooperation with others in the body of Christ. Through cooperation, we will go places in God that are impossible alone, and likewise, God will use us to push others into their destiny as well.

Verses 4–8

In the human body there are many parts and organs, each with a unique function. And so it is in the body of Christ. For though we are many, we've all been mingled into one body in Christ. This means that we are all vitally joined to one another, with each contributing to the others.

God's marvelous grace imparts to each one of us varying gifts. So if God has given you the grace-gift of prophecy, activate your gift by using the proportion of faith you have to prophesy. If your grace-gift is serving, then thrive in serving others well. If you have the grace-gift of teaching, then be actively teaching and training others. If you have the grace-gift of encouragement, then use it often to encourage others. If you have the grace-gift of giving to meet the needs of others, then may you prosper in your generosity without any fanfare. If you have the gift of leadership, be passionate about your leadership. And if you have the gift of showing compassion, then flourish in your cheerful display of compassion.

Cooperation in the Body of Christ

Paul begins his exhortation to unity by encouraging us to first have an honest evaluation and then to choose vital cooperation. The first ensures our humility, and the next ensures our ability to give to and receive from others within the family of God. We need one another, and none of us, no matter how spiritual or wise, is meant to make it on our own.

You are where you are right now because of the people in your life who have contributed to your life journey. Your mentors, pastors, teachers, fathers, mothers, counselors, and friends have all been paintbrushes in the hand of God as he has created the masterpiece of your life.

Loving Participation

This is where the "rubber meets the road," so to speak, in our progression into Christlikeness. How do you treat others? The answer to this question is the measure of your spirituality, no matter how gifted or knowledgeable you may be. Anything less than sincere love is less than the measure of Jesus.

Verses 9–16

Let the inner movement of your heart always be to love one another, and never play the role of an actor wearing a mask. Despise evil and embrace everything that is good and virtuous.

Be devoted to tenderly loving your fellow believers as members of one family. Try to outdo yourselves in respect and honor of one another.

Be enthusiastic to serve the Lord, keeping your passion toward him boiling hot! Radiate with the glow of the Holy Spirit and let him fill you with excitement as you serve him.

Let this hope burst forth within you, releasing a continual joy. Don't give up in a time of trouble, but commune with God at all times.

Take a constant interest in the needs of God's beloved people and respond by helping them. And eagerly welcome people as guests into your home.

Speak blessing, not cursing, over those who reject and persecute you.

Celebrate with those who celebrate, and weep with those who grieve. Live happily together in a spirit of harmony, and be as mindful of another's worth as you are your own. Don't live with a lofty mind-set, thinking you are too important to serve others, but be willing to do menial tasks and identify with those who are humble minded. Don't be smug or even think for a moment that you know it all.

True Spiritual Maturity

You can have all the titles, degrees, and accolades, but the truth is *you are only as spiritual as you are loving.* Love is the litmus test. Can you pass that test? The body of Christ is God's beautiful, holy, and treasured family. We are all at different stages of spiritual development, but we are all on time because we are under the blood of Jesus. Functioning healthily and lovingly within God's family is our assignment and our privilege. We must embrace this assignment, loving what God loves with all of our heart. Are you longing for more of Jesus? You will find him within his people. He is YAHWEH-Shammah, "the Lord is there." Where? In his people.

Right Relationships with Those Outside (Romans 12:17–21)

Harmony in Relationships

Well, take a deep breath and prepare to say "ouch" before you read these next few verses. Paul gives us powerful and clear instructions to keep us on course in life. It is certain that as we navigate our journey, there will be many opportunities to hold a grudge against others or to get even when someone wrongs us. The struggle is real. However, we can overcome because Jesus has already given us the victory. Through him, we can and will "defeat evil with good" (v. 21).

Verses 17–21

> Never hold a grudge or try to get even, but plan your life around the noblest way to benefit others. Do your best to live as everybody's friend.
>
> Beloved, don't be obsessed with taking revenge, but leave that to God's righteous justice. For the Scriptures say:
>
> "Vengeance is mine, and I will repay," says the Lord.
>
> And:

> If your enemy is hungry, buy him lunch!
> Win him over with kindness.
> For your surprising generosity will awaken his
>   conscience,
> and God will reward you with favor.

Never let evil defeat you, but defeat evil with good.

Grudges, Offense, and Vengeance

Do Christians need sound teaching about topics as dark and sinister as revenge and unforgiveness? Yes, we certainly do. Being alive on the earth guarantees us many opportunities to be offended. As the people of God, and certainly within the community of believers, we do not have the right to hold grudges or to take revenge.

"Defeat Evil with Good"

The concluding principle is so powerful: don't let evil defeat you; instead, you defeat evil by doing good. You will win every battle in this way. The greater One lives in you, and he is love. Love conquers evil every time. Win your victories by taking the "high road." The low road is quarreling, defending yourself, and getting even. It may seem easier, but it cannot take you to where God wants you to be. Choosing love is choosing the life he has destined you for.

These are the standards Paul gives us:

- No grudges
- No getting even
- No taking revenge
- No yielding to evil
- Plan ways to benefit others
- Be a friend to everyone
- Feed your hungry enemy
- Show your enemy generosity
- Win your enemy over with kindness

- Defeat evil with good

Let's Go Deeper!

Questions

1. In 11:25, Paul speaks of a hardening of Israel. The Greek word for hardening, *porosis*, can also mean "stubbornness," an unwillingness to learn something new. How did Israel display stubbornness to John the Baptizer, Jesus their Messiah, and the initial preachers of the gospel of grace? Do we at times also struggle with stubbornness when God wants to teach us something new? What are some "new things" God has taught you, and how did you resist at first? What can you learn from this that will help you grow and flourish into more new things?

2. According to 11:29, "God's...gifts...are never rescinded," and this can also be translated: "The grace-gifts and calling of God are void of regret and without change in purpose." Read Isaiah 27:9 and Jeremiah 31:33–34 and describe God's faithful dealings with his people.

3. Paul appeals to us in 12:1 in this way: "Beloved friends, what should be our proper response to God's marvelous mercies?" An important question is posed, so spend some time meditating on "God's marvelous mercies," such as your adoption into God's family, physical healing, forgiveness,

and grace. Make a list and then answer Paul's profound question: What should your response be?

4. Reformation means setting something back on the right course. According to 12:2, how will you experience a complete reformation? What is your part in ensuring your alignment with God's perfect will?

5. Romans 12:9–21 gives us a powerful standard and guideline for real Christianity. How will a healthy and accurate understanding of God's mercies (v. 1) equip you to live out the loving actions of verses 9–21?

Deeper Still!

Activations

Romans 12:1–2

The two verses cannot be overemphasized. If you haven't already, commit them to memory and to your lifelong pursuit. Within them, we find two important keys to living the life we are meant for as well as attaining our pursuit of true Christlikeness.

His Sacred Living Sacrifice

Living martyrdom is your high calling. Holding on to your life and fighting for your rights in any regard ensures a peace-less and fruit-less Christian journey. Surrender is not easy, but it is simple, and in it is *true worship* and the beautiful life you long for.

A Total Reformation of How You Think

This is the oh-so-practical side of Christianity. So, ask yourself the hard question: What are you doing daily to ensure your soul trans-formation? The change you need and long for depends completely on reforming your mind and thought life.

Let's Pray

> *Lord, I surrender all. I lay every piece of my life on your altar. You can have it all, Lord. I withhold nothing from you. I confess that my life is not my own. I am bought by your blood and meant for your pleasure. I give you all of me—body, mind, and will—as an act of sincere worship and devotion.*
>
> *Lord, today I commit to doing my part for bringing a total reformation to my thought life. Help me to prioritize the feeding of my mind and heart with truth and light, your Holy Word. I recognize that I make time for the things that are important to me, and so I ask that you would help me to make soul transformation and thought reformation of the utmost importance. In Jesus' name. Amen.*

Living in Unity

(Romans 13:1–14:12)

Right Relationships with Those in Authority (Romans 13:1–14)

Interacting with Others

We continue now in Paul's teaching on walking in love. This is the basic outline he followed for guiding us in how we interact with others:

- A healthy evaluation
- A vital cooperation
- A loving participation

Verses 1–10

Every person must submit to and support the authorities over him. For there can be no authority in the universe except by God's appointment, which means that every authority that exists has been instituted by God. So to resist authority is to resist the divine order of God, which results in severe consequences. For civil authorities don't intimidate those who are doing good, but those who are doing evil. So do what is right and you'll never need to fear those in authority. They will commend you for your good citizenship.

Those in authority are God's servants for the good of society. But if you break the law, you have reason to be alarmed, for they are God's agents of punishment to bring criminals to justice. Why do you think they carry weapons? You are compelled to obey them, not just to avoid punishment, but because you want to live with a clean conscience.

This is also the reason you pay your taxes, for governmental authorities are God's officials who oversee these things. So it is your duty to pay all the taxes and fees that they require and to respect those who are worthy of respect, honoring them accordingly.

Don't owe anything to anyone, except your outstanding debt to continually love one another, for the one who learns to love has fulfilled every requirement of the law. For the commandments, "Do not commit adultery, do not murder, do not steal, do not covet," and every other commandment can be summed up in these words:

"Love and value others the same way you love and value yourself."

Love makes it impossible to harm another, so love fulfills all that the law requires.

With Government

Romans 13 continues with the teaching on loving participation and begins with the right relationship that we as Christians are called to have with civil authorities. We mustn't think that our Christianity makes us opposed to, or even outside of, the authority of the government and its imperfect leaders. Jesus illustrated this when he spoke of paying taxes: "Jesus said, 'Precisely. The coin bears the image of the emperor Caesar, so you should pay the emperor his portion. But because you bear the image of God, you must give to God all that belongs to him'" (Mark 12:17).

All authority is established and ordained by God and deserves our honor and obedience. We must first obey God, but just as we give to God what is due him, we also give (taxes, honor, and more) to our rulers as is due them.

"Love and Value Others"

Paul sums up this important passage of instruction for living "debt free" toward those to whom we are to pay honor and respect by telling us to *simply love*. The golden rule is the standard, and it is powerful. We can't love and judge others at the same time. We must choose love, and when we do, God's grace will empower us to love as God loves. Paul gave Timothy, his spiritual son, clear and wise instruction on this important matter:

> Most of all, I'm writing to encourage you to pray with gratitude to God. Pray for all men with all forms of prayers and requests as you intercede with intense passion. And pray for every political leader and representative, so that we would be able to live tranquil, undisturbed lives, as we worship the awe-inspiring God with pure hearts. It is pleasing to our Savior-God to pray for them. He longs for everyone to embrace his life and return to the full knowledge of the truth...
>
> Therefore, I encourage the men to pray on every occasion with hands lifted to God in worship with clean hearts, free from frustration or strife. (1 Timothy 2:1–4, 8)

Verse 11

> To live like this is all the more urgent, for time is running out and you know it is a strategic hour in human history. It is time for us to wake up! For our full salvation is nearer now than when we first believed.

"To Live like This"

Paul is referring here to living in obedience to the laws and authorities set in place by God. An excellent life is a powerful testimony in this world of anger, racism, rebellion, and anarchy. We cannot be his witnesses unless our life reflects his virtue and values.

"Time Is Running Out"

Listen, Jesus is coming again, and our full salvation is nearer than the day we first met him. Are you living that way? It is easy to get sidetracked by life's difficulties and life's pleasures, so Paul gives us the needed warning: "It is time to wake up!" We don't have the luxury of living sloppy lives of sloppy grace. No, we are called to reflect *clearly* the views of our King and his kingdom. We are his ambassadors living in this world as strangers who represent a living Jesus to a dying world, and he is coming soon.

Verse 12

> Night's darkness is dissolving away as a new day of destiny dawns. So we must once and for all strip away what is done in the shadows of darkness, removing it like filthy clothes. And once and for all we clothe ourselves with the radiance of light as our weapon.

The Weapon of Light

You are clothed with Jesus! His glory is your covering and a weapon against the darkness. Think of that. Wherever you go, no matter how weak or dim you may *feel*, the truth is that you dispel the darkness. You are a light bearer and a glory dispenser. As you simply walk in the Spirit, one step at a time and one day at a time, you are bringing the kingdom with you every step of the way, fulfilling God's promise that says, "I will give you every place where you set your foot, as I promised Moses" (Joshua 1:3 NIV). God has empowered you and is equipping you to possess your promises in him, the inheritance of the beautiful life he has planned for you. Through your transformed life, the prophecy of Isaiah 60 is being fulfilled:

"Arise, shine, for your light has come, and the glory of the LORD rises upon you. See, darkness covers the earth and thick darkness is over the peoples, but the LORD rises upon you and his glory appears over you. Nations will come to your light, and kings to the brightness of your dawn" (vv. 1–3 NIV).

Verse 13

> We must live honorably, surrounded by the light of this new day, not in the darkness of drunkenness and debauchery, not in promiscuity and sensuality, not being argumentative or jealous of others.

No Jealousy

There is no need for competition in the body of Christ. We are all on equal footing. Walking, for all of us, requires reliance on the faithfulness and goodness of God. He is our balance, our guidance, our support, and our strength. None of us could fulfill our calling and run a worthy race except by God's grace alone. Therefore, competition and jealousy are nullified. We are those who fully recognize that we are needy and "poor in spirit." This mindset keeps us humble and fully dependent on God's grace. According to Jesus, being in touch with your spiritual poverty sets you up to receive the kingdom life and blessings. In fact, he said, "What happiness comes to you when you feel your spiritual poverty! For yours is the realm of heaven's kingdom" (Matthew 5:3). So, let your life message be this: Jesus is my life, my all in all.

Verse 14

> Instead fully immerse yourselves into the Lord Jesus, the Anointed One, and don't waste even a moment's thought on your former identity to awaken its selfish desires.

"Fully Immerse Yourselves"

Join and mingle yourself with Jesus. Soak in his love, his grace, his glory. Bliss is your inheritance. You are meant for life-union with the Anointed One. Immerse your day, your heart, your mind, your moments, your friendships, your money, and your time. Immerse it all into the Lord Jesus and don't waste even a moment on any lesser pattern of living.

Unity in the Midst of Diversity (Romans 14:1–12)

Receive One Another as God Has Received Us

God's beautiful family is amazingly diverse. Many nations, tribes, languages, and cultures make up the wondrous body of Christ. For this reason, the church is an opportunity for each one of us to mature—we must embrace each other's uniqueness and diversity. This requires love and grace. We are like a cluster of grapes because individually we are less powerful than we are collectively. The new wine is found in the cluster. The blessing and fullness of the Spirit is experienced and flows from our unity: "Here is what YAHWEH says, 'As new wine is found in the cluster, and someone says, "Don't destroy it, for there is a blessing in it"'" (Isaiah 65:8).

Verses 1–3

> Offer an open hand of fellowship to welcome every true believer, even though their faith may be weak and immature. And refuse to engage in debates with them concerning nothing more than opinions.
>
> For example, one believer has no problem with eating all kinds of food, but another with weaker faith will eat only vegetables. The one who eats freely shouldn't judge and look down on the one who eats only vegetables. And the vegetarian must not judge and look down on the one who eats everything. Remember, God has welcomed him and taken him as his partner.

A Gnat versus a Camel

Jesus once gave an interesting analogy about swallowing gnats versus swallowing camels (see Matthew 23:24). Obviously, swallowing a gnat is not pleasant, but it also is harmless. Swallowing a camel, however, is lethal. We should be sensible about what we make a "big deal" out of. Isn't this true in relationships? Unity, love, and true harmony will definitely require each of us to "gulp down" our personal opinions and preferences, swallowing our pride. This is what maturity will do. Immaturity will have us nitpicking and making mountains out of molehills in order to get our own way and prove ourselves right.

The Problem of Opinions

Your opinion will absolutely at some point (and likely, many points) contradict someone else's opinion in the church. It is in those moments that we must let go of pride, arrogance, and selfishness. Being right is overrated; it really is. Jesus bled and died—you can surely allow for the weaknesses and different viewpoints of your fellow believers. Here are two soul-straightening verses about our pride-filled opinions:

- "A fool is in love with his own opinion" (Proverbs 12:15).

- "Be free from pride-filled opinions, for they will only harm your cherished unity. Don't allow self-promotion to hide in your hearts, but in authentic humility put others first and view others as more important than yourselves" (Philippians 2:3).

A Love Feast of Christian Unity

Jesus was very clear: Christians will be *known by love for one another*. He said, "For when you demonstrate the same love I have for you by loving one another, everyone will know that you're my true followers" (John 13:35). Our unity cannot be broken any more than family members can change their DNA—we are family.

Just as the Lord fully accepted you when you first came to him with all your weaknesses and immaturity, so you are also called to accept your fellow believers *just as they are*...and not only *accept* but actually *celebrate*. We are a beautiful, diverse, multifaceted, and many-membered body. Let's celebrate one another's uniqueness!

Jesus Is Lord and Judge

Aren't you so thankful that the only one who is authorized to condemn or uphold you, the only one allowed to judge you, is the Lord Jesus Christ? No one, no person in the universe, has the right to judge your heart. Jesus alone reserves the right to judge his servants. And, oh, what a kind, merciful, and trustworthy judge is he!

Verses 4–12

Who do you think you are to sit in judgment of someone else's household servant? His own master is the one to evaluate whether he succeeds or fails. And God's servants will succeed, for God's power supports them and enables them to stand.

In the same way, one person regards a certain day as more sacred than another, and another person regards them all alike. There is nothing wrong with having different personal convictions about such matters. For the person who observes one day as especially sacred does it to honor the Lord. And the same is true regarding what a person eats. The one who eats everything eats to honor the Lord, because he gives thanks to God, and the one who has a special diet does it to honor the Lord, and he also gives thanks to God.

No one lives to himself and no one dies to himself. While we live, we must live for our Master, and in death we must bring honor to him. So dead or alive we belong to our Master. For this very reason the Anointed One died and was brought back to life again, so that he would become the Lord God over both the dead and the living.

Why would you judge your brothers or sisters because of their diet, despising them for what they eat or don't eat? For we each will have our turn to stand before God's judgment seat. Just as it is written:

"As surely as I am the Living God, I tell you:
'Every knee will bow before me
and every tongue will confess the truth
and glorify me!'"

Therefore, each one must answer for himself and give a personal account of his own life before God.

Jesus Is the Judge of Men's Hearts

Praise God that Jesus is the one who will be with us when we give an account:

There is not one person who can hide their thoughts from God, for nothing that we do remains a secret, and nothing created is concealed, but everything is exposed and defenseless before his eyes, to whom we must render an account.

So then, we must cling in faith to all we know to be true. For we have a magnificent King-Priest, Jesus Christ, the Son of God, who rose into the heavenly realm for us, and now sympathizes with us in our frailty. (Hebrews 4:13–14)

So, just as you would not want to stand uncovered and be subjected to judgment before mere mortals, neither should you want to uncover and judge anyone else. Breathe a sigh of relief, knowing that the one who is your judge is also your friend, lover, Savior, intercessor, Bridegroom, strengthener, and advocate.

The Diverse Body of Christ

God didn't break the mold when he made you because he didn't even use a mold. He dreamed of you in his loving heart and then created you for his delight. The psalmist said it this way: "You saw who you created me to be before I became me! Before I'd ever seen the light of day, the number of days you planned for me were already recorded in your book" (Psalm 139:16). God has never and will never be satisfied with a version of one of his beloved children that is a mere clone of someone or something else. No, he loves the true you, the real you, and he will bring you forth by his *grace*, into his *glory*, for the fullness of his purpose. And, when it is all said and done, you will look a lot like Jesus.

Grace Receivers and Grace Givers

If we have been so blessed and covered and empowered by God's grace, should we desire to also give that same grace to others? Indeed, we should, and we must. We represent Jesus in the earth. We are his body. We are his living epistles, his letters for others to read and know what God is really like. Are we representing him well? Are we showing the world a gracious Jesus who bears with the failings of the weak and covers a multitude of sin? Or are we displaying a different Jesus and a different gospel? We must *display* the grace we preach—in our words, our actions, and our relationships within the family of God. New baby Christians are watching, our children are watching, and the world is watching.

Let's Go Deeper!

Questions

1. According to Romans 13:1–7, what is the God-ordained duty of civil authorities? Is this duty worthy of respect? In our world, what negative results come from a lack of respect and honor for police, military, judges, elected officials, presidents, and other authorities?

2. Read 1 Timothy 1–8. When we see injustices enacted by those in authority, what is a powerful position to take?

3. According to Romans 13:1 and 7, what things are you *required* to give to governing authorities? Assess your heart and actions in this regard. As you make your "payments," do you do so as if in obedience to God and his Word? How will a right heart motivation and attitude help you?

4. What should Christians avoid according to 14:1? What is the problem with opinion-based debates?

5. Read 14:1–12 and describe what you believe Paul meant by this statement: "No one lives to himself and no one dies to himself" (v. 7).

Deeper Still!

Activations

The Debt to Love

We may enjoy the "dessert" sermons of Holy Spirit power and encouragement, but we so need these "peas and carrots" sermons of real-life, practical, Christlike living. These are not the passages to skim over. They are actually the opportunities for us to make real changes in our lives that will, in turn, bring real changes in the world around us. When Christians practice (not just preach) the gospel of grace, we become the salt and light believers that Jesus calls us to be:

> Your lives are like salt among the people. But if you, like salt, become bland, how can your 'saltiness' be restored? Flavorless salt is good for nothing and will be thrown out and trampled on by others.
>
> Your lives light up the world. For how can you hide a city that stands on a hilltop?…So don't hide your light! Let it shine brightly before others, so that your commendable works will shine as light upon them, and then they will give their praise to your Father in heaven. (Matthew 5:13–14, 16)

Let's take a holy moment and self-evaluate our life's message. How is your saltiness? How is your shininess? Jesus said, "Don't hide your light!" That means our light *can* be hidden. Is there anything—anger, unforgiveness, judgmental attitudes, self-pity, prejudice, pride, spiritual pride—blocking your light? Saltiness and brightness are parts of God's great plan for you. Live that beautiful life he intends.

Let's Pray

Father, I come humbly before your throne of grace and ask for mercy. Forgive me for the things and attitudes I have allowed to creep into my heart that are not like you. Forgive me for all anger, pride, selfishness, jealousy, competitiveness, judgmentalism, prejudice, and a "holier-than-thou" attitude. Forgive me for not making love the standard and goal in all my relationships. Realign my heart today, Lord. Realign me to your love and your Word. I lay down my pride, and I choose unity and love. Restore me and help me to truly be salt and light in my world. Amen.

LESSON 18

Love Is Key

(Romans 14:13–15:19)

Love One Another (Romans 14:13–23)

Love must be supreme. It is our goal because Jesus is love personified. The first eight chapters of Romans are about grace and glory, chapters 9 through 11 are about Israel, and starting in chapter 12, Paul turns a corner as he begins to exhort believers in godly and right relationships—with fellow believers, civil authorities, and even our enemies. Along those lines, here in chapter 14, Paul continues teaching the essential Christian call to love one another.

Our Lives Affect Others

This supreme call to love others does not always match conventional wisdom and certainly isn't in line with the attitudes and values of the world. It is a higher law and requires us to esteem others better than ourselves. Taking that higher road will not always make sense to our minds, but it will always make peace to our hearts. Remember, being right is not the goal; love is.

Verses 13–15

> So stop being critical and condemning of other believers, but instead determine to never deliberately cause a brother or sister to stumble and fall because of your actions.

I know and am convinced by personal revelation from the Lord Jesus that there is nothing wrong with eating any food. But to the one who considers it to be unclean, it is unacceptable. If your brother or sister is offended because you insist on eating what you want, it is no longer love that rules your conduct. Why would you wound someone for whom the Messiah gave his life, just so you can eat what you want?

Let Love Rule Your Conduct

There is a higher level of "rightness" beyond what is right or wrong—it is called *love*. Walking in love is right. Of course, we don't compromise on important gospel truth, but Paul's point concerning clean and unclean foods (which was relevant to his day) is a good example of a non-essential issue that should not cause division or unloving behavior in God's household.

Clean and Unclean Foods

Paul boldly says he has a personal revelation from the Lord about this issue; he knows that food is neither clean nor unclean. In other words, foods, in and of themselves, are not sinful or sin-causing. Peter received this same revelation in Acts 10:9–16 in which he plainly heard: "Nothing is unclean if God declares it to be clean" (Acts 10:15).

Both Peter and Paul had truth on their side. They were right about this issue of clean and unclean foods, yet here Paul teaches us an important principle: it is more important to be loving than to be right.

The Ones for Whom the Messiah Gave His Life

Another aspect of this point is that pride *destroys* and love *edifies*. Love bears with others' failings, weaknesses, differences. No, we never compromise on foundational truths, but we don't use our knowledge or "freedoms" to hurt or hinder someone else's faith. *Jesus died for all.* He is not putting up roadblocks or holding hoops for his people to jump through. He instead became the bridge to bring us to the Father. We need to do the same—be bridges, not stumbling blocks.

Relationships, Not Rules

Aren't you so glad God doesn't deal with you merely on the basis of rules? We always feel safe in his love and even his fatherly correction because we know it always and only comes from the place of true love. Let's make it our aim to provide that same loving, safe place for the people in our lives. This will naturally happen as we prioritize relationship and love over rules and being right.

Verses 16–18

> So don't give people the opportunity to slander what you know to be good. For the kingdom of God is not a matter of rules about food and drink, but is in the realm of the Holy Spirit, filled with righteousness, peace, and joy. Serving the Anointed One by walking in these kingdom realities pleases God and earns the respect of others.

The Kingdom Spirit Realm

The kingdom of God is in the realm of the Holy Spirit. Think about that. God's kingdom is holy and also governed by the Holy Spirit. This means that we, as kingdom ambassadors, are Spirit-led and Spirit-governed. We don't do as we please; we do what pleases the Spirit. As we do, we experience the righteousness, peace, and joy he brings: "Those who are motivated by the flesh only pursue what benefits themselves. But those who live by the impulses of the Holy Spirit are motivated to pursue spiritual realities. For the sense and reason of the flesh is death, but the mind-set controlled by the Spirit finds life and peace" (Romans 8:5–6).

Earn the Respect of Others

Our opinions, pet doctrines, "sacred cows," pride-filled rants, and holier-than-thou social media posts will probably never win over someone's heart. But love can! Love melts the cold heart, not arguments. Make love preeminent. Make love the goal, and then you will never fall into the trap of actually becoming a stumbling block to someone else. Let this powerful verse in Philippians be your holy pursuit: "Be free from pride-filled opinions, for they will only harm your cherished unity. Don't allow self-promotion to hide in your hearts, but in authentic humility put others first and view others as more important than yourselves" (Philippians 2:3).

We Help Each Other Grow

Looking for the best ways to help and serve others is the worthy goal of true ministry. You are meant to be a conduit of God's grace and blessing to others. Paul uses strong language here in these next verses to call us to account on this important issue, even admonishing us to "stop ruining the work of God" (Romans 14:20). It is time to evaluate whether we are building up or tearing down with our Christian service.

Verses 19–21

> So then, make it your top priority to live a life of peace with harmony in your relationships, eagerly seeking to strengthen and encourage one another. Stop ruining the work of God by insisting on your own opinions about food. You can eat anything you want, but it is wrong to deliberately cause someone to be offended over what you eat. Consider it an act of love to refrain from eating meat or drinking wine or doing anything else that would cause a fellow believer to be offended or tempted to be weakened in his faith.

Help, Don't Harm

We are to help each other, eagerly seeking to strengthen and encourage one another. Insisting on our own way and demanding that others adhere to our own opinions actually ruins the work of

God. That is heavy. Paul says it plainly here: "Make it your top priority" to live in peace and harmony with others.

"Ruining the Work of God"

Can it be? Is it possible that in our attempt to zealously serve God, we can actually destroy and tear down the lives that God himself is building up? The answer is simply yes. *Yes.* Therefore, we must not "insist on your own opinions about food" (v. 20) and other contentious issues that aren't essential salvation truths. Beloved, have your opinion and know what you believe. Hold on to your personal revelations—Peter and Paul did—but don't use them as tools to tear down the work of God.

Food

This was one of the "hot topics" of Paul's day in the church. In this passage, Paul is actually referring to eating food sacrificed to idols. Some thought it sinful; others did not. It was a matter of opinion and of conscience. It was not a matter of essential doctrinal truth.

Don't Force Your Opinions on Others

Oh, boy. Yes, he went there. Paul says it plainly and clearly: "Don't impose your [personal convictions] on others" (v. 22). This seems like something we shouldn't have to be told, but we do because— let's just face it—we love our own opinions. Again, the standard for our behavior is love for others, and being loving will often require us to close our mouths and open our hearts.

Verses 22–23

> Keep the convictions you have about these matters between yourself and God, and don't impose them upon others. You'll be happy when you don't judge yourself in doing what your conscience approves. But the one who has misgivings feels miserable if he eats meat, because he doubts and doesn't eat in faith. For anything we do that doesn't spring from faith is, by definition, sinful.

The Theology of Sin

This passage gives us an important definition of sin. What is sin? In this passage, sin is anything that doesn't come from faith. If you can't do something *in faith,* then don't do it; it is sinful. We obey the Lord in these matters, period. However, we don't impose our convictions on others, nor do we insist on personal liberties at the expense of hurting others. Again, love is the higher law. Love is the key to unity.

Bring Joy to One Another (Romans 15:1–7)

Living to Please Others

What is the mark of true spiritual maturity? In this next portion of Romans, Paul makes it very clear: the mature are those who "don't live to please themselves" (v. 1) but embrace the frailties of others. It isn't our knowledge, know-how, gifts, talents, or titles that show our spiritual growth. It is simply our love walk.

Verses 1–3

> Now, those who are mature in their faith can easily be recognized, for they don't live to please themselves but have learned to patiently embrace others in their immaturity. Our goal must be to empower others to do what is right and good for them, and to bring them into spiritual maturity. For not even the most powerful one of all, the Anointed One, lived to please himself. His life fulfilled the Scripture that says:
>
> > All the insults of those who insulted you fall upon me.

Spiritual Maturity

Jesus is our standard and our beautiful example. He was and is the most powerful and most intelligent One of all, yet he took our sins, failings, weaknesses, and frailties upon himself, incurring insults and rejection. *Let's be like Jesus.* He bends low to lift others up! He bends down to our level to help us: "Lord, bend down to listen to my prayer. I am in deep trouble. I'm broken and humbled, and I desperately need your help" (Psalm 86:1). Since he is so gracious with us, we can show this same grace to one another.

Pride and religion traffic in arguments, strife, opinions, and dogmatic debates, but love doesn't want to debate; it wants to bend over backward and build up believers. Love would rather look stupid than to wound or hurt another person. Love doesn't long to impose its beliefs on others or argue over ideas that are secondary, not primary to foundational theology. Love is primary, "for love is supreme and must flow through each of these virtues. Love becomes the mark of true maturity" (Colossians 3:14).

Verse 4

> Whatever was written beforehand is meant to instruct us in how to live. The Scriptures impart to us encouragement and inspiration so that we can live in hope and endure all things.

The Old Testament Instructions Substantiated

This is a clear instruction from the *New Testament* that the teachings of the *Old Testament* are good, instructive, encouraging, inspirational, hope-filled, and beneficial. Yes, we are new-covenant believers, but all of the Bible is for us to nurture our faith and help our spiritual growth. God is the same yesterday, today, and forever, and his Word endures forever.

Verses 5–7

> Now may God, the source of great endurance and comfort, grace you with unity among yourselves, which flows from your relationship with Jesus, the Anointed One. Then, with a unanimous rush of passion, you will with one voice glorify God, the Father of our Lord Jesus Christ. You will bring God glory when you accept and welcome one another as partners, just as the Anointed One has fully accepted you and received you as his partner.

Love Is the Perfect Bond

Love is the sum of all virtues and holds us together as the family of God (Colossians 3:14). The love theology of the book of Romans will help us in our oneness and safeguard us from disunity. We are, after all, varied, diverse, multifaceted, and many-membered. What holds this vast and wondrous body of Christ together? Love. This is the reason for Paul's passionate plea in Philippians where he said, "So I'm asking you, my friends, that you be joined together in perfect unity—with one heart, one passion, and united in one love. Walk together with one harmonious purpose and you will fill my heart with unbounded joy" (Philippians 2:2).

"Accept and Welcome One Another as Partners"

Those God has placed beside you in the building of his house are your teammates. We are living stones placed alongside one another...providentially and perfectly. This is a powerful picture for the interdependence, unity, and strength of the body of Christ: "You are rising like the perfectly fitted stones of the temple; and your lives have been built up together upon the foundation laid by the apostles and prophets, and best of all, you are connected to the Head Cornerstone of the building, the Anointed One, Jesus Christ himself!" (Ephesians 2:20). Peter also used this metaphor, exhorting us to "Come and be his 'living stones' who are continually being assembled into a sanctuary for God" (1 Peter 2:5).

So, those partners God has placed next to you may be rubbing you wrong, but that is actually for your good. Iron does indeed sharpen iron, and your teammates are sharpening you: "It takes a grinding wheel to sharpen a blade, and so one person sharpens the character of another" (Proverbs 27:17). They are polishing your rough edges and helping you grow and become more like Christ.

Avoid the "Porcupine Shuffle"

Porcupines have a habit in cold weather that is both funny and a bit sad. They will instinctively huddle together for warmth, but their cuddling will activate their quills. They involuntarily poke one another and then scatter back out into the cold. The cycle repeats over and over and over. This is, unfortunately, like many of us in God's family. We need one another and enjoy the warmth of unity…only until something or someone activates our sensitivities and causes us to break away in offense. We must cherish our unity above all, getting rid of touchiness, offense, rejection wounds, and over-sensitivity. *It is time to grow up.* There is so much more at stake than getting what you want or being "right."

Paul's Example of Power and Love (Romans 15:8–19)

Love-Empowered Ministry

True ministry is simply the overflow from our intimate connection to the Lord. As we soak in his love, love naturally flows out from us to those around us. If all that we do comes from God's love, he is ultimately glorified, and souls are always blessed.

Verses 8–12

I am convinced that Jesus, the Messiah, was sent as a servant to the Jewish people to fulfill the promises God made to our ancestors and to prove God's faithfulness. And now, because of Jesus, the non-Jewish people of the world can glorify God for his kindness to them, fulfilling the prophecy of Scripture:

Because of this I will proclaim you among the nations and they will hear me sing praises to your name.

And in another place it says:

"You who are not Jewish,
celebrate life right alongside his Jewish people."

And again:

> Praise the Lord, all you who are not Jews,
> and let all the people of the earth
> raise their voices in praises to him.

And Isaiah prophesied:

> "An heir to David's throne will emerge,
> and he will rise up as ruler
> over all the non-Jewish nations,
> for all their hopes will be met in him."

Jew and Gentile Joined

Paul includes within his call to Christian unity a call for unity between Jew and gentile—we are one in Christ. However, talk about different! It was truly miraculous for these two groups to become one in Christ, and yet that is exactly what God accomplished through the broken body of Jesus: "Ethnic hatred has been dissolved by the crucifixion of his precious body on the cross. The legal code that stood condemning every one of us has now been repealed by his command. His triune essence has made peace between us by starting over—forming one new race of humanity, Jews and non-Jews fused together in himself!" (Ephesians 2:15).

No Racism in the Kingdom

There is simply no place for racial division in God's family. We are one—diverse as we are—we are fused together through Christ. Love must override and win in every matter of diversity. *Love will overcome all.* As Jesus said, we will be known and recognized as his disciples because of our love for one another: "For when you demonstrate the same love I have for you by loving one another, everyone will know that you're my true followers" (John 13:35).

Love Is the Key

Love is the key to overcoming every prejudice and every difference that would normally divide and conquer us. This is the dominant message of these remaining chapters of Romans, and *it is all-important.* Fundamental to Christianity, in comparison to all other ideologies, philosophies, and religions, is love. God is love! His kingdom is filled with love. His people are ministers of love. Love is our primary mandate and mission, lest we get sidetracked.

Holy Spirit–Empowered Ministry

If you and I can "do ministry" on our own…perhaps it isn't really God's work but rather our own work. We can minister from Holy Spirit power or soul power. May this reality inspire us to lean on our Beloved all the more.

Verses 13–19

> Now may God, the fountain of hope, fill you to overflowing with uncontainable joy and perfect peace as you trust in him. And may the power of the Holy Spirit continually surround your life with his super-abundance until you radiate with hope!
>
> My dear brothers and sisters, I am fully convinced of your genuine spirituality. I know that each of you is stuffed full of God's goodness, that you are richly supplied with all kinds of revelation-knowledge, and that you are empowered to effectively instruct one another. And because of the outpouring of God's grace on my life to be his minister and to preach Jesus, the Anointed One, to the non-Jewish people, I have written rather boldly to you on some themes, reminding you of their importance. For this grace has made me a servant of the gospel of God, constantly doing the work of a priest, for I endeavor to present an acceptable offering to God; so that the non-Jewish people of the earth may be set apart and made holy by the Spirit of holiness.
>
> Now then, it is through my union with Jesus Christ, that I enjoy an enthusiasm and confidence in my ministry for God. And I will not be presumptuous to speak of anything except what Christ has accomplished through me.

For many non-Jewish people are coming into faith's obedience by the power of the Spirit of God, which is displayed through mighty signs and amazing wonders, both in word and deed. Starting from Jerusalem I went from place to place as far as the distant Roman province of Illyricum, fully preaching the wonderful message of Christ.

As Far as Illyricum

This distant province of the Roman Empire was approximately a thousand miles from Jerusalem. This gives us a clear picture of the extent of Paul's obedience to the great commission (Matthew 28:18–20). He describes his travels with these words, "I went from place to place...fully preaching the wonderful message of Christ." Imagine the gospel being spread *fully* for a thousand miles. In our day, that would be a true feat; in Paul's day, it was nearly miraculous. This amazing pioneer of the gospel message left a beautiful "trail" of new churches in his travels, new believers, and new hearts on fire for Jesus.

"Fully Preaching"

Paul's description of "fully preaching" is to declare the gospel by the power of the Holy Spirit with "mighty signs and amazing wonders, both in word and deed" (v. 19). This is our example. The gospel is not a mere philosophy or quaint idea to ponder; *it is power*. It is revealed, proclaimed, and preached in mighty signs and amazing wonders, and this was a significant aspect of Paul's ministry.

To fully preach the gospel we must include the supernatural power of the Holy Spirit. This is, in fact, the fullness of the great commission Jesus gave us:

> And he said to them, "As you go into all the world, preach openly the wonderful news of the gospel to the entire human race! Whoever believes the good news and is baptized will be saved, and whoever does not believe the good news will be condemned. And these miracle signs will accompany those who believe: They will drive out demons

in the power of my name. They will speak in tongues. They will be supernaturally protected from snakes and from drinking anything poisonous. And they will lay hands on the sick and heal them." (Mark 16:15–18)

Last Days Ministry

Verses 18–19 of Romans 15 give us a power-packed picture of what last days ministry looks like: people come to faith in Christ by the power of the Spirit displayed in mighty signs and wonders in word and in deed.

- *Word*—There are signs and wonders *in word*. God will use his messengers to show forth his miracle power: "For example, if you have a speaking gift, speak as though God were speaking his words through you" (1 Peter 4:11). Powerful and thunderous preaching is God's method, "for in his wisdom, God designed that all the world's wisdom would be insufficient to lead people to the discovery of himself. He took great delight in baffling the wisdom of the world by using the simplicity of preaching the story of the cross in order to save those who believe it" (1 Corinthians 1:21).

- *Deed*—Yes, signs will follow those who believe! That is the standard for New Testament ministry. We are those who know our God and do great exploits (Daniel 11:32). God has not changed, and he is a miracle-working God. How does he do his miracles? Through you and me: "Now wherever you go, make disciples of all nations, baptizing them in the name of the Father, the Son, and the Holy Spirit. And teach them to faithfully follow all that I have commanded you. And never forget that I am with you every day, even to the completion of this age" (Matthew 28:19–20).

We have so much to look forward to and so much to get excited about! Doom and gloom is not the forecast—*glory is*. Get your hopes up and dream with God. Ask him to reveal his kingdom of righteousness, peace, and joy *through your words and through your deeds*. He can, and he will.

Let's Go Deeper!

Questions

1. What was Paul's goal and purpose in writing this portion of Romans? Was his goal met in your own heart and life? How so?

2. According to 14:19 and 15:2, what should be the top priority for every believer in regard to relationships? Is it yours? What are some ways you could make it a greater priority?

3. Eating or not eating certain foods was one of the "hot topics" in the church of Paul's day. In Romans 14:13–21, Paul references food sacrificed to idols. Some thought it sinful to eat this food; others did not. It was a matter of opinion and of conscience. What are some similar topics in the church today? How does this teaching in Romans counsel you concerning them?

4. According to Romans 15:1, what is the mark of true spiritual maturity? We can also look at this conversely. What, therefore, is the mark of spiritual immaturity? How can you grow in this area?

5. Romans 15:15–19 gives us a clear picture of the powerful last days church ministry that is modeled by Paul the apostle. Read those verses once more and then write down the description they give for true and effective ministry.

Deeper Still!

Activations

Avoiding the "Porcupine Shuffle"
[Refer to this example from the lesson.]

We must cherish our unity above all, getting rid of touchiness, offense, rejection wounds, and over-sensitivity. It is time to grow up!

How is your love walk, dear saint? Have you been doing the "porcupine shuffle"? For many of us, it seems easier to withdraw and isolate than to deal with the deeper issues. What are those issues? Usually:

- Painful past experiences
- Unhealed rejection wounds
- Fear of abandonment and rejection

- Unforgiveness
- A root of bitterness
- Judgmental and critical attitudes

Do you recognize in yourself any of those common issues? Within the family of God, these things are exposed (quills out!) but also healed—unless we retreat into old habits. Are you ready to break out of old habits and into the freedom of love?

Let's Pray

Father, I want to grow up and go forward into all that you have planned for me. I recognize that I have allowed certain attitudes and behaviors that are clearly wrong and unloving to remain in my life. I want to follow in the steps of Jesus who lived selflessly and lovingly. Lord, I've got some ways that are not based in love, and I repent. I repent of _____ (list them out one by one). I don't want to isolate or repel others any longer because I know you have called me to be a vessel of your love. Fill me, Lord, with a fresh baptism of your love and fire, and at the exact moment when my "quills" react, help me to deny myself, take up my cross, and follow you. Amen.

Paul's Final Remarks

(Romans 15:20–16:27)

Paul's Example of Faithful Obedience
(Romans 15:20–21)

Verses 20–21

> It is my honor and constant passion to be a pioneer who
> preaches where no one has ever even heard of the Anointed
> One, instead of building upon someone else's foundation.
> As the Scriptures say:
>
>> Those who know nothing about him will clearly see
>> him,
>> and those who have not heard will understand.

Paul, the Pioneer
No doubt, everyone had opinions about where Paul should preach,
how he should preach, and certainly what he should preach, and
it is the same for each of us. As we go forth in life and ministry to
fulfill our individual callings, we will have to stay true, as Paul did,
to our heavenly mandate.

Paul longed to take the gospel to places where it had never
been heard. This was his passion. We still need these pioneer-
hearted preachers in our day. There are still unreached places and

people groups. God will harvest his church from every people, nation, tribe, and tongue. We have reached every people and nation but not every tribe and every tongue. The gospel still must go out— this is still our mission and mandate. One day, it will be fulfilled, for this is the song of the redeemed in heaven:

> They were all singing this new song of praise to the Lamb:

> Because you were slaughtered for us,
> you are worthy to take the scroll and open its seals.
> Your blood was the price paid to redeem us.
> You purchased us to bring us to God
> out of every tribe, language, people group, and nation.
> You have chosen us to serve our God
> and formed us into a kingdom of priests
> who reign on the earth. (Revelation 5:9–10)

Paul's Ministry (Romans 15:22–33)

Paul's Intention to Visit Rome

In the following passage, Paul gives a bit of what we might call a missionary newsletter, sharing a ministry update and itinerary. Along with telling of his plan to deliver an offering gathered from among the believers in Macedonia and Greece to the church in Jerusalem, he assures the church in Rome that he longs to come to them. He desires to spend some time of ministry with them and also "be spiritually refreshed by [their] fellowship" (v. 32).

Verses 22–33

> My pursuit of this mission has prevented me many times from visiting you, but there is now nothing left to keep me in these regions. So many years I have longed to come and be with you! So on my way to Spain I hope to visit you as I pass through Rome. And after I have enjoyed fellowship with you for a while, I hope that you would help

me financially on my journey. But now I'm on my way to Jerusalem to encourage God's people and minister to them.

I am pleased to inform you that the believers of Macedonia and Greece have made a generous contribution for the poor among the holy believers in Jerusalem. They were thrilled to have an opportunity to give back to the believers in Jerusalem. For indeed, they are deeply grateful for them and feel indebted because they brought them the gospel. Since the ethnic multitudes have shared in the spiritual wealth of the Jewish people, it is only right that the non-Jewish people share their material wealth with them.

So, when I have completed this act of worship and safely delivered the offering to them in Jerusalem, I will set out for Spain and visit you on my way there. I am convinced that when I come to you, I will come packed full and loaded with the blessings of the Anointed One!

That's why I plead with you, because of our union with our Lord Jesus Christ, to be partners with me in your prayers to God. My dear brothers and sisters in the faith, with the love we share in the Holy Spirit, fight alongside me in prayer. Ask the Father to deliver me from the danger I face from the unbelievers in Judea. For I want to make sure that the contribution I carry for Jerusalem will be favorably received by God's holy ones. Then he will send me to you with great joy in the pleasure of God's will, and I will be spiritually refreshed by your fellowship.

And now may the God who gives us his peace and wholeness be with you all. Yes, Lord, so let it be!

"Fight alongside Me in Prayer"

Paul certainly appreciated and valued monetary assistance, but we can see in this passage the even greater value he placed on the partnership of prayer. He went so far as to say, "I plead with you...to be partners with me in your prayers to God" (v. 30). Paul had plans! He had big, Holy Spirit–inspired plans to do important work in God's kingdom. However, he understood that he could never accomplish them alone. He needed God's power and the support of God's people to accomplish God's plans.

Paul's Friends (Romans 16:1–27)

There are actually *thirty-seven people* mentioned by name in Paul's final words to the Romans in this amazing letter. Thirty-seven supporters, partners, fellow messengers, fellow laborers, and friends. This is significant and worthy of our study. Think of this: each one of these friends' names is forever—for all eternity—memorialized in the Word of God. Therefore, we must infer they were exceptional and remarkable.

Who were these people whom Paul honored, needed, and loved? They were loving, beautiful servants of the Lord. They comprised both men and women who carried and treasured the gospel light. They are worthy of our attention and thought.

In a sense, these special friends actually bring Paul "down to earth" for us. He was a *real* person who lived his allotted days on the earth as we all have and will. In the course of his life, Paul was not a "loner" or super-spiritual, flitting from city to city, holding nice gospel crusades. No, he lived a difficult life and walked a journey of much victory as well as much suffering. Yet, he had great joy and great friends along the way. Some of his dear friends are, thankfully, revealed to us here in Romans 16 so that we can study and learn from them.

Paul Sends His Loving Greetings

Just imagine being one of these dear saints who had the awesome privilege to co-labor with and serve the apostle Paul. We, of course, have the privilege of hindsight and can see the full scope of the magnitude of their spiritual legacy—but they didn't. None of them wrote books in the Bible, and most of them are only known to those who have actually studied this sort of postscript to Paul's letter to the Romans. They were simply serving Jesus their King. Yet, they share in the same reward as Paul. He could never have gotten this letter to Rome himself; he needed Phoebe. He didn't physically write this letter himself; he needed Tertius his copyist. And so on. Paul, in these final words, helps us all to see how important and meaningful just one obedient heart is in God's glorious kingdom.

Verses 1–15

> Now, let me introduce to you our dear and beloved sister in the faith, Phoebe, a shining minister of the church in Cenchrea. I am sending her with this letter and ask that you shower her with your hospitality when she arrives. Embrace her with honor, as is fitting for one who belongs to the Lord and is set apart for him. So provide her whatever she may need, for she's been a great leader and champion for many—I know, for she's been that for even me!

> Give my love to Prisca and Aquila, my partners in ministry serving the Anointed One, Jesus, for they've risked their own lives to save mine. I'm so thankful for them, and not just I, but all the congregations among the non-Jewish people respect them for their ministry. Also give my loving greetings to all the believers in their house church.

> And greet Epenetus, who was the first convert to Christ in the Roman province of Asia, for I love him dearly.

> And give my greetings to Miriam, who has toiled and labored extremely hard to benefit you.

> Make sure that my relatives Andronicus and Junia are honored, for they're my fellow captives who bear the distinctive mark of being outstanding and well-known apostles, and who were joined into the Anointed One before me.

> Give my regards to Ampliatus, whom I love, for he is joined into the Lord.

And give my loving greetings to Urbanus, our partner in ministry serving the Anointed One, and also to Stachus, whom I love.

Don't forget to greet Apelles for me, for he's been tested and found to be approved by the Anointed One.

And extend warm greetings to all those of Aristobolos's house church.

Give my love to my relative Herodion, and also to all those of the house church of Narcissus, for they too are joined into the Lord.

Please greet Tryphena and Tryphosa, for they are women who have diligently served the Lord.

To Persis, who is much loved and faithful in her ministry for the Lord, I send my greetings.

And Rufus, for he is especially chosen by the Lord. And I greet his mother, who was like a mother to me.

I cannot forget to mention my esteemed friends Asyncritus, Phlegon, Hermes, Patrobas, Hermas, and all the brothers and sisters who meet with them.

Give my regards to Philologus, Julia, Nereus and his sister, and also Olympas and all the holy believers who meet with them.

Paul Greets and Commends His Friends

- **Phoebe:** This woman had a great effect on Paul's life. He calls her "dear and beloved sister." Paul describes Phoebe with the Greek word *prostatis*, which means "champion" and "the one who goes first, a leading officer, presiding over many." This woman was not just a deaconess. Her heroic faith and nobility set her apart. To be labeled a *prostatis* would require that she be very influential. She likely was quite wealthy as well, using her wealth to fund charitable works and to support the gospel and gospel messengers.

- **Prisca and Aquila and Their House Church:** This remarkable couple had a special place in Paul's heart. He loved and admired them. They were Paul's co-laborers. Paul affirmed them and, with them, other traveling ministers who live a life of itinerant gospel work. They had a church that met in their house. Prisca was a diminutive form of Priscilla ("long life"). She and her husband Aquila ("eagle") were tent-makers like Paul. They were not only business part-ners but also partners with him in ministry. See Acts 18:2, 18, 26; 1 Corinthians 16:19; 2 Timothy 4:19.

- **Epenetus:** This man was the first Turk to come to faith in Christ. Paul honors him and says, "I love him dearly." His name means "praiseworthy."

- **Miriam (Mary):** Paul particularly lauds Miriam's extreme toil and labor. Her name essentially gives the meaning of exaltation and honor. She was a notewor-thy woman of God.

- **Andronicus and Junia:** These were Paul's rela-tives and were imprisoned with him. They bore the mark of being well-known apostles. This is notable because Junia was a woman. This is an instance of female apostles in the Word of God. Typically, women are allocated to children's or women's minis-try and missionary work—the argument being that only men are allowed to teach. In the two places where Paul actually refers to restricting women (in Corinth and Ephesus), there was a regional issue of the worship of Diana (Roman goddess). The temple worship involved women priests; many of whom were also prostitutes. When these women were newly converted, they brought their goddess worship and similar women-led worship experiences with them. The restriction given by Paul was necessary for these *specific churches* only because of their *specific regional culture.* This restriction was for the women newly converted from Diana worship, not for women in general, and certainly not for Junia, who was noteworthy and "outstanding among the apostles." Photine is another notable woman preacher who clearly was not restricted in ministry. (You can research her life and works.)

- **Ampliatus:** Ampliatus was a common name given to slaves, and it means "large one." The Eastern Orthodox Church recognizes him as one of the seventy disciples whom Jesus sent out. He is believed to have become the bishop of Bulgaria.

- **Urbanus:** Urbanus was also a common name given to slaves. It means "polite one."

- **Apelles:** *Apelles* means "called one."

- **Stachus:** *Stachys* means "head of grain." He is said to have been one of the seventy disciples Jesus sent out. He eventually became the bishop of Byzantium.

- **Aristobolos and His House Church:** By implication, those connected to Aristobolos were his "house church." *Aristobolos* means "best counselor." Traditionally he is known as one of the seventy disciples Jesus sent out, and he brought the gospel to Britain.

- **Herodion:** Herodion's name means "heroic." He was traditionally considered one of Jesus' seventy disciples. He later became the bishop of Neoparthia (Iraq), where he was beaten to death by the Jews but was resurrected and continued to preach the gospel. It is believed that he was eventually beheaded in Rome on the same day Peter was martyred.

- **Narcissus and His House Church:** Although nearly every translation adds the word *household*, it is not found in the text. By implication, this would be those meeting as a church in his house. Narcissus' name means "astonished" (or "stupefied"). Some have identified him as a close friend of Emperor Claudius.

- **Tryphena and Tryphosa:** *Tryphena* means "living luxuriously." Some have identified her as Antonia Tryphaena (10 BC—AD 55), the princess of the Bosporan Kingdom of eastern Crimea, connected to the queen of Thrace. This would mean that she was royal and wealthy. Tryphosa can also mean "living luxuriously" or "triple [three-fold] shining." Some scholars believe that Tryphena and Tryphosa were twin sisters born into royalty.

- **Persis:** *Persis* means "to take by storm." She was a woman from Persia (Iranian background) who was a godly servant and passionate follower of Jesus.

- **Rufus:** *Rufus* means "red." It is believed he was the son of Simon of Cyrene (Libya), who helped Jesus carry his cross to Calvary. See Mark 15:21.

- **Asyncritus:** *Asyncritus* means "incomparable." The Orthodox Church recognizes him as an apostle. He became the bishop of the church of Hyrcania (Turkey). In this verse, Paul joins five men together. They could have represented the five-fold ministry of Ephesians 4:11, or they may have been leaders of house churches, for there were others who were "with" them and connected to them.

- **Phlegon:** *Phlegon* means "burning one." He was considered to be one of the seventy disciples Jesus sent out. The Orthodox Church recognizes him as an apostle who became the bishop of Marathon in Thrace.

- **Hermes:** *Hermes* means "preacher of the deity." He was considered to be one of the seventy sent out by Jesus and later became the bishop of Dalmatia.

- **Patrobas:** *Patrobas* means "fatherly" (paternal). He likewise was one of the seventy sent by Jesus and later became the bishop of Neapolis (Naples).

- **Hermas and His/Their House Church:** Hermas was one of the seventy and later became the bishop of Philippopolis (Bulgaria). There are interesting traditions surrounding Hermas. It is said that he was a very wealthy man but fell into poverty because of his sins. He was visited by an "angel of repentance," who accompanied him for the rest of his life until he was martyred. There are writings known as "The Shepherd of Hermas" that some scholars attribute to him.

- **Philologus:** *Philologus* means "talkative." He was recognized by the Orthodox Church as an apostle of Christ. It is likely that Julia was his wife and Nereus and his sister were their children (listed below). Philologus and Olympas apparently had a measure of influence over a number of "holy believers" in the faith. The majority of the people named in this chapter were not Jewish, and many of their names indicate that they were former slaves. God can bless and anoint anyone who turns to him in faith.

- **Julia:** (See above.)

- **Nereus:** (See above.)

- **Olympas and Their House Church:** *Olympas* means "heavenly." The Orthodox Church recognizes Olympas as an apostle who was mentored by Peter and was beheaded the same day Peter was martyred in Rome.

Verse 16

Greet each other with a holy kiss of God's love. All the believers in all the congregations of the Messiah send their greetings to all of you.

"A Holy Kiss"

This references the precious love of Jesus that truly binds our hearts together as one and as family. The "kiss" is the kiss of Song of Songs, the kiss of God upon our heart. We receive his kiss of love, and we freely give his love to others within his household.

Paul's Final Instructions

Here Paul gives a final warning: "Watch out for those who cause divisions and offenses among you" (v. 17). As a true spiritual father, he cautions his dear children to put on their Satan-crushing shoes of peace (Ephesians 6:15) to stand against that which is a truly insidious trap—the lure of deceivers looking to pull people to themselves instead of pointing them to Christ and Christlikeness.

Verses 17–20

And now, dear brothers and sisters, I'd like to give one final word of caution: Watch out for those who cause divisions and offenses among you. When they antagonize you by speaking of things that are contrary to the teachings that you've received, don't be caught in their snare! For people like this are not truly serving the Lord, our Messiah, but are being driven by their own desires for a following. Utilizing their smooth words and well-rehearsed blessings, they seek to deceive the hearts of innocent ones.

I'm so happy when I think of you, because everyone knows the testimony of your deep commitment of faith. So I want you to become scholars of all that is good and beautiful, and stay pure and innocent when it comes to evil. And the God of peace will swiftly pound Satan to a pulp under your feet! And the wonderful favor of our Lord Jesus will surround you.

Under Your Feet

This word for "pound" is *suntribo,* and it means "to pound into jelly." What a picture! The God of peace is going to do the pounding, but he is going to do it under *your* feet. Your mandate is to crush Satan. Satan bruised Jesus on the cross as was prophesied in Genesis 3: "And I will put enmity (open hostility) between you and the woman, and between your seed (offspring) and her Seed; He shall [fatally] bruise your head, and you shall [only] bruise His heel" (Genesis 3:15 AMP). But Jesus' church is crushing Satan and destroying his works until the full restoration of all things. You have Satan-crushing feet! You are not a victim. You are the victor through Christ!

Verse 21

My ministry partner, Timothy, sends his loving greetings, along with Luke, Jason, and Sosipater, my Jewish kinsmen.

Paul's Partners: Timothy, Luke, Jason, Sosipater

- **Timothy:** Timothy was a spiritual son and ministry partner to the apostle Paul. See Acts 16:1–3.

- **Luke:** Or "Lucius." This seems to be the Luke who wrote Luke and Acts, but there remains considerable debate surrounding who that "Luke" may be.

- **Jason:** Jason also appears in Acts 17, where he opened his home to Paul, Silas, and Timothy while they were in Thessalonica. Tradition states that Jason was one of the seventy disciples sent out by Jesus and was appointed the bishop of Tarsus by Paul. According to church tradition, he became the bishop of Iconium.

- **Sosipater:** According to church tradition, he was recognized as one of the seventy disciples and became the bishop of Iconium.

Verse 22

(I, Tertius, am the one transcribing this letter for Paul, and I too send my greetings to all of you, as a follower of the Lord.)

Tertius, the Scribe

- **Tertius:** Tertius, the copyist for Paul, was recognized in church history as one of the seventy disciples of Jesus. He became the bishop of Iconium after Sosipater and was eventually martyred.

Verses 23–24

My kind host here in Corinth, Gaius, likewise greets you, along with the entire congregation of his house church. Also, the city administrator Erastus and our brother Quartus send their warm greetings.

May the grace and favor of our Lord Jesus, the Anointed One, continually rest upon you all.

And Everyone Else!

- **Gaius and His House Church:** This is most likely the Gaius whom Paul baptized (1 Corinthians 1:14) and who became a ministry partner with Paul (Acts 19:29). *Gaius* means "happy," "jolly."
- **Erastus:** Erastus was a political appointee who was undoubtedly of a high social status in the city of Corinth. His duties would have included being the treasurer of the city. Church tradition holds that he

was one of the seventy disciples of Jesus and that he served as a minister (deacon) of the church in Jerusalem and later in Paneas. An excavation in Corinth uncovered a street with an ancient inscription dated to the first century AD. It reads: "Erastus… laid the pavement at his own expense." His name means "loveable."

- **Quartus:** Quartus is also recognized in church history as one of the seventy disciples sent by Jesus. He became the bishop of Beirut. Nikolai Velimirovic wrote that Quartus suffered greatly for his faith and won many converts to Christ through his ministry.

Paul Praises God

In these final verses, Paul concludes by giving his praise and honor to God. He is so thankful for his friends and fellow servants, but his ultimate thanks and trust belong to the Lord.

Verses 25–26

I give all my praises and glory to the one who has more than enough power to make you strong and keep you steadfast through the promises found in my gospel; that is, the proclamation of Jesus, the Anointed One. This wonderful news includes the unveiling of the mystery kept secret from the dawn of creation until now. This mystery is understood through the prophecies of the Scripture and by the decree of the eternal God. And it is now heard openly by all the nations, igniting within them a deep commitment of faith.

The Mystery Revealed

What is this mystery Paul refers to? He gives a hint in this letter to the Romans. It is the mystery of the sons and daughters of God being unveiled, the mystery all of creation is standing on tiptoe to see: "I am convinced that any suffering we endure is less than nothing compared to the magnitude of glory that is about to be unveiled within us. The entire universe is standing on tiptoe, yearning to see the unveiling of God's glorious sons and daughters!" (Romans 8:18–19). This mystery is the unveiling that the Holy Spirit and Jesus our King are interceding for—the hope of glory, Christ in us, true Christlikeness being unveiled in the church. Grace is powerfully at work in you and me right now to bring forth this unveiling. *Grace is bringing you into glory.*

Verse 27

> Now to God, the only source of wisdom, be glorious praises for endless ages through Jesus, the Anointed One! Amen!
>
> (Paul's letter was transcribed by Tertius in Corinth and sent from Corinth and carried to Rome by Phoebe.)

"Now to God"

What a fitting ending to such a magnificent biblical treatise. Throughout this epistle, Paul laid out, powerfully and systematically, what many consider to be the clearest discourse on the Christian faith. The letter to the Romans is such a gift to us as Christ's followers. How enriched and strengthened we are through this great work, and Paul concludes it by giving all the credit and praise to "God the only source of wisdom." Romans is brilliant because it is inspired. Thus, we receive it as from God, not mere men, and to him be all the "glorious praises for endless ages through Jesus, the Anointed One!"

Let's Go Deeper!

Questions

1. What is something you learned in this lesson that perhaps you never realized before? What portion or point in this lesson affected you the most and why?

2. Here in Paul's closing portion of his letter to the Romans, we get a glimpse into his life and ministry through those he names as companions, co-laborers, and friends. What does this reveal to you about Paul, about ministry, and about God?

3. The main themes of Romans are grace and glory. How did your understanding of grace increase through this study? What did you learn about how glory is the ultimate purpose of grace?

4. What is grace to you?

5. What does it mean to you personally that you have been declared "not guilty"? (See Romans 5:16 and 8:33.) How can you share this wonderful news with others?

Deeper Still!

Activations

Paul's purpose in writing the letter of Romans was to make the case for salvation by grace alone, through faith alone, in Christ alone. He spent eight truly amazing chapters building that case and then boldly announced that the case is closed: "So now the case is closed. There remains no accusing voice of condemnation against those who are joined in life-union with Jesus, the Anointed One" (Romans 8:1).

The case is well and truly closed, dear friend. Jesus paid it all, and there is nothing more to add to his full salvation. As we have learned in Romans: *grace plus anything else is no longer grace.*

Hopefully, through this study, you have been made aware of any ways in which you may have trusted in your own ability, goodness, works, or merit rather than fully leaning on Jesus and his grace. It is my prayer that you let go of those false foundations and go forward, building only on the bedrock of grace. Grace is more than enough. It silences all accusing voices, and it will bring you fully into the glory of God: Christlikeness!

Let's Pray

Father, how grateful we are for your Holy Word. Your Word is life to us. We are thankful that you have made us the recipients of your grace and love and that you have declared us eternally "not guilty." We will stand before you one day, Lord, but not in our own righteousness or goodness and not to give an account for our sin. We will stand clothed in your righteousness as ones redeemed with sacred blood, the blood of Jesus. Thank you, Lord, for calling us, justifying us, and transforming us from one brighter level of glory to another (2 Corinthians 3:18). Thank you for your grace that is taking us to glory! Amen.

About the Authors

BRIAN & CANDICE SIMMONS have been described as true pioneers in ministry. Their teaching and spiritual gifts have opened doors into several nations to bring the message of authentic awakening and revival to many. For many years, they have labored together to present Christ in his fullness wherever God sends them.

After a dramatic conversion to Christ in 1971, Brian and Candice answered the call of God to leave everything behind and become missionaries to unreached peoples. Taking their three children to the jungle tropical rain forest of Central America, they planted churches for many years with the Paya-Kuna people group.

After their ministry overseas, Brian and Candice returned to North America, where they planted numerous ministries, including a dynamic church in New England (US). They also established Passion & Fire Ministries, under which they travel full-time as Bible teachers in service of local churches throughout the world.

Brian and Candice are co-authors of numerous books, Bible studies, and devotionals that help readers encounter God's heart and experience a deeper revelation of God as our Bridegroom-King, including *The Blessing, The Image Maker, The Sacred Journey, The Wilderness,* and *Throne Room Prayer.*

Brian is also the lead translator of The Passion Translation®. The Passion Translation (TPT) is a heart-level translation that uses Hebrew, Greek, and Aramaic manuscripts to express God's fiery heart of love to this generation, merging the emotion and life-changing truth of God's Word.

Brian and Candice have been married since 1971 and have three children as well as precious grandchildren and great-grandchildren. Their passion is to live as loving examples of a spiritual father and mother to this generation.